Better living through
economics

Better Living through Economics

BETTER LIVING
THROUGH ECONOMICS

Edited by

John J. Siegfried

HARVARD UNIVERSITY PRESS
Cambridge, Massachusetts
London, England
2010

Library of Congress Cataloging-in-Publication Data

Better living through economics / edited by John J. Siegfried.
p. cm.
Includes bibliographical references and index.
ISBN 978-0-674-03618-5
1. Economics—Research. I. Siegfried, John J.
HB74.5.B48 2010
330—dc22   2009028098

Contents

Better Living through Economics

Introduction

John J. Siegfried

This book illustrates the fundamental contributions of economic research to important public policy decisions. The examples are from the past half century. It may surprise many people to learn that it was economics research that built the foundation for eliminating the military draft in favor of an all-volunteer army in 1973, for passing the Earned Income Tax Credit in 1975, for deregulating airlines in 1978, and for adopting the Pension Protection Act of 2006 that switched the default option to participate in 401(k) retirement plans. Other important but less discrete changes in policy have also resulted from economic research, including a new approach to monetary policy that has moderated economic fluctuations substantially, a reduction of trade impediments so that countries can exploit their natural (comparative) advantages better, and the adoption of tradable emissions rights, which have enabled us to improve our living environment without sacrificing more goods and services than necessary.

The value of the improved policies documented in this volume is likely hundreds of billions of dollars. The diffusion of inflation targeting among monetary authorities around the world and the widespread adoption of liberalized trade regimes alone have made it possible for residents of many countries to enjoy higher economic growth rates than would otherwise have been attainable. Virtually all the policies described in these chapters have improved the welfare of many individuals. Through their effects on income and wealth they have indirectly reduced mortality and improved health, welfare, and happiness.

Of course, policy changes that, on average, make more people better off than worse off seldom make everyone better off. Consequently, a proper welfare analysis requires interpersonal utility comparisons. Are those who are made better off made sufficiently better off to outweigh the losses imposed on those who end up worse off? The traditional approach to this question has been to use the compensation principle. That is, do the winners gain enough that they can, at least conceptually, compensate the losers sufficiently to make the losers no worse off than they would have been absent the policy change and still leave themselves with a residual gain? If the answer is yes, then, at least in theory, the policy change could be constructed to make some people better off while making no one worse off. Absent such considerations as envy and other relative income issues, the policy change might then be declared a "good thing." Unfortunately, however, matters are not quite so simple. Whether, in fact, compensation actually must be paid, or whether it is sufficient that it could be paid, even though in fact it is not paid, remains controversial. The chapters in this volume, by and large, ignore such distributional considerations. To do otherwise would drag the analysis into a morass it could hardly escape.

Contributions to human welfare in the biological, medical, engineering, and electronics fields usually move from research to consumers through private-sector initiatives. Those contributions tend to be well documented through either our system of patents or academic endeavors to document systematically the history of science. In contrast, contributions to human welfare in economics often, but not always, move from research results to consumers through government policy decisions, and the steps from innovation to the adoption of economics to policy decisions remain a mystery. Even those who use the tools and contributions frequently do not know their source. From time to time the contributions from economics are so singularly visible that their origins are made obvious. The capital-asset pricing model (developed by William Sharp, Harry Markowitz, and Merton Miller), the Black-Scholes option pricing model, index mutual funds (developed by Burton Malkiel), and the use of auctions to deal with overbooked airline flights (William Vickrey, Alfred Kahn, and Elizabeth Bailey) are prominent examples. However, for the most part, the contributions of economics to our daily lives go unrecognized.

It is the thesis of this volume that economics has made enormous contributions to human welfare, even if it is sometimes difficult to identify precisely the individual pioneers. The examples range over many fields of economics, including monetary economics, international trade, industrial organization and regulation, public economics, labor economics, behavioral economics, game theory, natural resource economics, and the economics of poverty.

The selections in this volume constitute only a few illustrations of the many contributions that economic research has made to improvements in public policy. Many others could have been included: the role of game theory in the Cold War's mutually assured destruction (MAD) strategy, congestion pricing of highways, improvements in national income accounting, peak-load pricing by public utilities, the benefits of youth education, or the migration from fixed to flexible exchange rates, to name just a few of the more obvious ones.

Interestingly, only a few of the contributions outlined here have been financed or promoted through the private sector. Economics tends to differ from the other sciences in that the basic science is a nearly pure public good, with little private value. Patents, copyrights, or other benefit-internalizing institutions, therefore, cannot capture the value of innovation. As a result, the funding of much of the basic science in addition to the policy applications has been by governments, and especially by the National Science Foundation (NSF). Indeed, a majority of the chapter authors have been or currently are NSF grantees (including Bailey, Blank, Krueger, Laibson, Moffitt, Plott, Roth, Taylor, and White).

Much of the research that transformed the way government statisticians measure price was sponsored by the NSF, including grants to Michael Boskin, Erwin Diewert, Robert Gordon, Zvi Griliches, Jerry Hausman, Dale Jorgenson, Robert Pollak, and Sherwin Rosen. The Canada Council also supported Diewert's research. Of course, government statistical agencies themselves, especially the U.S. Bureau of Labor Statistics, conducted much research on price measurement.

The research on poverty in the chapters on welfare reform and the Earned Income Tax Credit (EITC) relied heavily on investments by the NSF in data, particularly the Panel Study of Income Dynamics (PSID), a unique, nationally representative sample of U.S. households that covers the socioeconomic characteristics of families over a full life cycle and provides intergenerational data for those families. The Department of Health and Human Services and the National Institutes of Health, as well as the Annie E. Casey Foundation and the Smith-Richardson Foundation, were important supporters of early research on the EITC.

NSF funding of research by John Ledyard, John McMillan, Paul Milgrom, Charles Plott, Alvin Roth, and Robert Wilson and his collaborators led to basic advances in auction theory, matching models, and experimental methodology that are highlighted in the chapters on the spectrum auction, hospital-residents and school-student matching, and Charles Plott's introductory overview. The basic science provided a tool kit for designing allocation methods that meet specific needs. David Gale and Lloyd Shapley's fundamental contribution to matching problems was funded in part by the U.S. Office of Naval Research. The Federal Communications Commission's staff was intimately involved in designing the spectrum auctions. Government funding contributed to the great spectrum auction in a second important way: the auction probably would never have taken place if the Federal Communications Commission had not been able to test it first. John Ledyard, Charles Plott, and David Porter conducted tests at the California Institute of Technology's experimental laboratory. The Cal Tech laboratory was established by the first-ever major NSF instrumentation award in the social sciences.

The improved macroeconomic performance of the U.S. and other economies over the past twenty-five years is due at least in part to changes in monetary policy that reflect what John Taylor calls in his chapter the "Great Awakening in monetary research." Most key contributors to the great awakening enjoyed U.S. government support, including Finn Kydland, Robert Lucas, Edmund Phelps, Edward Prescott, Thomas Sargent, John Taylor, and Neil Wallace. The NSF funded the Carnegie/Rochester Conference Series in Public Policy, the Brookings Panel on Economic Activity, and the National Bureau of Economic Research (NBER) Macroeconomics Annual—forums where pathbreaking academic research could be presented and disseminated quickly to government decision makers. Moreover, numerous NSF grantees, including Ben Bernanke, Olivier Blanchard, Stanley Fischer, Anne Krueger, Kenneth Rogoff, Joseph Stiglitz, Lawrence Summers, and Janet Yellen later became decision makers and influential advisors in central banks and international financial institutions. The U.S. Agency for International Development and the NBER funded research by Jagdish Bhagwati and Anne Krueger that concluded that open trade policies are economically efficient.

The U.S. government provided much of the financial support for the progress in economic theory that spawned deregulation in the transportation industry and related antitrust reforms. Academic economists Timothy Bresnahan, Jeremy Bulow, William Comanor, Kenneth Elzinga, Richard Gilbert, George Hay, Michael Katz, Willard Mueller, Janusz Ordover, Daniel Rubinfeld, F. M. Scherer, Carl Shapiro, Leonard Weiss, Lawrence White, and Robert Willig, among others, were responsible for redefining and implementing new policies while they served in temporary assignments at the Department of Justice and the Federal Trade Commission (FTC). Both the Antitrust Division of the Department of Justice and the FTC's Bureau of

Economics contain large staffs of professional economists who have conducted economic research on competition policy for decades. With assistance from the Ford Foundation, the Brookings Institution supported Richard Caves's 1962 effort to organize economics thinking about the airline industry in *Air Transport and Its Regulators,* George Eads's research on local service airlines, and Jim Miller and George Douglas's pathbreaking research published in 1974 on the trade-off between service quality and price in the airline industry. Core research by Elizabeth Bailey, William Baumol, John Panzar, and Robert Willig on contestability, which concluded that airline markets could operate competitively so long as entry was quick and inexpensive, was conducted at Bell Laboratories.

Peculiarly, academic economists without external funding conducted most of the pioneering research on the economic costs of the military draft. Eventually, however, President Richard Nixon appointed the President's Commission on an All-Volunteer Armed Force to study the transition from military conscription to a voluntary army. This commission, as well as its staff, was well populated with economists. In 1970 it recommended that the draft be replaced by a volunteer military.

The use of transferable permits to control pollution was based on pioneering research by NSF grantee Wallace Oates in the 1980s on markets for pollution control. The NSF has also supported David Laibson's basic research in behavioral finance and influential theoretical work on behavioral economics by Matthew Rabin. Major funding for the application of behavioral economics principles to policy changes in the Pension Protection Act of 2006 came from the National Institute on Aging under the auspices of the National Institutes of Health.

This volume begins with an overview by Charles Plott, followed by descriptions of the role of economics in fostering twelve specific policy changes. The chapters explain how economics progresses when patterns are recognized and verified through repeated independent research, and how economics works its way into the political system until eventually improvements occur.

Overview:
Highlights of the Benefits of
Basic Science in Economics

Charles R. Plott

This chapter rests on two theses. The first is that basic research in economics has had a profound effect on our way of life. Implicit in this thesis is the suggestion that the social value of the contributions of economics compares well with the contributions of basic research in any field of science. Remarkably, the contributions in economics have been accomplished with only a tiny fraction of the levels of research support given other sciences.[1]

The second is that the first thesis is not widely accepted. Few members of the scientific community and an even smaller proportion of the general public have any knowledge at all of what economics is about or what it has accomplished. Indeed, a widely held presumption exists that basic research in economics is not as productive as basic research in other sciences. This chapter questions that presumption by using an approach to the benefits of economics that differs from tradition. First, I will look far into history, which is the approach used by other sciences. Although the lag time from discovery to application in economics is very short by scientific standards, one should think in terms of many decades when one is searching for the impact of basic research. Consequently, for the development of this chapter I take the longer perspective. Second, I will look broadly. Typically, economists overlook the specialized disciplines that fall within the broad framework of economics. Finance, operations research, many parts of management, and law are good examples that could be classified as part of the economic sciences and certainly share in the development and use of basic science. This chapter casts a wide net. Third, I avoid holding economics to unrealistic standards. Unfortunately, economics tends to be evaluated in terms of success in attaining economic goals set by society or by a political process, and such goals are often unattainable. By contrast, and following the lead of other sciences, this chapter will turn to progress in the direction of selected, long-standing, social goals as opposed to success in attaining them. In that regard, it is important to note that the applications goals of economics are far more complex than those of the other sciences. No other science aspires to such difficult goals as influencing an entire economy or even controlling a single market. Typical basic research in other sciences focuses on much simpler tasks, such as activity that takes place at the level of test tubes (or much smaller sites), and typically the success of the science is judged in terms of progress, as opposed to some goal completely attained. A typical mistake is to evaluate economics research in terms of whether some lofty goal has been achieved (such as removing unemployment, inflation, or collusion in markets) and in doing so to impose a standard that no science could meet. Thus, the focus of this chapter is on progress.

In reviewing the examples, three things should be remembered. First, many of the uses of economics are associated with policy analysis, which by its nature is permeated with politics and conflicting values. Applications of science cannot remove these aspects. Second, the problems are hard and the science is incomplete. Judgments based on opinions alone, as well as mistakes, are to be expected. Congressional committees, supporting staffs, regulatory authorities, management, and others who shoulder the responsibility for difficult decisions make the judgments, and the science should not be blamed when mistakes are made. The role of science is supportive, offering options and identifying trade-offs, but it is seldom decisive. It is one thing to have basic principles to guide models of complex processes, but it is another thing to work out the implications of the models under a complex of conditions where the model is to be applied. The science cannot be held accountable for how it is used or mistakes made when it is used. Third, most of the basic science in economics has been a stepchild of applications.[2] Basic results are not integrated, and successful applications are not identified in relation to the underlying science. As a result, the connections of applications to economics and the basic scientific foundations are typically neither documented nor advertised. The public never knows the source of the benefits it enjoys.

Observations

This chapter is organized around eleven observations, each of which focuses on broad areas that touch everyone either directly or indirectly. The observations are followed by documentation and discussion. Together, these observations provide support for the first paragraph of this chapter.

1. *The application of principles of economics is integrated into all regulatory policies, including commerce, financial sectors, public finance, competition, energy, health, utilities, transportation, and communication; governmental policies and even the basic structure of the law itself have been dramatically improved through scientific advances in economics.*

In regulation and competitive policies, the products of economics research are pervasive. Our economy is built on the idea that competition can protect the consuming public, and how that competition is managed has an effect on all prices, new products, and the ability of businesses to produce income. Economics research touches almost every aspect of every life in the United States.

The dynamics of policy changes frequently mirrors the progress of economics research. This is not to say that long lags and big mistakes are not possible or that politics plays no part, but in economics, policy changes are often motivated by research results. A reasonable reading of history can hold that the deregulation revolution was precipitated in part by books written by John Meyer and colleagues,[3] a book on airlines by James Miller and George Douglas,[4] and Alfred Kahn's 1970 treatise *The Economics of Regulation.*[5] These led directly to airline and railroad deregulation and (with others) to telecommunications deregulation and electricity deregulation. This is not to say in retrospect that every aspect of these complex social decisions was correct, but only that the tools to approach such complex problems are at the heart of basic economics research. These examples alone touch everyone in the United States.

In many cases, because of the nature of the engineering and institutional technology, competition cannot be implemented, and monopoly remains. In these cases, the basic insights resulting from economics research can again be found. Marginal cost pricing as a methodology for regulating monopoly prices can be traced directly to basic economic principles. In more complex environments, such as electricity, in which demand occurs during some peak period, theory suggests that pricing according to the time of day can bring about cost-reducing coordination of demand. Peak-load pricing is an ancient concept recognized in the 1880s by Arthur Hadley (later the president of Yale) and formalized by Peter Steiner, among others, in the 1950s. The French were the first to implement it in electricity; much of one issue of the *American Economic Review* in the late 1950s was devoted to a work by Marcel Boiteaux on the French experience. Now peak-load pricing is considered in every major regulated industry in the United States and is implemented in select instances by many industries. The use of midweek announcements of low fares on routes with excess capacity by the airlines is another easily understood example of using prices to attain efficiencies. Moreover, the airlines have been leaders in using marginal costs together with demand assessments in designing routing systems, setting prices, and scheduling flights.

The broad understanding of the implications of principles of competitive behavior and how it can be channeled by appropriate policies has led to major differences in the design of policies in the United States from those in other parts of the world. For example, in the United States economists opposed implementation of the European approach to achieving rapid technological progress, that is, anointing a national champion monopoly enterprise to do the job. No doubt the high-tech venture-capital industry that has shaped so many lives would have emerged with or without economists, but the policy judgments that flowed from the science at least helped avoid the skewing of incentives that held back the emergence of vibrant high-tech start-up markets in Europe, to Europe's present disadvantage.

Principles of economics were remarkably important in the emergence of an analytically based antitrust policy around the turn of the twentieth century. Jeremiah Jenks of Cornell drafted Theodore Roosevelt's early policy statements on antitrust, and the Bureau of Corporations, the predecessor of the Federal Trade Commission's Bureau of Economics, provided the analytic foundation for the Standard Oil, American Tobacco, DuPont, and other early antitrust cases. More recently, economics research has played a decisive role in reorienting merger enforcement toward an efficiency-oriented approach. In this approach, a more dynamic perspective is adopted that enables long-term interrelationships to be taken into account in assessing merger and pricing policies. This long-run, general-equilibrium perspective is derived directly from economic analysis and research. This understanding of the nature of economic efficiency and its measurement has had profound effects on both antitrust and regulatory perspectives and policies.

The prices found in markets reflect many variables, and the control of prices has implications that are difficult to detect when many of the variables are hidden from view. Price controls frequently can have very undesirable consequences, and how and where to look for these consequences requires models based on principles of economics. Research by Ken Arrow,

Calvin Roush, Joe Kalt, and Paul MacAvoy, among others, showed and measured hidden and indirect problems that resulted from the U.S. oil and gas price-control schemes of the 1970s. The removal of the controls ultimately led to more rational allocation of resources in those markets. More recently, the subtle and potentially major implications of price controls have been found in the research of Henry Grabowski and John Vernon, among others, who showed that attempts to control pharmaceutical prices are likely to have serious detrimental long-term effects on innovation and product development.

Evidence of the importance of economics research to regulation and the law is not confined to the classical areas of regulation and regulatory policy. In 1945 no major law school had courses on law and economics. Today every major law school has such courses, taught by tenured economists. Many of the nation's important judges have attended workshops on law and economics conducted by economists.

Similarly, in 1945 the economics of health was not a subfield of economics. Today it is a veritable industry that produces hundreds of applied and theoretical research articles each year. This research concerns the nature of health organizations, the liability of practitioners, the methodology used by insurers, and the structure of the organizations in which the health industry exists. Policy debates regarding the efficiency gains associated with alternative forms of production arrangements, such as health management organizations, are leavened by substantive research on the efficiency and pricing consequences of such arrangements. Similarly, discussions regarding how to deal with the nation's uninsured population are guided by economic principles. The prominent national health insurance experiment of the 1980s provided information about how consumers alter their health-care choices when confronted with economic incentives in the form of coinsurance and deductibles. These insights are now relied on in medical-care pricing arrangements both in the private sector and in public health-care plans.

Basic research has been extended far beyond simple markets and market relationships to the structure of organizations themselves and how different organizational forms function to serve the public. Research on policy has moved from the nature of the rules alone to include the nature of the organization that makes the rules. The understanding of economic organization has been vastly transformed during the past twenty-five years by making a more prominent place for the cognitive and behavioral attributes of human actors (effectively supplanting the fiction of "economic man") and by joining law, economics, and organization in a genuinely interdisciplinary fashion. The upshot is that the older theory of economic organization in which technology was virtually determinative and organizational variety was interpreted as presumptively anticompetitive has been supplanted by a theory in which a place has been made for each generic mode of organization—firm, market, public bureau, and nonprofit. Because each has distinctive strengths and weaknesses, the costs of overreaching and using a "favored" mode to excess are better appreciated.

This broad research agenda has had massive ramifications for several broad areas. (1) In antitrust enforcement organizational variety is now perceived to operate often in the service of economy, and the preconditions for monopoly have been carefully delimited. (2) Excesses of regulation have been identified, and deregulation has not been prescribed across the board but in a discriminating way. (3) The roles of information, information technology, and intellectual property rights are recognized and factored into the theory of the high-performance economy. (4) The study of efficient contracting has been prominently featured in the evolving science of economic organization, whence the law takes its place in the theory. (5) Of special importance to the efficacy of contracting is the condition of credibility, which is jointly determined by the condition of the political-judicial-bureaucratic environment and the efforts of the parties to craft bilateral credible commitments. (6) The foregoing research on contracts has relevance, moreover, not merely to a high-performance economy (where management consulting firms have been relying on new developments in the theory of economic organization) but also in less developed and developing countries, including especially those undergoing economic reform.[6]

There are no measurements of the ultimate impacts of all the avenues through which basic economics research on competition policy has found its way into the lives of people. However, the data that exist suggest that the impact has been to transform whole industries. For example, the reduction of economic regulation in airlines, trucking, railroads, and telecommunications has reduced prices dramatically and has led to a greater variety of products.[7]

2. *A deeper scientific understanding of the complex relationships among our monetary institutions, our fiscal institutions, and economics' responses to their decisions and policies helped reduce the frequency and magnitude of recessions in the United States. The problems of inflation and unemployment are better understood in terms of such relationships, and that understanding has been used to help avoid the costly and harmful instances of such episodes.*

The fruits of economics are used almost daily by everyone who reads the business pages of a newspaper. The concepts of "gross domestic product"

(GDP) and "the money supply" seem commonplace and rooted in common sense. However, even the best-read citizens do not appreciate the fact that the formal definition and use of these concepts, which dictate some of the most important aspects of our lives and life experiences, are the results of years of patient scientific work. Improvements are made constantly.

Without some measure of national income or the nation's output, it would be impossible to craft any effective macroeconomic policy designed to combat inflations and depressions. The origin of the current structure of the national accounts probably can be traced back to the work of Ezra Seaman in the middle of the nineteenth century.[8] However, it was not until the Great Depression and World War II focused scientific attention and led to the development of elements of models of the complex interactions within a whole economy that the system of national accounts as we know them today was developed and widely accepted. Although many economists contributed to their development, the major innovations were made by Simon Kuznets and George Jaszi.[9] These measures have been the subject of continuous evolution and improvement with accumulation of data and the advances of theory.

Indeed, all the major statistical concepts and measures that are used to guide both macroeconomic policy and millions of decisions within private businesses—measures that are now regularly developed and published by the nation's statistical agencies—have their roots in economic theory and analysis. Examples are such familiar and important measures as the unemployment rate, the level of fixed reproducible capital and its use, concepts and measures of productivity and productivity growth, and estimates of the growth and usage of human capital stock. The heavy reliance of the Federal Reserve Board, the Bureau of Economic Analysis, and the Bureau of Labor Statistics on economic analysis and economists is testimony to this contribution.

One of the greatest and most visible accomplishments of a better understanding of macroeconomic relationships has been the remarkably improved performance of the U.S. economy in past decades. The last twenty-five years of the twentieth century in the United States was a period of unprecedented economic stability, including the two longest peacetime expansions in American history, as well as low inflation and low interest rates. This contrasts greatly with the fifteen years of economic instability before this period, which were marked by high inflation and five recessions. By developing a better understanding of the relationship between monetary policy and the economy, economics research helped bring about this impressive turnaround. This research included work on expectations, the effects of incentives on price and wage setting, and the costs of inflation and disinflation. Two discussions of the contributions of economics research on monetary policy during this period contain good summaries.[10] Not many years ago national leaders could be heard advocating an increase in the money supply to reduce inflation, a policy that is known now to have the opposite effect. Indeed, economics has dramatically changed the way we live and the policies that are advocated. The world will always experience economic challenges stemming from the changing dynamics of institutions, organizations, regulations, and resources. The attempts to understand sources and remedies to the current world financial difficulties are calling on a full range of understanding derived from economic principles. The basic science of economics research appears to be the single source of tools, alternatives, and understanding about how new and unwanted challenges might be met.

Economics is changing rapidly as new theories, methodologies, and tools are produced. Over the years the field of economics has taken full advantage of the rapidly expanding capacity for electronic computation. Today the scientific community has large-scale econometric models and large-scale microeconomics-based growth models. These tools are used to help industry and government forecast the economy and analyze both short- and long-term policy impacts. The Auerbach-Kotlikoff Dynamic Life Cycle Simulation Model is one example.[11] This model, which aggregates the microeconomic behavior of individual households and firms, is being used by the Congressional Budget Office to understand the micro- and macroeconomic impacts of tax reform and Social Security reform. Similarly, the Federal Reserve Board and the Congressional Budget Office rely on a variety of both macro- and microeconometric models in analyzing the interactions among budgetary actions, money-supply and interest-rate movements, individual decisions, and the performance of the macroeconomy.

3. Many of the principles that govern the delicate interdependencies that exist in free-market systems have been uncovered. The understanding of these interdependencies resulting from economics research serves as the framework for the crafting of policies with major implications such that even small percentage gains of economic efficiency hold vast benefits for the people of the United States and the world.

One of the great intellectual achievements of economics research has been to develop a rigorous formulation of an economic system that captures the interdependencies among competing products, prices, production processes, input costs, wages, and the millions of other variables that characterize any economy. With this achievement has come a deep understanding of the nature and sources of market values, which are a product of the interactions in the whole system and not simply of the variables as seen by an isolated individual within the system. This has led to an understanding of the sources of wealth, the nature of risk, and how activities in one part of the world can ultimately be felt in other parts. The framework has been constructed, and current research is focused on translating it into operational detail.

Perhaps one of the most visible applications of the general theory has been in the field of international trade. The theory of international trade has uncovered many deep principles that form our understanding of how complex systems of interdependent economies work. Perhaps the most fundamental is the principle of comparative advantage. This principle holds that countries have a tendency to specialize in and trade the goods in which they have comparative advantage. This specialization will lead to the greatest overall efficiency. From a policy perspective, the principle of comparative advantage stresses that countries should concentrate on the activities that they do best relative to other activities that they could do. Whether some other country does the activities better is irrelevant. If each country follows its own comparative advantage and if there is free international trade, the outcome will be the greatest overall well-being in terms of the world's aggregate wealth. The operation of this principle has major implications for modern economies. Take, for example, the Eastern European countries that are in transition from communist to market economies. What should these countries produce? The theory of comparative advantage says that they should produce the goods that they are relatively good at producing. How do we know what goods these are? If the countries engage in free international trade and channel competition such that internal markets work properly, then the right goods will be produced. David Ricardo discovered this principle in the early 1800s, but its expansion and elaboration are products of modern research (Murray Kemp and Ronald Jones). The principle does not say that the government should do nothing. On the contrary, it says that there are natural tendencies and that the most productive policies are those that will be harmonious with them.

The theory of comparative advantage underpins the modern notion that free international trade is important for the health of the world economy. Research done in the past twenty years has solidified these ideas and produced a consensus within the scientific community that is spreading to the general public that free markets and, in particular, free international markets are in everyone's best interest. This has led to a number of highly visible results. The founding of the General Agreement on Tariffs and Trade

(GATT) (which has now become the World Trade Organization) has led to fifty years of significant reductions in existing barriers to trade and has resulted in a dramatic increase in international trade and an accompanying increase in prosperity. For example, the spectacular growth of the Asian economies has been linked to this openness. In addition, there has been an explosion of regional free-trade agreements such as the European Economic Community (EEC) and the North American Free Trade Agreement (NAFTA), which have further stimulated the growth of international trade.

Current research is examining the implications of the theory under conditions of rapid change and associated economic pressures for adaptation under uncertainty. Nobody questions that the pace of change is rapid today. As electronic trading, electronic banking and insurance, telecommunications, and trade in services become more important, it will be academic research that will guide policy makers in reshaping institutions to deal with this rapidly changing environment.

Along with trade liberalization have come dramatic changes in international payments systems in the past three decades. The Bretton Woods system has given way to systems of flexible exchange rates that have facilitated this spectacular record of growing international trade. Academic research by Milton Friedman and others proved extremely influential in leading to this change. Currently, research continues into how to make this system work better. For example, the European Union's creation of a single currency, the euro, is a spectacular change that has had and continues to have far-reaching effects. Years of academic research produced a body of knowledge that enabled policy makers to understand the effects of this dramatic change, and this research will be invaluable in dealing with the difficulties that arise in the future as the system expands and evolves.

It is undeniable that the world is changing at a very rapid pace. Given this reality, it is increasingly important that basic academic research be strongly supported. In order that policy makers can adapt rapidly to changing circumstances, they need a body of research to help them understand this increasingly complex world.

4. The potential for a compatible existence of the environment with other aspects of our economy is being unveiled. Scientific research in economics is revealing strategies for safeguarding the environment while minimizing the compromise with economic efficiency and productivity.

The concepts of benefits and costs are so ingrained in policies regarding the environment that few realize that cost-benefit analysis is a product of economics research. The central concepts of externalities and public goods to capture the relationships among environmental variables and other economic variables are discoveries of the 1950s and were further developed in the 1960s. Indeed, early formulations of the principles can be found in the basic research of Pigou in the 1920s[12] and in the writings of Coase in the early 1960s.[13] The research of today has integrated these concepts and has applied them to the design of environmentally friendly policies based on a realization that many environmental problems arise from inappropriate and inefficient definitions and assignments of property rights. Indeed, it is the special role of rights that distinguishes environmental activity from those activities that are ordinarily left to the private sector. A few years ago only the research literature recognized the "problem of the commons" as an instance of institutional failure in need of better definitions of rights. Now recognition of institutional failure is commonplace and can be found in many instances of policies in which access to and use of natural resources are issues, ranging from fishing to the use of parks.

Classical cost-benefit analysis measures the value placed on an item by the social costs of producing the item and the value of the item as reflected in the prices that people are willing to pay. The environment, by its very nature, does not meet this market test. Yet trade-offs among resource uses are implicit, and a need exists to find methods for identifying the value of environmental concerns in relation to the value of the resources needed to support them. On the one hand, the environment is valued, but, on the other hand, the resources required to maintain the environment are also valued, especially in the sense that those resources could be used to produce other badly needed things. Economic analysis to identify and measure the social benefits and social costs of alternative approaches is central to the design of many of our most effective and efficient policies.[14]

Research in recent years has demonstrated the successful development of technology to retrieve preference information from actual behavior. Even though the "environment" is not something that an individual can purchase at a store, the value placed on the environment can be identified with the choices that people make in everyday life. Both travel costs[15] and hedonic price methods, which employs features of things purchased in a market, are used to impute value to environmental variables.[16] These methods are part of the growing application of a revealed-preference approach to nonmarket valuation.[17]

In addition, rather remarkable advances in the technique of contingent valuation have been made. This technique employs advanced survey and questionnaire methods to coax out revelations of individual willingness to pay for changes in the levels of various public goods (such as water quality) that can be influenced by public policy. This technique is increasingly used both by government agencies and in litigation to assess the economic damages that have been caused by discharges and other activities that lead to decreased environmental quality.

In the late 1960s and early 1970s the idea of using marketable permits for pollution control was being worked out in mathematical and theoretical economic journals. That such instruments might be successfully applied was the product of pure theory and the most basic research. Few policy decision makers found the ideas appealing. No one was interested, but in the years that followed, the ideas quickly became refined, and as early as the late 1960s and mid-1970s policy proposals were beginning to surface.[18] Once again, in economics the time from discovery to application was very short by scientific standards. Cap-and-trade policies began to emerge to control hunting, fishing, and other activities in the area of resource economics.

In 1975 the U.S. Environmental Protection Agency began to experiment with an economic incentive approach known as the Emissions Trading Program, which included a limited system of tradable permits. As experience and theory advanced, it became clear that the predictions derived from economics about the benefits in comparison with classical command-and-control systems worked. Today tradable permits have been developed for a number of environmental problems; the most visible permits were enacted in the Clean Air Act Amendments of 1990, which established tradable permits in a market auction run by the Chicago Board of Trade. The states have also been active, as is demonstrated by the California Regional Clean Air Incentives Market (RECLAIM). Currently, markets are proposed to control greenhouse gases, as established by the Climate Change Convention that went into force on March 21, 1994. Similarly, following the Kyoto Conference, economists have developed models that can mitigate some of the fears that nations have about implementing economic incentive arrangements for environmental control; these approaches are now subject to intensive scrutiny throughout the world and hold great potential for controlling behaviors that lead to environmental warming. Although the success of such an ambitious, worldwide program has yet to be determined, and many unknowns exist, the importance of the underlying science cannot be questioned.[19]

Such policy successes are crafted from mountains of technical, mathematical, and experimental work. In this work, the guiding concepts of efficiency were made precise, and techniques were developed to introduce the forms of the trading instruments (the permits) into classical models so the underlying science could be applied. There was a need to fashion and direct incentives, and models had to be developed to determine what could and what could not be advocated on purely efficiency grounds. Experimental work was used to test the market principles on which the policies were based. New dimensions of policy, such as the banking of permits, the overlap of permit applicability, and even the architectures of the markets themselves, were the subjects of years of academic research before they found their way into policy implementation. The result is an immensely important class of social tools that help remove the problems of pollution without destroying the industries that produce it. This social tool kit would not exist without basic scientific research in economics.

5. Modern communications technologies and computational technologies have produced new methods of channeling competition and have the potential to replace expensive, traditional bureaucratic and administrative processes.

Perhaps the most dramatic illustration of the power of economics research in combination with communications and computational technology has been the electromagnetic spectrum license sales of the Federal Communications Commission (FCC). The sales not only have produced billions of dollars for the U.S. Treasury but also have managed to distribute the licenses more quickly and much more cheaply than at any other time in history. Basically, the classical administrative processes for choosing firms that could operate licenses were abandoned in favor of auctioning off the licenses. The benefit-capturing auction architectures developed in the United States have been mimicked around the globe.

The idea that broadcast licenses could be auctioned and that the outcome would be in the public interest was first advanced in the economics literature in the 1970s. This proposal was suggested along with other proposals for allocating public property, such as the idea that airport access could be distributed by marketable permits rather than regulatory review. The general theory applied to both the FCC licenses and airport landing rights is very similar to the theory used for the development of emissions permits in the environmental field. As might be expected, a system of regulatory review was in place at the time of all proposed applications. Thus, it was necessary to determine that auctions could be designed to perform the same functions as the administrative processes while achieving greater efficiency in execution and distribution. In addition, collusion possibilities needed to be studied, as well as other behaviors that are of concern when competition is used as a replacement for administration. The resulting need was to design new forms of auctions that differed dramatically from anything that had existed before in history.

During the early 1970s laboratory experimental methods in economics were generalized and extended. The most basic discovery of how markets could be studied under laboratory conditions was made by Vernon Smith in the late 1950s,[20] and basic discoveries about public goods and alternative allocation mechanisms were made in the early 1970s,[21] although publication delays masked the relationship between discovery and publication. By the mid-1970s laboratory methods had already found their way into business applications[22] and regulatory applications.[23] By the late 1970s a merger between theory and experiments was instrumental in changing the way in which airport access was organized in the United States.[24] The speed with which basic research in economics can become translated into important applications is clear from this example. The impact of laboratory experimental methodology has grown to include major decisions regarding the environment such as Southern California's RECLAIM.[25] Modern laboratory experimental methods played a key role in the United Nations negotiations of the Kyoto conventions.[26] The impact of basic laboratory research affects our way of living in subtle and surprising ways, from the pricing of natural gas transmission[27] to the allocation of vital organs to ailing individuals[28] to the management of fascinating space exploration.[29]

Perhaps the most visible consequence of this research is the FCC auctions, which were designed from first principles of economics and game theory. They were tested experimentally before they were implemented. Implementation took place in stages, beginning with small auctions and progressing to more complex ones.[30] At each stage the results were reviewed, and the rules and procedures were revised in their light. By all accounts the results were successful, with benefits that far exceed all research funding for economics summed over all of history. Again, the benefits of small amounts of funding for basic research in economics are clear, and the speed with which basic research in economics becomes translated into applications is remarkable by scientific standards.

6. *The organization, efficiency, and overall functioning of business, governmental, and military enterprises have been vastly improved through the application of methods from the disciplines of economics, operations research, statistics, and the decision sciences. Techniques for cost minimization, scheduling, forecasting, strategy development, and control have produced the most successful economic machine known to history.*

When the U.S. military operation Desert Storm in Iraq in 1991 was reviewed, the popular press was quick to identify logistical efforts, including supply deployment, equipment inventories, and troop dispatch, as key elements of this success, which had an overwhelming impact on lives around the globe. However, the newspapers did not mention the fact that the fundamental tools used in these tasks were the products of basic scientific attention in economics and related disciplines. Without this research our world would be much different.

The development of tools to facilitate and support complex decisions has long been an area of economics and its sister disciplines, operations research and decision theory. Tools such as input-output analysis, linear programming, and nonlinear programming were the subject of decades of refinements and interpretation before the very visible applications found today. Many of our industries could not function without them. Airline schedules, the search engines visible on the Internet, and the structure of assembly lines and major production facilities (from refineries and plastics to cookies) are all heavily in debt to these tools.[31]

Tools for forecasting are applied wherever decisions are made. The development of an understanding of when forecasting tools can and cannot be applied, together with improvements of the mathematical tools, involves an integration of the fields of statistics with the field of econometrics. When applied to economic and industrial environments, improvements in forecasts can save billions of dollars in costs. Techniques that were at the frontiers of research only a few years ago can now be found integrated into the most common computer program packages and are used in thousands of business applications.

Strategic analysis is derived from the mathematical theory of games. One might think that its use is reserved for the military, but in fact it is used pervasively as an industrial tool by managers who interact strategically in competitive environments. Mistakes in business can be costly not only to a business but also to its customers, its employees, and the economy as a whole. Mistakes can be a result of simply failing to map and understand the decisions of competitors. Sometimes people think of business as war, a zero-sum game in which gains to one are necessarily losses to someone else. A basic insight from the most basic economics principles is that all can gain in economics, and vehicles that facilitate those gains come from game theory.

7. *Industrial economics and organizational psychology, human factors, and economic sociology have helped identify the elements that make better working environments and strengthen productivity. By anticipating the magnitude and consequences of population-growth trends and international immigration, these sciences have helped organizations increase the efficiency of their operations while accommodating the culturally diverse labor force in the United States.*

Developments in organization theory and economic psychology have led to a revolution in personnel policies and the techniques used to organize complex interactive environments. The enormous number of consultants working with large firms and governmental agencies, and the demand for their services, attest to the efficiency gains that they generate. The "team" concept of organizing production follows directly from the insights of game theory and incentive arrangements developed by economics research and is among the most visible and most widely applied manifestations of this research. Some observers cite such organizational changes as underpinning the very long stretch of productivity growth that we have experienced.

In addition, models developed by economic demographers have enabled us to measure the nature and the economic impacts of immigration, including the contributions that immigrants have made to the development of a number of service and high-technology sectors in the U.S. economy. Basic research on the determinants of migration has enabled economists and policy makers to reconcile the desires of potential migrants to enter the nation with the labor-force needs of potential employers of immigrants. This basic theory has, for decades, put the spotlight on the nature of immigration policy in the United States and has led to the application of economic criteria in decisions regarding how many immigrants and what composition of immigration will best serve the national interest.

Theoretical and empirical advances in forecasting demographic trends (including migration) are central to adopting efficient policies and policy changes. For example, demographic models growing out of economic analysis play an important role in establishing bounds around demographic forecasts that underlie the Social Security system, the cost implications of an aging population for the health-care sector, and the long-run changes in the composition of demands on production sectors as the population changes its age and ethnic composition.

8. The location and relocation of economic activity are fundamental to the economic health of entire regions of our country and our cities. Research in regional economics and economic geography has served to improve the efficiency of these processes, thereby benefiting hundreds of thousands of people.

Space and location play a special role in economic relationships. A major discovery was that spatial configurations tend to be structured to minimize the cost of transportation and communication. That discovery led to valuable contributions from regional economics and geography with surprising applications. Few realize that the maps used for almost every purpose from cities to highways to weather are substantially influenced by the basic science that is the focus of these disciplines. Currently, these disciplines are challenged to provide some understanding of the implications of the Internet and the dramatic reductions in communications costs.

Economic location studies owe much to the idea of the functional region, first proposed in the 1920s. Interest in understanding the functional relationships among phenomena in regional space led to the mapping of a wide range of variables that became critical to sound policy making and scientific understanding. For example, the insights that land-use maps provided about changing land-use patterns have been applied in the development of land-use plans at scales ranging from the local to the national. In the scientific arena efforts to map such variables as precipitation and evaporation have been at the heart of efforts to understand and model the dynamics of the climate system. In the more purely economic arena a concern with interdependencies among phenomena in regional space has led to the development of models that help explain regularities in both settlement patterns and land-use patterns (e.g., central place theory). Comparing real-world circumstances with expected regularities allows us to recognize efficiencies and inefficiencies, as well as the role that noneconomic forces may play in the production of particular patterns of settlement and land use.

Studies in economic geography also address such fundamental questions as how and why commodities, money, and information flow from place to place; what characteristics of a place cause it to do better or worse than other places; and how political and economic developments can affect the comparative success of regions. The utility of the latter question is demonstrated in a study by Ann Markusen and colleagues of the relationship between regional economic growth in the United States and patterns of military expenditure. Military spending during times of "hot wars" (World War II, the Korean War, and the Vietnam War) had a very different geographic impact than did military spending during periods dominated by the Cold War. Such studies shed light on the differential impact of different public spending initiatives, with important implications for future decisions on the regional allocation of public defense monies. A host of other studies in economic geography help us understand why some regions do better than others under particular conditions, and how the mix of social, political, and material attributes of places can affect the potential success of particular businesses.[32]

In health care, good decisions about where a particular service should be located must take into consideration the spatial organization of people, health problems, and related services. By focusing attention on location efficiencies, geographic studies have pointed to specific ways of providing needed health-care services cost-effectively. Regional economics and geographic studies have also helped us understand where diseases develop and how they spread (e.g., AIDS).

Environmental change and our understanding of it are touched by the research. Regional and geographic studies of both the spatial distribution of phenomena and their relationship in places have shed critical light on the ways in which humans are transforming the environment. Studies on the flow of plutonium in the Rio Grande River system, for example, were critical to tracing sources of plutonium contamination. On a larger scale, work by geographers to understand the spatial relationships between climate and vegetation patterns is playing a critical role in efforts to reconstruct the Quaternary climate record, a necessary step in assessing the degree to which current human activities may be producing global warming.

9. Employment, the job-creation process, the job-location process, and the process of attracting employees are fundamental to the income-producing capacity of any economy. These processes have been dramatically improved by scientific work in economics.

Millions of choices relevant to the most efficient use of labor and capital resources are made on an ongoing basis by private firms, nonprofit organizations, and governments. These choices involve how many and what kind of workers to hire, where to locate and how to size production facilities, and how to organize the relationship between production facilities in various locations. All these choices involve balancing at the margin the costs and benefits of various options.

Business firms and government agencies regularly make use of economic planning instruments and knowledge that derive from research in labor economics and managerial economics done in the post–World War II period. Indeed, "human capital" concepts of organizational planning can be traced directly to the groundbreaking work of Jacob Mincer and Gary Becker in labor economics in the early postwar period.

Similarly, deliberations about options for welfare reform policies that might encourage welfare recipients to enter the workforce and basic research regarding the effectiveness of a variety of programs and policies in increasing work, wages, and productivity played a central role in policy debates. Much of this research relied on social experimental analysis and involved measuring the social benefits and costs of alternative work-oriented policies. It seems doubtful that the draconian 1996 welfare reform legislation could have been as successful as it appears to have been without the insights and knowledge from this early research—insights that leavened the policy discussion leading to passage and implementation of the legislation.

10. *Savings rates have been declining, and there are grave concerns about the future of the Social Security system, which is the largest form of support for many households whose members are approaching retirement. The labor-force participation of older Americans has decreased dramatically in recent decades, even as the population is living longer. Behavioral, economics, and social scientists are pinpointing the effects of public and private pensions, the availability of health insurance, and changes in morbidity and disability on retirement decisions while mapping possible system reforms and assessing their implications for different groups of Americans.*

Few people are aware of the tools that are used to protect our savings. Great strides in the field of finance, based on basic research in decision theory and econometrics, have revolutionized the way in which our savings are managed and how risk is reduced. These improvements not only provide security for an aging population but also help remove burdens on public institutions. For evidence, one needs to look no further than the keys of a handheld financial calculator to find concepts and terms that existed only in the most technical economic journals a few years ago.

Today the portfolios of the largest mutual funds are managed through such concepts. Indeed, the very benefits that can be gained from a mutual fund are derived from the principles that were exposed in the scientific literature of the 1960s and 1970s. Not only can the management techniques and the structure of the organizations that manage savings be traced to this literature, but the market instruments they use, such as options and other finely crafted financial instruments that are central tools for reducing risk, are products of the same body of science.

Another example with a major impact is indexation, which can be traced directly to economic theory. In January 1997 the U.S. government issued its first indexed bonds at the initiative of Lawrence Summers. But indexed labor contracts and the like go further back. The theory of indexation is central to these policies, and the Bureau of Labor Statistics is changing the way it computes the Consumer Price Index to take account of criticisms that follow from the application of economic theory (the Boskin Commission Report, 1996). The principles developed by this theory have very wide implications and uses that extend from mortgage underwriting to Fannie Mae and Freddy Mac, including use by banks that are now decreasing reliance on online appraisals in favor of automated valuation models (AVMs), which are based on econometric models, and computerized instant property valuations. As a result, mortgage underwriting is becoming automated and instant.

While theory and tools to protect our savings have been the subject of research, so have the deep issues of our demographic and economic trends and their policy implications. Over the past decade the U.S. national saving rate, defined as (a) the sum of total net output (GDP minus depreciation) less total (government and private) consumption divided by (b) total net output has averaged roughly half the rate observed in the 1950s and 1960s. Our lower rate of saving has meant a lower rate of domestic investment and therefore a slower rate at which our nation adds to its stock of plant, equipment, and residential structures. This capital represents the tools with which America's workers work. The more tools America's workers have and the better they are, the more our workers can produce and, therefore, earn. Although the U.S. economy was growing rapidly near the turn of the twentieth century, the overall U.S. economic growth record since the early 1970s has been poor. So too has been the record of real wage improvements among America's workers.

Such complex tendencies have many interacting causes, and the scientific effort to untangle them has led to some very surprising possibilities. As documented by Gokhale, Kotlikoff, and Sabelhaus,[33] the decline in U.S. saving can be traced, in large part, to the massive intergenerational redistribution that has been associated with the expansion of Social Security and Medicare. Their study bears witness to the predictions of Franco Modigliani's life-cycle theory of saving that the young save and the old dissave and that taking from young savers to give to old spenders will raise aggregate consumption and lower national saving.

The hypothesis that differences exist in the behavior of generations has important policy implications and has produced the concept of generational accounting.[34] Close to thirty countries around the world are now doing generational accounting, to a large extent at the governmental level. Generational accounting indicates which generations will pay the government's bills. In so doing, it determines whether current fiscal policy is sustainable and affordable.

Many economists are now working in the area of Social Security reform. The theoretical foundations were laid by Paul Samuelson and Peter Diamond. Recent proposals for Social Security reform by John Shoven, Henry Aaron, and Martin Feldstein have been central to the recent debate. Economics research has both highlighted the unfunded liability problem and suggested several solutions.

11. *Economic theory contributes to an understanding of the causes and consequences of poverty. Although acceptable policies for the eradication of poverty remain a challenge, economics has been the major source of suggestions.*

The persistence of poverty in spite of affluence and economic growth is a long-standing social concern to which substantial scientific research efforts have been devoted, especially by economists and sociologists. Perhaps more than in any other area, the interaction between policy makers and social scientists has produced both improved social policy and substantial research breakthroughs. A distinct field of poverty research developed in response to the government's announcement of the War on Poverty in the mid-1960s, and, in turn, major scientific advances by poverty researchers have guided the evolution of social and welfare policy since then.[35]

Major advances in databases (for example, large cross-sectional surveys, such as the Current Population Survey of the Bureau of the Census, and panel surveys, such as the Michigan Panel of Income Dynamics) and computer technology led to substantial progress in measuring the variables that reflect access to resources and needs. These measurements are necessary both to identify the number and composition of the poor and to gauge the level of and trends in economic inequality. The initial crude measures of poverty were replaced with a measure that was rooted in economic theory and relied on accurate measurement of the sources of being of living units of various sizes and compositions. These efforts led to the nation's official poverty measure, adopted in 1969.[36]

Numerous analyses of the economic structure of the nation's social insurance and welfare systems yielded estimates of labor-supply and savings disincentives, and the recognition of this trade-off between efficiency and equity drove the search for policy reforms and redesign that would maintain antipoverty effects while reducing these adverse efficiency incentives. This research underlay major policy shifts in the 1980s and 1990s that culminated in the "welfare-to-work" emphasis of current policy. The findings on efficiency effects of income support, together with the distributional (or antipoverty) effects of policy measures, provided the underpinning for debate on numerous policy reform proposals, which ranged from President Nixon's Family Assistance Plan to President Jimmy Carter's Program for Better Jobs and Income and further from the negative income tax and credit income tax plans to the current welfare-to-work reform. Each of these proposals engaged the efforts of poverty researchers who played important roles in estimating the labor-supply and savings effects of proposals, their probable impacts on family structure, fertility, and regional output patterns, and the incidence and composition of poverty.

This empirical research, which relied on large databases, often of a longitudinal nature, led to major insights regarding social mobility, the attainment of economic status, and the dynamics of income flows and change. Because of this research, analysts, policy makers, and citizens also came to understand education and training as investments, with productivity returns that equal or exceed the returns on investments in machines and equipment. In addition, the effects of discrimination and segregation in labor and in housing markets on both national productivity and poverty served to leaven national debates about how to mitigate these problems.

In addition to providing the knowledge and database for developing and designing efficient social policies, this research led to important advances in social science that spilled over into numerous other areas. As a result of concern about the ability of policy interventions to reduce poverty, a new and distinct approach to social research known as policy analysis and evaluation research developed. The basic economic concepts of social benefits and costs were refined and applied to human resource and income-support interventions, and social cost-benefit analysis became a standard tool for assessing public-sector interventions.

A variety of basic econometric methods were also developed in response to the problems that were encountered in the drive of researchers to understand the behavioral effects of social policy interventions, including selectivity adjustment methods and structural modeling techniques. These methods are now widely adopted in scientific research on human subjects in a variety of disciplines. A particular research method, social experimentation, adopted the control-experimental random-assignment concepts of the natural sciences and applied them to policy interventions in the social area—negative income taxation, health insurance, housing allowances, and education and training programs. This method has now become standard in designing or proposing public policy initiatives and reforms in areas far afield from the poverty problem—for example, education policy, housing policy, and utility pricing policy—and is increasingly used in assessing changes in firm organization and workforce development.

Microdata simulation modeling is a computer-based process of estimating the effects on individuals and families, and on their behaviors, of policy interventions. It is a research tool with far-reaching consequences that has grown out of the poverty research effort. With the development of large representative sample surveys of the U.S. population after 1960 came the ability to apply the rules and structure of income-transfer, taxation, and regulatory initiatives to each sampled observation (and hence to various population groups or the entire nation) in estimating the distribution of income changes and behaviors resulting from any policy change. This research method has become increasingly sophisticated, incorporating dynamic structures and behavioral responses. Many such methods and models now exist and are used regularly by the U.S. Treasury, the Department of Health and Human Services, the Social Security Administration, and the Congressional Budget Office to assess the efficiency and distributional effects of policy proposals in a variety of dimensions.

The application of this field's economic and social research evaluations to policy interventions distinguishes the United States from much of Western Europe, where welfare-state interventions also absorb large amounts of resources, but without the evidence necessary to assess efficiency, behavioral, and distributional effects. The superior performance of the U.S. labor market in productivity and job creation relative to that of other large welfare states is, in part, attributable to these constant efficiency analyses of policy interventions by economic and social science researchers. This hands-on applied research approach is largely nonexistent in other nations and has been made possible only through the public support of the basic research on which the methods rest.

Concluding Remarks

This chapter takes a defensive posture. That the products of basic research in economics are not well recognized outside the field of economics seems rather obvious. For example, the funding levels for basic research in economics are pitifully low, with research support for the average Ph.D. in economics being but a tiny fraction of the research support found in other sciences (Table O.1 and Figure O.1). The National Science Foundation's budget for economics has been flat for decades even though the overall NSF budget has increased steadily (Figures O.2 and O.3). Indeed, in real terms the budget for economics has had no growth since the early 1990s even though funding for other sciences has experienced healthy and steady increases. One might think that economics basic research receives funding from other sources outside the NSF. However, economics does not receive the benefits of well-staffed and funded programs elsewhere in governmental agencies, while the other sciences enjoy large levels of support from many agencies. To put this in perspective, each year other sciences receive more funding than economics has received in the history of the world, and this lopsided level of funding has existed for decades.

In terms of benefits per dollar spent on research and certainly in terms of the benefit of the marginal dollar spent on research, economics must be the most valuable of all sciences. Yet there is no chorus of testimony or news articles singing praises. No one calls attention to economics discoveries and the benefits they give to the public. No one is demanding more research support. On the contrary, economics is often given the pejorative label of a "soft science," suggesting that progress is not as important or as likely as in the "real" sciences. I suspect that this stigma is tolerated by economists simply because they themselves do not understand what their profession has accomplished. I hope that this chapter and others like it will help correct this situation.

Table O.1 Basic research funding, NSF and all federal sources, and Ph.D. degrees granted by field of study

Field	1980				1989				2004			
	Ph.D.s	NSF $ (ooo)	Federal, all sources $ (ooo)	Federal, $ per Ph.D. $ (ooo)	Ph.D.s	NSF $ (ooo)	Federal, all sources $ (ooo)	Federal, $ per Ph.D. $ (ooo)	Ph.D.s	NSF $ (ooo)	Federal, all sources $ (ooo)	Federal, $ per Ph.D. $ (ooo)
Engineering	2,479	89,372	465,228	188	4,526	175,784	1,138,797	251	5,775	193,790	2,171,711	376
Mathematics	744	27,166	66,835	90	861	73,229	169,696	197	1,076	193,159	479,075	445
Astronomy and astrophysics	121	34,487	279,420	2,309	113	82,305	541,021	4,788	165	202,087	765,356	4,639
Physics	862	95,593	668,155	775	1,165	159,784	1,383,049	1,187	1,186	219,214	1,904,521	1,606
Chemistry	1,538	68,385	256,922	167	1,971	121,007	526,668	267	2,127	177,284	775,963	365
Earth, atmosphere, and marine	628	253,223	522,560	832	738	416,256	993,408	1,346	686	663,060	2,022,913	2,949
Computer/information science	218	20,603	46,215	212	612	67,068	148,481	243	948	532,332	712,183	751
Biology	3,803	148,567	1,185,974	312	4,106	266,627	2,752,249	670	5,939	450,073	7,222,801	1,216
Psychology	3,098	11,875	84,206	27	3,209	12,450	200,532	62	3,327	2,871	979,225	294
Economics[a]	846	10,297	40,010	47	1,035	9,404	38,001	37	1,069	17,803	47,992	45
Political science[b]	607	3,544	7,493	12	541	3,280	6,376	12	946	5,981	6,736	7
Anthropology	370	6,812	14,234	38	324	8,375	13,069	40	531	9,856	12,875	24
Sociology[c]	663	4,300	25,377	38	494	2,853	47,211	96	599	4,409	48,578	81
Other SS[d]	475	11,891	60,456	127	559	11,189	63,455	114	993	123,344	303,110	305

Sources: Early Release of Summary Statistics on Science and Engineering Doctorates, NSF, March 1990. Federal Funds for Research and Development, Federal Obligations for Research by Agency and Detailed Field of Science and Engineering: Fiscal years 1970–2003, NSF.

a. Economics, econometrics, urban studies, public policy.

b. Area studies, government, political science, international relations.

c. Criminology, sociology, general social sciences.

d. Geography, history of science, linguistics, statistics. SS NEC.

Compiled for Testimony of the Economic Science Association, Public Choice Society, Southern Economics Association, and the Western Economics Association International for the NSF BBS Task Force Looking to the Twenty-first Century.

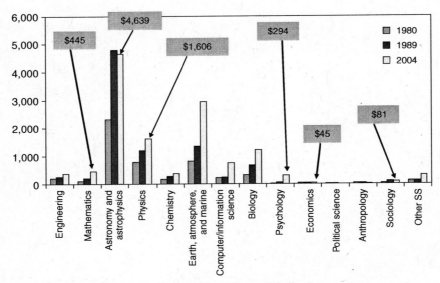

Figure O.1 Funding per graduating Ph.D. from all federal sources

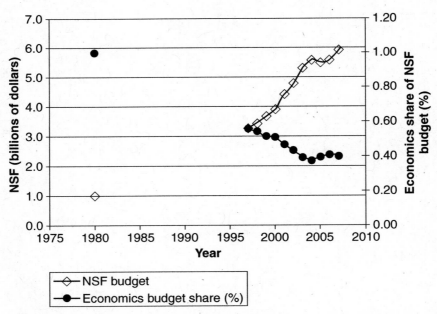

Figure O.2 NSF budget (billions of dollars) and economics NSF budget as a percentage of the NSF budget

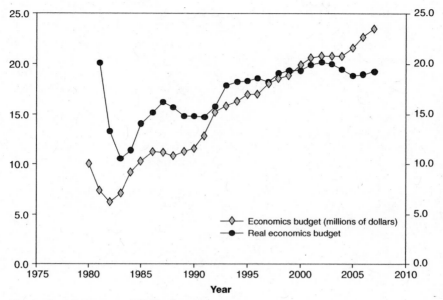

Figure O.3 Economics NSF budget over time

Notes

This chapter was constructed from the responses of several economists who, a few years ago, were asked to help make a case for economics that might be put before Congress. The details reported here are really theirs. Indeed, they should be listed as coauthors. I would like to acknowledge and thank these scholars: Bob Bordley, Lance Davis, Bob Haveman, Larry Kotlikov, Alec Murphy, Ray Riezman, Steve Shavell, Mike Sherer, Robert Shiller, John Taylor, and Oliver Williamson.

1. The social, behavioral, and economic sciences collectively represent about half of the nation's scientific community. That half of the community receives less than 3% of the National Science Foundation (NSF) budget, the primary source of research funds, and economics receives about 0.5%, but each year the benefits from economics research alone easily surpass many times the entire NSF annual budget for all sciences.
2. This can be particularly unhealthy because the most basic issues, those with high risk and broad, unfocused, and long-term implications, cannot be pursued. Furthermore, research with potentially undesirable implications from the point of view of funding sources might even be discouraged.
3. John Robert Meyer, Merton J. Peck, and Charles Zwick, *The Economics of Competition in the Transportation Industries* (Cambridge: Harvard University Press, 1959).
4. Late 1960s or early 1970s.

5. Alfred E. Kahn, Economics of Regulation: Principles and Institutions (New York: Wiley, 1970).

6. See Oliver Hart, *Firms, Contracts and Financial Structure* (Oxford: Clarendon Press, 1995); in addition to Oliver Williamson, *The Economic Institutions of Capitalism* (New York: Free Press, 1985); and Paul Milgrom and John Roberts, *Economics, Organization and Management* (Englewood Cliffs, N.J.: Prentice Hall, 1992).

7. Clifford Winston, "Economic Deregulation: Days of Reckoning for Microeconomists," *Journal of Economic Literature* (1993) 31(3):1263–89.

8. Ezra C. Seaman, *Essays in the Progress of Nations* (New York, 1852).

9. See, for example, Simon Kuznets, "National Income," in Edwin R. A. Seligman, ed., *Encyclopedia of the Social Sciences* (New York: Macmillan, 1993), 11:204–224; and M. Gilbert and George Jaszi, "National Product and the Income Statistics as an Aid to Economic Problems," *Dun's Review* (1944): 9–11, 32–38.

10. See Thomas Sargent, *The Conquest of American Inflation* (Princeton, N.J.: Princeton University Press, 1999), and John B. Taylor, "Monetary Policy and the Long Boom," *Review of the St. Louis Federal Reserve Bank*, December 1998: 3–12.

11. See Alan J. Auerbach and Laurence J. Kotlikoff, *Dynamic Fiscal Policy* (Cambridge: Cambridge University Press, 1987).

12. A. C. Pigou, *The Economics of Welfare* (London: Macmillan, 1920).

13. R. Coase, "The Problem of Social Cost," *Journal of Law & Economics* 3:1–44 (2007).

14. Presidential Executive Orders for Benefit Cost Analysis EO12291 and EO12866 are clear examples. The use of cost-benefit analysis in evaluating the relicensing of dams is required by the Electric Consumers Protection Act (1986). The use of the same tools is part of the legislation crafted in the Thompson-Levin Regulatory Reform Bill on the evaluation of federal regulations (S. 981). More than a dozen states have mandated cost-benefit analysis for the evaluation of their rules (see Robert W. Hahn, *In Defense of the Economic Analysis of Regulation* [Washington, D. C.: AEI Press, 2005]).

15. See Smith, V. K., and Y. Kaoru, "Signal or Noise: Explaining the Variation in Recreation Benefit Estimates." *American Journal of Agricultural Economics* (1990) 72:419–433; Smith, V. K., and J. C. Huang, "Can Markets Value Air Quality? A meta-analysis of hedonic property value models." *Journal of Political Economy* (1995) 103(11):209–227; Walsh, Johnson, and McKean, "Benefit Transfer of Outdoor Recreation Demand Studies, 1968–1988," *Water Resources Research* 28(3): 707–713.

16. There are many uses of these methods in tax assessment, litigation, cost-benefit analysis, and compensation for injuries to property. The *Appraisal Journal* contains many examples.

17. Myrick A. Freeman III, *The Measurement of Environmental and Resource Values: Theory and Methods* (Washington, D.C.: Resources for the Future, 1993); Joseph A. Herriges and Catherine L. Kling, eds., *Valuing Recreation and the Environment: Revealed Preference Methods in Theory and Practice* (Northampton, Mass.: Edward Elgar, 1999); J. B. Braden and C. D. Kolstad,

eds., *Measuring the Demand for Environmental Quality* (New York: North-Holland, 1991); V. Kerry Smith, *Estimating Economic Values for Nature: Methods for Non-market Valuation* (Cheltenham, United Kingdom: Edward Elgar, 1996).

18. J. H. Dales, *Pollution, Property and Prices* (Toronto: University of Toronto Press, 1968).

19. D. J. Dudek and J. Palmisano, "Emissions Trading: Why Is This Thoroughbred Hobbled?" *Columbia Journal of Environmental Law* 13(2) (1998): 217–256; R. W. Hahn, "Economic Prescriptions for Environmental Problems: How the Patient Followed the Doctor's Orders," *Journal of Economic Perspectives* 3(2) (1989): 95–114; R. W. Hahn and G. L. Hester, "Marketable Permits: Lessons from Theory and Practice," *Ecology Law Quarterly* 16 (1989): 361–406; R. W. Hahn and G. L. Hester, "Where Did All the Market Go? An Analysis of EPA's Emission Trading Program," *Yale Journal of Regulation* 6(1) (1989): 109–153; T. H. Tietenberg, *Emissions Trading: An Exercise in Reforming Pollution Policy* (Washington, D.C.: Resources for the Future, 1985); T. H. Tietenberg, "Economic Instruments for Environmental Regulation," *Oxford Review of Economic Policy* 6(1) (1990): 17–33.

20. Vernon L. Smith, "An Experimental Study of Competitive Market Behavior," *Journal of Political Economy* 70(2) (April 1962): 111–137.

21. M. Firoina and Charles R. Plott, "Committee Decisions under Majority Rule: An Experimental Study," *American Political Science Review* 72 (June 1978): 575–598.

22. Mike Levine and Charles R. Plott, "Agenda Influence and Its Implications," *Virginia Law Review* 63(4) (May 1977): 561–604.

23. Charles R. Plott and James Hong, "Rate Filing Policies for Inland Water Transportation: An Experimental Approach," *Bell Journal of Economics* 13 (Spring 1982): 1–19.

24. D. Grether, R. M. Isaac, and Charles R. Plott, "Alternative Methods of Allocating Airport Slots: Performance and Evaluation" (paper prepared for the Civil Aeronautics Board, Polinomics Research Laboratories, Pasadena, Calif., 1979); published as *The Allocation of Scarce Resources: Experimental Economics and the Problem of Allocating Airport Landing Slots* (Boulder, Colo.: Westview Press, 1989).

25. Dale Carlson, Charles Forman, John Ledyard, Nancy Olmstead, Charles Plott, David Porter, and Anne Sholtz, "An Analysis and Recommendation for the Terms of the RECLAIM Trading Credit" (South Coast Air Quality Management District, April 1993); Dale Carlson, Charles Forman, Nancy Olmstead, John Ledyard, David Porter, and Anne Sholtz, "An Analysis of the Information and Reporting Requirements, Market Architectures, Operational and Regulatory Issues, and Derivative Instruments for RECLAIM," (South Coast Air Quality Management District, July 1993).

26. Richard Baron, "Emission Trading: A Real Time Simulation," Paper presented at COP6, The Hague, IEA.AIE, November 13–24, 2000.

27. Charles R. Plott, "Research on Pricing in a Gas Transportation Network," Office of Economic Policy Technical Report no. 88-2, Federal Energy Regulatory

Commission (Washington, D.C., July 1988); Kevin McCabe, Stephen Rassenti, Stanley Reynolds, and Vernon Smith, "Market Competition, and Efficiency in Natural Gas Pipeline Networks," *Natural Gas* 6(3):23–26, October 1989.

28. Alvin E. Roth, Tayfun Sönmez, and M. Utku Ünver, "Kidney Exchange," *Quarterly Journal of Economics* 119(2) (May 2004): 457–488.

29. David Porter and Randi Wessen, "Market-Based Approaches for Controlling Space Mission Costs: The Cassini Resource Exchange," *Journal of Reduced Mission Operations Costs* 1(1): 9–25, March 1998.

30. For an account of this process, see John McMillan, "Selling Spectrum Rights," *Journal of Economic Perspectives* 8(3): 145–162; for an account of the use of experimental methods in this process, see Charles R. Plott, "Laboratory Experimental Testbeds: Application to the PCS Auction," *Journal of Economics and Management Strategy* 6(3) (Fall 1997): 605–638.

31. Of the thousands of applications, dozens have been videotaped and are publicly available at www.informs.org/Edelman. Examples of these are integrated planning techniques (at the U.S. Postal Service, Johnson County Public Schools, Chinese Planning and World Bank, and Pacific Lumber); inventory management (at Hewlett-Packard, IBM, and Electric Power Research Institute); linear programming (at United Airlines, Pacific Lumber, and Harris Corporation); logistics management (at IBM); marketing strategy (at AT&T); multicriteria decision making (at the U.S. Army, IBM, the Egyptian government, Marriott, and the Netherlands Rikswaterstraat); network optimization (at Procter & Gamble, AT&T, Bellcore, and NYNEX); optimization (at GRT, CITGO, Mobil, and the San Francisco Police Department); process control (at Cerestar); queuing (at New York City, the New Haven Fire Department, and L.L. Bean); risk analysis (at the National Aeronautics and Space Administration [NASA] and the Department of Energy [DOE]); scheduling models (at Pacific Gas and Electric and Blue Bell); simulation modeling (at Reynolds Metals and Monsanto); stochastic programming (at Electrobras and Cepel Brazil); supply chain management (at IBM); and transportation research (at the French National Railroad, the Military Airlift Command, and the Israeli Air Force). Countless other applications are recorded in the journal *Interfaces*.

32. Ann Markusen Peter Hall, Scott Campbell, and Sabina Deitrick *The Rise of the Gunbelt: The Military Remapping of Industrial America* (New York: Oxford University Press, 1991). Other useful references include National Research Council, *Rediscovering Geography: New Relevance for Science and Society*, Rediscovering Geography Committee, Board on Earth Sciences and Resources, Commission on Geosciences, Environment, and Resources, National Research Council (Washington, D.C.: National Academy Press, 1997); Susan Hanson, ed., *Ten Geographic Ideas That Changed the World* (New Brunswick, N.J.: Rutgers University Press, 1997); Susan Hanson, ed., *Geography's Inner Worlds: Pervasive Themes in Contemporary American Geography* (New Brunswick, N.J.: Rutgers University Press, 1992); and Paul Krugman, *Geography and Trade* (Cambridge, Mass.: MIT Press, 1991).

33. Gokhale, Jagadeesh, Laurence J. Kotlikoff, and John Sabelhous, "Understanding the Postwar Decline in U.S. Saving: A Cohort Analysis," in William Brainard

and George L. Perry, eds., *Brookings Papers on Economic Activity* 1 (1996): 315–390.

34. See Laurence J. Kotlikoff, *Generational Accounting* (New York: Free Press, 1992), and Alan J. Auerbach, Laurence J. Kotlikoff, and Will Leibfritz, eds., *Generational Accounting around the World* (Chicago: University of Chicago Press, 1999).

35. The interaction between basic research, applied research, and policy making in this area is discussed in Robert Haveman, *Poverty Policy and Poverty Research: The Great Society and the Social Sciences* (Madison: University of Wisconsin Press, 1987).

36. Nobel Prize winner James Tobin stated the following about the development of this official national economic indicator: "Adoption of [this] specific quantitative measure . . . will have durable and far-reaching political consequences . . . So long as any families are found below the official poverty line, no politician will be able to . . . ignore the repeated solemn acknowledgments of society's obligation to its poorer members." James Tobin, "Raising the Incomes of the Poor," in Kermit Gordon, ed., *Agenda for the Nation* (Washington, D.C.: Brookings Institution, 1970), 83.

COMMENT

Daniel S. Hamermesh

Charles Plott's synthesis is an insightful, useful summary of the general issues and specific chapters included in this volume. There is little to criticize in it—indeed, its magisterial expanse makes it nearly impervious to specific criticism. Instead, herein I discuss conditions under which economic ideas can affect policy and demonstrate the breadth of these applications in terms of the locus rather than the types of policies.

I should first note that the relationship between economic thought and policy is inherently different from that between the "hard" sciences and invention. For example, John Bardeen, Walter Brattain, and William Shockley were clearly responsible for the transistor that led directly to the "silicon age"; but no single economist and no single economic article can legitimately be identified as responsible for a particular policy change. Even George Stigler's apologia (1976) for economics, based on John Maynard Keynes's intellectual contributions that underlay the post–World War II reduction of the variance of aggregate activity, perhaps claims too much for a single researcher's ideas. Indeed, much of our success works through "the application of principles of economics," as Plott notes. These are simple principles, the things we teach in Econ 1, but anyone who has spent time in government knows how (fortunately apparently decreasingly) foreign they are to most people and how useful they are in restructuring policy debates.

Let me illustrate by examples of the areas where economic ideas might have the greatest influence on federal policy. One policy I was involved in was the New Jobs Tax Credit of 1977, a marginal credit that offered a large subsidy on employers' federal unemployment tax if they expanded employment beyond 102% of the previous year's level. As an antirecession job-creation measure, President Carter had proposed a small cut in the Federal Insurance Contributions Act (FICA) tax—essentially a subsidy to all employment. Recognizing the substitution effects of a subsidy at the margin, Senator Lloyd Bentsen, who led the legislative battle for this idea, was able to get this superior alternative to that proposed by Carter's economic advisors enacted. President Obama proposed essentially the same program during his 2008 campaign, but it was dropped from his legislative agenda, apparently because liberals objected to offering credits to employers, even though these would have expanded employment.

Another success story is the use of experience rating of unemployment insurance (UI) benefits, through differential taxation of employers depending on the costs they generate for the UI system, to reduce employment fluctuations by reducing incentives for layoffs. Although this idea is associated with the work of Marty Feldstein in the 1970s, it goes back to the 1920s when UI was first being discussed in the United States. It led many states to expand the range of UI tax rates and affected the discussions about financing unemployment compensation in such countries as Denmark and the Netherlands.

Both of these ideas were in areas where no policy had been established. Contrast those situations with that of the minimum wage, first adopted in the United States in 1938, on which labor economists have probably published more than on any other labor-market policy. While Card and Krueger (1995) achieved the pinnacle of political recognition in a speech by President Bill Clinton, their work had no more influence on policy than did the massive amount of research by other economists showing the detrimental employment effects of minimum wages. Because of the entrenchment and political symbolism of minimum wages, economic arguments have been used to support preconceived political positions, not to generate policy. In general, the best opportunity to affect policy does not arise in discussions of modifying existing policies, but when new policies are being developed.

Almost all of this volume and of Plott's comments are "inside the Beltway"—they deal with federal policies and programs. All also deal with legislation and regulation. Yet much of the influence of economics research has been at state and local levels, and much has been in policy that is constructed implicitly—through judicial precedent. In the former genre, consider school choice and vouchers. Proposed by Milton Friedman (1955), these policies have been increasingly discussed in policy debates at the state level and have been instituted in a few states and cities. Smoking bans were rare in the 1950s but are now widespread in the United States and other rich countries. Although they are no doubt partly the result of the income superiority of good health, Coasian notions of property rights have affected their structure.

Perhaps the best application of a single idea to legal precedent is the notion of hedonics in valuing lost earnings, based on Rosen (1974), but clearly going back to Adam Smith. Although the idea has met with substantial resistance in courts, it is still very active and will no doubt be used repeatedly in the future. Even something as mundane as my research on beauty (Hamermesh and Biddle 1994) has been picked up by attorneys in numerous cases involving lost earnings; and Borjas's work on the impacts of immigration (e.g., Borjas 1999) has recently been used as the intellectual basis of a growing number of class-action suits by native workers competing for jobs with illegal immigrants in large firms.[1]

Although basic research in economics, both theoretical and empirical, has demonstrably more than paid for itself in the practical realms of federal legislation, state and local legislation, and legal precedent, in the end our biggest contributions are the inchoate effects that we have on the public psyche and public debate. Over the past fifty years political debates involving economic issues have become more rarified: terms and concepts that were not known even to economists before 1929 are today familiar to all intelligent laypeople. These ideas are conveyed through the courses that we teach, particularly the introductory courses taken by most college students; but at some remove they stem from our basic research.

Despite these successes we have a long way to go. One despairs, for example, at people's views about the impact of immigration.[2] I am quite convinced, however, that new basic ideas eventually prove their worth— there is a reverse Gresham's law of economic ideas—and they do this because they are beautiful and because economists are and will continue to be concerned about explaining them to the public, both in classrooms and in the media.

Notes

1. E.g., Williams v. Mohawk Indus., Inc., 411 F.3d 1252 (11th Cir. 2005).
2. See *Economist*, December 15, 2007, 36.

References

Borjas, George J. "The Economic Analysis of Immigration." In Orley Ashenfelter and David Card, eds., *Handbook of Labor Economics,* vol. 3A. Amsterdam: Elsevier, 1999.

Card, David, and Alan B. Krueger. *Myth and Measurement.* Princeton, N.J.: Princeton University Press, 1995.

Friedman, Milton. "The Role of Government in Education." In Robert Solo, ed., *Economics and the Public Interest.* New Brunswick, N.J.: Rutgers University Press, 1955.

Hamermesh Daniel S., and Jeff E. Biddle. "Beauty and the Labor Market." *American Economic Review* 84 (December 1994): 1174–1194.

Rosen, Sherwin. "Hedonic Prices and Implicit Markets." *Journal of Political Economy* 82 (January 1974): 34–55.

Stigler, George J. "Do Economists Matter?" *Southern Economic Journal* 42 (January 1976): 347–354.

COMMENT

Daniel Newlon

I would like to congratulate Charles Plott on making a persuasive case for the benefits of economics research and the need for increased funding of basic economics research. His chapter and the other chapters in this volume on better living through economics provide a service to the economics profession. But this case could be more persuasive if his chapter downplayed invidious comparisons with other sciences and placed more emphasis on advances in basic science in economics that took place after the National Science Foundation started supporting basic economics in 1960.

The claim that "no other science aspires to such difficult goals as influencing an entire economy or even controlling a single market" will irritate rather than persuade other scientists that economics is an important basic science. This controversial statement (are studies of human biology, ecological systems, or the atmosphere, for example, less complicated than the study of markets?) detracts from the chapter. The case for economics as a useful science rests not on how complex its goals are but on how successful it is in reaching those goals. Later in his chapter Plott presents striking and disturbing (to an economist) comparisons of investment in basic science by the federal government in economics and other scientific disciplines. But physical and natural scientists would probably find it reasonable that more would be spent on their fields of science because of the expensive laboratory equipment needed for most basic research in them. To be more convincing, the chapter needs to show how the relatively small amount of funding for basic research is distorting economics and keeping it from realizing its full potential.

Plott's chapter takes a longer perspective because the lag from discovery to application often takes many decades. This long-term perspective works well in making the case for economics as a field of science based on robust principles and theories with useful applications but less well in making the case for more funding for basic research because the NSF started funding economics only in 1960. Plott mentions the research of only two of the thirty-eight Nobel laureates and none of the twenty-three John Bates Clark Medal winners supported by the NSF.

Let me illustrate how Plott's chapter could have made a more persuasive case for NSF funding of basic science by using one of his examples. In Plott's second observation he describes how basic research in macroeconomics led to dramatic improvements in macroeconomic policy, but he does not discuss the fundamental research of NSF grantees and eventual Nobel laureates Robert Lucas, Edward Prescott, Finn Kydland, and Edmund Phelps that transformed macroeconomics. NSF grantees also provided new policy instruments for central banks such as the Taylor rule, a monetary-policy rule that prescribes how much the central bank should adjust the nominal interest rate in response to changes in inflation and macroeconomic activity. And Ben Bernanke went directly from doing basic research supported by the NSF on inflation targeting to managing the Federal Reserve. New ideas, new tools, and people with grants from a small NSF program help improve long-run performance, i.e., higher economic growth, less unemployment, and lower inflation for the United States and for many other countries, and also help combat financial and economic crises.

The value of economics is widely recognized. Economists are sought for influential positions in government, academics, and business. Universities compete with each other to strengthen their research and teaching programs in economics. Undergraduate enrollments in economics have never been higher. But funding for basic economics research barely keeps pace with inflation. Why? This reflects at least in part our training in economics. We are all too aware of the societal costs of rent seeking and mistakenly treat arguments for more funding for basic economics research as lobbying. These chapters on better living through economics show us the way to be more effective advocates for our discipline.

Note

The views expressed in this comment are the personal views of an economist. They do not necessarily represent the views of the National Science Foundation or the U.S. government.

CHAPTER ONE

The Evolution of Emissions Trading

Thomas H. Tietenberg

Over the past thirty-plus years the use of transferable permits to control pollution has evolved from little more than an academic curiosity to the centerpiece of the U.S. program to control acid rain and international programs to control greenhouse gases. What explains this remarkable transition? How was the approach shaped by economic theory and empirical research?

Early History

By the late 1950s both economists and policy makers had formed quite well-developed and deeply entrenched visions of how pollution-control policy should be conducted. Unfortunately, these two visions were worlds apart.

Economists viewed the world through the eyes of Pigou (1920). Professor A. C. Pigou had argued that in the face of an externality, such as pollution, the appropriate remedy involved imposing a per-unit tax on the emissions from a polluting activity. The tax rate would be set equal to the marginal external social damage caused by the last unit of pollution at the efficient allocation. Faced with this tax rate on emissions, firms would internalize the externality. By minimizing their own costs, firms would simultaneously minimize the costs to society as a whole. According to this view, rational pollution-control policy involved putting a price on pollution.

Policy makers, on the other hand, preferred controlling pollution through a series of legal regulations ranging from controlling the location of polluting activities to the specification of emissions ceilings.

The result was a standoff in which policy makers focused on quantity-based policies (Kelman 1981) while economists promoted price-based remedies (Kneese and Schultze 1975). During the standoff the legal regimes prevailed. Taxes made little headway.

In 1960 Ronald Coase published a remarkable article in which he sowed the seeds for a different mind-set (Coase 1960). Claiming that Pigou's analysis had an excessively narrow focus, Coase argued that if property rights were made explicit and transferable, the market could play a substantial role not only in valuing these rights but also in assuring that they gravitated to their best use. To his fellow economists Coase pointed out that a property rights approach allowed the market to value the property rights (as opposed to the government in the Pigouvian approach). To policy makers Coase pointed out that the then-existing legal regimes provided no incentives for the rights to flow to their highest-valued use.

It remained for this key insight to become embedded in a practical program for controlling pollution. John Dales (1968) pointed out its applicability for water, and Tom Crocker (1966) did the same for air.

Theoretical Foundations

The appeal of emissions trading comes from its ability to achieve a pre-specified target at minimum cost even in the absence of any regulator information on control costs. Under this system permits are either auctioned off or distributed among emitters on the basis of some criterion such as historical use. As long as marginal abatement costs differ, incentives for trade exist. Firms with high marginal abatement costs buy permits from firms with low marginal costs until the market clears and the demand for permits equals the fixed supply.

Although the general properties of the system had been correctly anticipated by Dales and Crocker, it remained for Baumol and Oates (1971) to demonstrate them formally. Interestingly, their original article is not about a marketable permits system but rather about a charge system designed to meet a predetermined environmental target. Nonetheless, because the mathematics is perfectly equivalent for the two cases, the result derived for a charge system immediately was recognized as relevant for emissions trading.

Baumol and Oates proved that a uniform charge would result in meeting the predetermined environmental target cost-effectively. This was important because it implied that the control authority had to impose only a single tax rate on all polluters for the allocation of control responsibility to be achieved at minimum cost. Because all profit-maximizing firms would equate their marginal control costs to this uniform charge, marginal control costs would necessarily be equalized across emitters, precisely the condition required for a cost-effective allocation.

The main practical difference between the two approaches, however, was how the "correct" price would be determined. Although any price would result in equal marginal costs, only one price would be consistent with meeting the prespecified standard. In a tax and standards system this price would be found iteratively, through trial and error. In the marketable permits system the price would be established by the interaction of the demand for and supply of permits in the market. Not only would the control authority have no role in setting the price, but prices would be determined immediately, avoiding a long iterative procedure.

Baumol and Oates's results apply only in a special case—when all emissions from all emitters have the same impact on the environmental target (Tietenberg 1973). When the target involves meeting an ambient concentration standard, this special case has become known as the "uniformly mixed" case. One prominent example involves climate-change gases, because all emissions have the same impact on the environmental target regardless of the location from which they are emitted. The Baumol-Oates theorem is also valid when the environmental target is defined in terms of aggregate emissions rather than pollutant concentrations.

In many other cases, however, the location of the emissions does matter. In these cases the contribution of any unit of emissions to the environmental target (say, an ambient standard that sets a concentration limit at a particular location in the air or water) will depend on its location. All other things being equal, sources closer to the receptor are likely to have a larger impact than those farther away. For these cases neither a single tax rate nor a single permit price will suffice. Differentiation of rates among sources is necessary.

Montgomery (1972) proved the existence of a cost-effective permit-market equilibrium in this more complicated case. In general, those sources that have higher marginal impacts on the environmental target need to pay higher prices per unit of emissions, which can be implemented by having separate permits for each receptor location (Tietenberg 1973). When the environmental target is defined in terms of pollutant concentrations in the ambient air (as it is in most countries), the permits can be defined in terms of allowable concentration units. Although the emissions allowed by each permit would degrade the concentration at the associated receptor location by the same amount, each permit would allow differing amounts of emissions depending on the location of the emitter vis-à-vis the receptor. Each permit would authorize lower emissions for those emitters having a greater impact on the receptor location for each unit of emissions.

The Command and Control Policy Context

Stripped to its essentials, the U.S. approach to pollution control before the adoption of emissions trading, which remains partially intact today, relied on a command-and-control approach to controlling pollution. Ambient standards, which establish the highest allowable concentration of the pollutant in the ambient air or water for each conventional pollutant, represent the targets of this approach. To reach these targets, emission or effluent standards (legal discharge ceilings) are imposed on a large number of specific discharge points, such as stacks, vents, outfalls, or storage tanks.

The political acceptability of a cost-effectiveness, quantity-based approach grew as the difficulties with the command-and-control approach became more apparent. Both cost-effectiveness and a quantity-based approach seemed more consistent with, and a less radical departure from, traditional environmental policy. Existing pollution targets could be retained.

The Push for Reform

A pivotal point in the reform movement occurred when empirical cost-effectiveness studies showed that it was possible to reach the predetermined standards at a *much* lower cost than was the case with the traditional command-and-control regime. This remarkably consistent finding, produced for a number of different pollutants and geographic settings, offered the politically salable prospect of either achieving the existing environmental objectives at a much lower cost or obtaining a much higher level of environmental quality for the same expenditure. Theory proved that command-and-control regulation typically was not cost-effective, but empirical work demonstrated that the degree of inefficiency was very large indeed. This work suggested that the gains from reform would be large enough to outweigh the transition costs.

The Evolution of Emissions Trading

The Offset Policy: The Problem Becomes the Solution

The political opportunity to capitalize on these economic insights came in 1976.[1] By then it had become clear that a number of regions, designated "nonattainment" regions by the Clean Air Act, would fail to attain required ambient air-quality standards by the deadlines mandated in the act. Because further economic growth appeared to make the air worse, which was contrary to the intent of the statute, the Environmental Protection Agency (EPA) was faced with the unpleasant prospect of prohibiting many new businesses (those that would emit any of the pollutants responsible for nonattainment in a region) from entering these regions until the air quality met the ambient standards.

Prohibiting economic growth as the means to resolve air-quality problems was politically unpopular among governors, mayors, and many members of Congress. The EPA was facing a potential revolution. At this point, of necessity, the EPA considered its options. Was it possible to address the air-quality problem while facilitating further economic growth?

It was possible, as it turned out, and the means to achieve these apparently incompatible objectives involved the creation of an early form of emissions trading. Existing sources of pollution in the nonattainment area were encouraged to reduce their emission levels below the current legal requirements voluntarily. Once the EPA certified these excess reductions as "emission-reduction credits," they became transferable to new sources that wished to enter the area.

New sources were allowed to enter nonattainment regions provided they acquired sufficient emission-reduction credits from other facilities in the region that total regional emissions were lower (not just the same) after entry than before. (This was accomplished by requiring new sources to secure credits for 120% of the emissions they would add; the additional 20% would be "retired" as an improvement in air quality.) Known as the "offset policy," this approach not only allowed economic growth while improving air quality, the original objective, but also made economic growth the vehicle for improving the air. It turned the problem on its head and made it part of the solution.

It was not long before the federal government began to expand the scope of the program by allowing credits to be banked and permitting existing sources to trade with other existing sources. In this program not only was the government required to certify each reduction before it qualified for credit, but also credit trades were generally approved by the control authority on a case-by-case basis. Not surprisingly, the huge transaction costs associated with this level of government involvement limited the effectiveness of the program, leading one pair of commentators to subtitle an article about this program "Why Is This Thoroughbred Hobbled?" (Dudek and Palmisano 1988).

Tackling Acid Rain: The Sulfur Allowance Program

The most successful version of emissions trading to date has been its use in the United States to control electric utility emissions that contribute to acid rain. Under this innovative approach, allowances to emit sulfur oxides were allocated to individual plants, and the amount of authorized emissions was reduced in two phases so as to assure a reduction of 10 million tons in emissions from 1980 levels by the year 2010.

Perhaps the most interesting political aspect of this program was the role of trading in the passage of the acid-rain bill. Although reductions of acid-rain precursors had been sought in a succession of bills during the first two decades of Clean Air Act legislation, none had passed into law. With the inclusion of an emissions-trading program for sulfur in the bill, the compliance cost was reduced sufficiently to make passage politically possible.

Sulfur allowances form the heart of this tradable-permit program. An allocation formula determines the distribution of allowances to specified utilities. Each allowance, which provides a limited authorization to emit one ton of sulfur, is defined for a specific calendar year, but unused allowances can be carried forward into future years. They are fully transferable not only among the affected sources but even to individuals who may wish to "retire" the allowances, thereby denying their use to authorize emissions.

Emissions in this controlled sector cannot legally exceed the levels permitted by the allowances (allocated plus acquired). An annual year-end audit balances emissions with allowances. Utilities that emit more than is authorized by their holdings of allowances face a substantial per ton penalty and must forfeit allowances worth an equivalent number of tons in the following year.

This program has several innovative features that were influenced by analysis, but in the interest of brevity I will mention only one—assuring the availability of allowances by instituting an auction market. Although allowances can be transferred either by private sale or in the annual auction, historically the problem with private sales was that prices were confidential, so transactors operated in the dark. Because of an absence of knowledge not only about potential buyers and sellers but also about prices, transaction costs were high; the lack of price transparency inhibited effective emissions trading.

The EPA facilitated this market by instituting an auction market run by the Chicago Board of Trade. During the negotiations utilities fought the idea of an auction because they knew that it would raise their costs significantly. Whereas under the traditional means of distributing allowances utilities would be given the allowances free of charge, under an auction they would have to buy these allowances at the full market price, a potentially significant additional financial burden.

To gain the advantages an auction offers for improving the efficiency of the market while not imposing a large financial burden on utilities, the EPA established what has become known as a zero-revenue auction (Hahn and Noll 1982). Each year the EPA withholds from its allocation to utilities somewhat less than 3% of the allocations and auctions these off. In the auction these allowances are allocated to the highest bidders, and successful buyers pay their actual bid price (not a common market-clearing price). The proceeds from the sale of these allowances are refunded to the utilities from which the allowances were withheld on a proportional basis. Although this auction design is not efficient because it provides incentives for inefficient strategic behavior (Hausker 1992; Cason 1993), the degree of inefficiency is apparently small (Ellerman et al. 2000).

Emissions Trading in the Kyoto Protocol on Climate Change

In December 1997 industrial countries and countries with economies in transition (primarily the former Soviet republics) agreed to legally binding emission targets for greenhouse gases at the Kyoto Conference. The Kyoto Protocol became effective in February 2005. It authorizes three cooperative implementation mechanisms that involve tradable permits—Emissions Trading, Joint Implementation, and the Clean Development Mechanism.

- Emissions Trading (ET) allows trading of "assigned amounts" (the national quotas established by the Kyoto Protocol) among countries listed in Annex B of the protocol, primarily the industrialized nations and the economies in transition.
- Under Joint Implementation (JI) Annex B parties can receive emission-reduction credit when they help finance specific projects that reduce net emissions in another Annex B country. This "project-based" program is designed to exploit opportunities in Annex B countries that have not yet become fully eligible to engage in the ET program.

- The Clean Development Mechanism (CDM) enables Annex B countries to finance emission-reduction projects in non–Annex B countries (primarily developing countries) and to receive certified emission reductions (CERs) for doing so. These CERs can then be used along with in-country reductions to fulfill "assigned amount" obligations.

These programs have, in turn, spawned others. Even individual companies are involved. BP, an energy company, has established company-wide goals and an intracompany trading program to help individual units within the firm meet those goals. Despite the fact that the United States has not signed the Kyoto Protocol, even American companies, states, and municipalities have accepted caps (some voluntary and some mandatory) on carbon dioxide (CO_2) and methane emissions and are using emissions trading to help meet those goals. The first mandatory program to control CO_2 in the United States, the Northeast's Regional Greenhouse Gas initiative (RGGI), took effect on January 1, 2009.

The European Emissions Trading System (EU ETS)

The largest emissions-trading program for climate change has been developed by the European Union (EU) to facilitate implementation of the Kyoto Protocol (Kruger and Pizer 2004). The EU program covers twenty-five countries, including the ten "accession" countries, most of which are former members of the Soviet bloc. Its first three years, from 2005 through 2007, constituted a trial phase. The second phase coincides with the first Kyoto commitment period, beginning in 2008 and continuing through 2012. Subsequent negotiations will specify future details.

Initially, the program covers only CO_2 emissions from four broad sectors: iron and steel, minerals, energy, and pulp and paper. All European installations in these sectors larger than established thresholds, some 12,000 in all, are included in the program.

Lessons about Program Effectiveness

Economic principles have been used to design these programs, and economic analysis has helped shape their evolution and assess their success. Two types of studies have been used to evaluate cost savings and air-quality impacts: ex ante analyses, which depend on computer simulations, and ex post analyses, which examine the actual implementation experience.

The vast majority, although not all, of the large number of published ex ante studies have found command-and-control outcomes to be significantly more costly than the lower-cost alternative (Tietenberg 2006). Although detailed ex post analyses are relatively rare, two detailed evaluations of the sulfur allowance program have been conducted (Carlson et al. 2000; Ellerman et al. 2000). Although both found that considerable cost savings had been achieved in meeting the air-quality goals following the implementation of the program, their interpretation of the sources of these savings differs. While Ellerman and colleagues found substantial savings due to the structure of the sulfur allowance program, Carlson and colleagues attributed a larger share of the lower costs to factors they saw as exogenous to the trading program (declines in the price of low-sulfur coal and improvements in technology that lowered the cost of fuel switching).

Conventional wisdom holds that emissions trading lowers costs but has no affect on air quality, but that seems to be an oversimplification. In retrospect, we now know that the feasibility, level, and enforcement of the emissions cap can all be positively affected by the introduction of emissions trading. In addition, emissions trading may trigger environmental effects from pollutants that are not covered by the limit. Although most of these external effects are desirable (such as the associated reduction in mercury emissions when coal-fired plants switch to natural gas), some are detrimental (such as the leakage effects that occur when polluting plants relocate to avoid the regulation) (Tietenberg 2006).

In general, air quality has improved substantially under emissions trading. For some programs, the degree to which credit for these improvements can be attributed solely to emissions trading (as opposed to exogenous factors or complementary policies) is not completely clear.

For early credit programs, such as the offset policy, the magnitude of the positive air-quality increases and cost savings has been smaller, and the achievements have occurred more slowly than anticipated by the original proponents. Constraints imposed on early credit programs by an excessively cautious bureaucracy took their toll. Fortunately, the number and intensity of these constraints have tended to diminish over time as familiarity with this approach increases bureaucratic comfort with it.

Lessons for Program Design

Baseline plus Credits versus Cap and Trade

Emissions trading programs fit into one of two general categories: credit programs or cap-and-trade programs.

- Credit trading, the approach taken in the offset program (the earliest program), allows emission reductions above and beyond baseline legal requirements to be certified as tradable credits.
- In a cap-and-trade program a total aggregate emissions limit (the cap) is defined and then allocated among users. Compliance is established by simply comparing actual use with the assigned firm-specific cap as adjusted by any acquired or sold permits.

Establishing the baseline for credit programs in the absence of an existing permit system can be challenging. For example, the basic requirement in the Clean Development Mechanism component of the Kyoto Protocol is "additionality." Deciding whether reductions are "additional" (as opposed to reductions that would have occurred anyway) requires establishing a baseline against which the reductions can be measured.

Defining procedures that assure that the baselines do not allow unjustified credits is no small task. A pilot program for Activities Implemented Jointly, a form of joint implementation which was established at the first Conference of the Parties in 1995, demonstrated the difficulties of assuring additionality. Requiring proof of additionality was found to impose very high transaction costs, as well as introducing considerable ex ante uncertainty about the actual reductions that could be achieved (Schwarze 2000). By imposing a cap that can be directly compared with actual emissions, cap-and-trade programs avoid this complication and reduce transaction costs significantly.

Price Volatility, Caps, and Safety Valves

In contrast to an alternative policy such as environmental taxation, which provides some assurance of stable prices, in the face of "shocks" a cap can lead to politically unacceptable permit price increases. For example, participants in an emissions-trading program in the greater Los Angeles area (known as the Regional Clean Air Incentives Market, RECLAIM) experienced a very large unanticipated demand for power that could be accommodated only by increasing the output from older, more polluting plants. Supplies from the normal sources of power, including imported hydropower from the Pacific Northwest, were severely diminished by a variety of circumstances. The large increase in demand for emissions permits resulting from the need to bring these "dirty" plants on line, coupled with the fixed supply of permits, caused permit prices to soar in a way that had never been anticipated.

To gain the political support needed for implementation, modern emissions-trading programs have had to deal with participant concern about volatile prices. The general prescription is to allow a "safety valve" in.the form of a predefined penalty that would be imposed on all emissions over the cap once prices exceeded a predefined threshold (Jacoby and Ellerman 2004). This per-unit penalty would typically be lower than the sanction imposed for noncompliance during normal situations (when compliance would be much easier). In effect, this penalty would set the maximum price that would be incurred in the pursuit of environmental goals in unusually trying times. Safety valves can also be accompanied by a price floor (Pizer, 2004; Newell et al., 2005).

In the case of RECLAIM, when permit prices went over a predefined threshold, the program was suspended until the control authorities figured out what to do, and an alternative (substantial) fee per ton was imposed in the interim. The revenue was used to subsidize additional alternative emissions reductions, typically from sources not covered by the cap (Harrison 2002).

Initial Allocation Method

Most operating systems either exclusively or mainly allocate permits free of charge to the program participants on the basis of some criterion (historical authorized emissions, for example). Free distribution has advantages and disadvantages. Research on how preexisting distortions in the tax system affect the efficiency of the chosen policy instrument demonstrates that the ability to use revenue from the sale of permits to reduce these distortions (rather than giving them to users) can enhance the efficiency of the system by a large amount.[2] That conclusion, of course, supports the use of revenue-raising instruments such as taxes or auctioned permits rather than free distribution (Goulder et al. 1999; Parry et al. 1999).

How revenues are distributed, however, also affects the relative attractiveness of alternative approaches to environmental protection from the point of view of various stakeholders. To the extent that stakeholders can influence policy choice, using free distribution in general and prior use in particular as allocation criteria has increased the implementation feasibility of emissions trading (Svendsen 1999). This historical experience, however, need not be decisive for the future because the empirical evidence suggests that the amount of revenue needed to hold users harmless during the change is only a fraction of the total revenue available from auctioning (Bovenberg and Goulder 2001). Allocating all permits free of charge is therefore not inevitable in principle, even when political feasibility considerations affect the design.

Basing the initial allocation on prior use can also promote inefficient strategic behavior. An initial allocation based on historic use creates an incentive to intensify emissions before the implementation date (to qualify for a larger initial allocation). In emissions trading this effect has generally been minimized by basing initial allocations on a combination of activity levels, which are historically based, and emission rates per unit of activity based on standard good-practice norms (Raymond, 2003).

Economic research (Parry et al. 2006) has also demonstrated that auctioned allowances can have more desirable distributional properties than freely distributed allowances. In response to this new evidence on both the efficiency and the distributional advantages of auctioned permits, several states in a new emissions-trading program to control carbon emissions in the Northeast (the Regional Greenhouse Gas Initiative) have committed to auctioning off 100% of their allowances. The revenues are typically used to promote energy efficiency or renewable energy resource development, strategies that tend to lower the future trajectories of allowance prices.

Spatial Aspects

Traditional theory presumes that the commodity being traded is homogeneous. In practice, without homogeneity, emission trades can confer external benefits or costs on third parties, resulting in allocations that do not maximize net benefits.

One example of an external effect involves pollutants where the location of the emission, as well as the amount of the emission, matters. Spatial issues arise whenever the transfer could alter the point of emission. Although, as noted earlier, optimal permit systems can theoretically be defined to address spatial issues, in practice they have not been used because of their inherent complexity. Practical solutions for incorporating source location into an emissions-trading program to deal with these spatial issues is a difficult but manageable proposition (Tietenberg 1995).

One possibility involves dividing the control region into zones. However, zonal permit systems that can be initiated with plausible amounts of information are typically not very effective (Tietenberg 2006, chap. 4). When permits cannot be traded across zonal boundaries, the cost penalty can be very sensitive to the initial allocation of zonal caps. Studies suggest that no conventional rule of thumb for allocating the required emissions reduction among zones comes close to the cost-effective allocation.

An alternative strategy, now also common, involves the creation of trading rules that govern individual transactions. One trading-rule strategy, known locally as "regulatory tiering," applies more than one regulatory regime at a time. In the sulfur allowance program sulfur emissions are controlled both by the regulations designed to achieve local ambient air-quality standards and by the sulfur allowance trading rules. All transactions have to satisfy both programs. Thus trading is not restricted by spatial considerations (national one-for-one trades are possible), but the use of acquired allowances is subject to local regulations protecting the ambient standards. Unlike programs that restrict all transactions or employ a much stricter cap to prevent spatial concentration peaks (known as "hot spots"), this approach prohibits only the few transactions that would result in a hot spot. Ex ante empirical analysis of this approach suggests that regulatory tiering may well have been an effective compromise (Atkinson and Tietenberg 1982).

The Temporal Dimension

Ex post evaluations have revealed that the temporal aspects of emissions-trading provisions have been quite important for both lowering costs and promoting quicker reductions. Emissions-trading systems can incorporate temporal flexibility by allowing banking, borrowing, or both. *Banking* means holding a permit beyond its designated date for later use or sale. *Borrowing* means using a permit before its designated date.

The economic case for this flexibility is that it allows sources to time their abatement investments optimally. Flexibility in timing is important not only for reasons that are unique to each firm but also for reasons that relate to the market as a whole. When everyone makes control investments at the same time, it strains the supply capacity of the system and drives input prices up.

When only the aggregate stock of emissions over some period matters, the price of permits would normally rise at the rate of interest, and the holders would automatically choose to use them in the manner that minimizes the present value of abatement costs. Decentralized decision making in this case would be compatible with social objectives. Special temporal controls would be counterproductive.

When a single aggregate emissions cap is not sufficient to protect against damage from concentration peaks, timing becomes a separate control variable. Situations where the damaging effects of peak concentrations are important open the door to a potentially important market failure (Kling and Rubin 1997). Although firms have an incentive to minimize the present value of abatement cost, they do not have an efficient incentive to minimize the present value of all costs, including the damage caused by hot spots. In general, the resulting incentive is to delay abatement (abating too little during the early periods and concentrating too much abatement later).

Delaying abatement, however, is not always the optimal choice for the firm, even in an unrestricted permit market. When over time marginal abatement costs rise, marginal production costs fall, aggregate emission targets decline, or output prices rise, firms have an incentive to bank rather than borrow permits. In the sulfur allowance program, because of the ability to bank emissions, firms reduced emissions early (when concentrations were high) and increased them later (when concentrations were lower). In this case banking clearly reduced concentrations and reduced costs (Ellerman et al. 2000).

Concluding Comments

Emissions trading provides a good example of the "pendulum" theory of public policy. In the early 1970s emissions trading was considered an academically intriguing but ultimately impractical idea. It had trouble getting on the national agenda. Reformers had few successes.

However, that changed once the expectations created by economic analysis had been confirmed on the ground by the sulfur allowance program. It demonstrated not only the feasibility of the approach but also its effectiveness. Emboldened by success, expectations and enthusiasm started to outrun reality.

In the final stage, the one I believe we are now in, reality is beginning to reassert itself. My sense is that both policy makers and academics are beginning to realize not only that emissions trading has achieved a considerable measure of success, but also that it has specific weaknesses. It has also been interesting to observe the growing prominence of auctioned permits, moving the whole enterprise much closer to the economic point of view that prevailed at the outset.

Economic analysis has helped us understand that not all emissions-trading programs are equal. Some designs are better than others. Furthermore, one size does not fit all. Emissions-trading programs can (and should) be tailored to each specific application.

The evidence suggests that although emissions trading is no panacea, well-designed programs that are targeted at pollution problems appropriate for this form of control are beginning to occupy an important and durable niche in the evolving menu of environmental policies. This economic idea has come of age.

Notes

1. Because of limitations of space, only a small sampling of the operating programs can be mentioned here. Emissions trading has been used in many other

contexts, including the RECLAIM program in the greater Los Angeles area (Hall and Walton 1996), the program to phase out lead in gasoline (Nussbaum 1992), the NOx Budget Trading Program in the Northeast (Farrell 2001), reducing or eliminating ozone-depleting chemicals (Stavins and Hahn, 1993) emissions averaging of industrial toxics (Anderson 2001), and controlling particulates in Santiago, Chile (O'Ryan 1996; Montero et al. 2002).
2. One example is the use of these revenues to allow a lowering of income tax rates, thus reducing the distortions associated with taxing income.

References

Anderson, R. C. (2001). *The United States Experience with Economic Incentives for Pollution Control*. Washington, D.C.: National Center for Environmental Economics.

Atkinson, S. E., and T. H. Tietenberg (1982). "The Empirical Properties of Two Classes of Designs for Transferable Discharge Permit Markets." *Journal of Environmental Economics and Management* 9(2): 101–121.

Baumol, W. J., and W. E. Oates (1971). "The Use of Standards and Prices for Protection of the Environment." *Swedish Journal of Economics* 73: 42–54.

Bovenberg, A. L., and L. H. Goulder (2001). "Neutralizing Adverse Impacts of CO_2 Abatement Policies: What Does It Cost?" In *Behavorial and Distributional Effects of Environmental Policy*, ed. C. E. Carraro and G. E. Metcalf. Chicago: University of Chicago Press: 45–85.

Carlson, C., D. Burtraw, M. Cropper, and K. Palmer (2000). "Sulfur Dioxide Control by Electric Utilities: What Are the Gains from Trade?" *Journal of Political Economy* 108(6): 1292–1326.

Cason, T. N. (1993). "Seller Incentive Properties of EPA's Emission Trading Auction." *Journal of Environmental Economic Management* 25(2): 177–195.

Coase, R. (1960). "The Problem of Social Cost." *Journal of Law & Economics* 3(October): 1–44.

Crocker, T. D. (1966). "The Structuring of Atmospheric Pollution Control Systems." In *The Economics of Air Pollution*, ed. H. Wolozin. New York: W. W. Norton & Co., 61–86.

Dales, J. H. (1968). *Pollution, Property and Prices*. Toronto, University of Toronto Press.

Dudek, D. J., and J. Palmisano (1988). "Emissions Trading: Why Is This Thoroughbred Hobbled?" 13(2): 217–256.

Ellerman, A. D., P. L. Joskow, R. Schmalensee, J-P. Montero, and E. Bailey (2000). *Markets for Clean Air: The U.S. Acid Rain Program*. Cambridge, U.K.: Cambridge University Press.

Farrell, A. (2001). "Multi-lateral Emission Trading: Lessons from Inter-state NOx Control in the United States." *Energy Policy* 29(13): 1061–1072.

Goulder, L. H., I. W. H. Parry, R. C. Williams III, and D. Burtraw (1999). "The Cost-Effectiveness of Alternative Instruments for Environmental Protection in a Second-Best Setting." *Journal of Public Economics* 72(3): 329–360.

Hahn, R. W., and G. L. Hester (1989). "Where Did All the Markets Go? An Analysis of EPA's Emission Trading Program." *Yale Journal of Regulation* 6(1): 109–153.

Hahn, R. W., and R. G. Noll (1982). "Designing a Market for Tradeable Emission Permits." In *Reform of Environmental Regulation*, ed. W. A. Magat. Cambridge, Mass.: Ballinger, 119–146.

Hall, J. V., and A. L. Walton (1996). "A Case Study in Pollution Markets: Dismal Science vs. Dismal Reality." *Contemporary Economic Policy* 14(2): 67–78.

Harrison, D., Jr. (2002). "Tradable Permits for Air Quality and Climate Change." In *The International Yearbook of Environmental and Resource Economics, 2002/2003*, ed. T. Tietenberg and H. Folmer. Cheltenham, U.K.: Edward Elgar, 311–372.

Hausker, K. (1992). "The Politics and Economics of Auction Design in the Market for Sulfur Dioxide Pollution." *Journal of Policy Analysis and Management* 11(4): 553–572.

Jacoby, H. D., and A. D. Ellerman (2004). "The Safety Valve and Climate Policy." *Energy Policy* 32(4): 481–491.

Kelman, S. (1981). *What Price Incentives? Economists and the Environment*. Westport, Conn.: Greenwood Publishing Group.

Kling, C., and J. Rubin (1997). "Bankable Permits for the Control of Environmental Pollution." *Journal of Public Economics* 64(1): 99–113.

Kneese, A. V., and C. L. Schultze (1975). *Pollution, Prices, and Public Policy*. Washington, D.C.: Brookings Institution.

Kruger, J. A., and W. A. Pizer (2004). "Greenhouse Gas Trading in Europe—The New Grand Policy Experiment." *Environment* 46(8): 8–23.

Montero, J. P., J. M. Sanchez, and R. Katz (2002). "A Market-Based Environmental Policy Experiment in Chile." *Journal of Law & Economics* 45(1, pt. 1): 267–287.

Montgomery, W. D. (1972). "Markets in Licenses and Efficient Pollution Control Programs." *Journal of Economic Theory* 5(3): 395–418.

Newell, R., W. Pizer, and J. Zhang (2005). "Managing Permit Markets to Stabilize Prices." *Environmental & Resource Economics* 31(2): 133–157.

Nussbaum, B. D. (1992). "Phasing Down Lead in Gasoline in the U.S.: Mandates, Incentives, Trading and Banking." *In Climate Change: Designing a Tradeable Permit System*, ed. T. Jones and J. Corfee-Morlot. Paris: Organization for Economic Co-operation and Development, 21–34.

O'Ryan, R. (1996). "Cost-Effective Policies to Improve Urban Air Quality in Santiago, Chile." *Journal of Environmental Economics and Management* 31(3): 302–313.

Parry, I. W. H., H. Sigman, M. Walls, and R. C. Williams III (2006). "The Incidence of Pollution Control Policies." In *The International Yearbook of Environmental and Resource Economics, 2006/2007*, ed. T. Tietenberg and H. Folmer. Cheltenham, U.K.: Edward Elgar, 1–42.

Parry, I. W. H., R. C. Williams, and L. H. Goulder (1999). "When Can Carbon Abatement Policies Increase Welfare? The Fundamental Role of Distorted Factor Markets." *Journal of Environmental Economics and Management* 37(1): 52–84.

Pigou, A. C. (1920). *The Economics of Welfare*. London: Macmillan.

Pizer, W. A. (2002). "Combining Price and Quantity Controls to Mitigate Global Climate Change." *Journal of Public Economics* 85(3): 409–434.

Raymond, L. (2003). *Private Rights in Public Resources: Equity and Property Allocation in Market-Based Environmental Policy.* Washington, D.C.: Resources for the Future.

Schwarze, R. (2000). "Activities Implemented Jointly: Another Look at the Facts." *Ecological Economics* 32(2): 255–267.

Seskin, E. P., R. J. Anderson, Jr, and R. O. Reid (1983). "An Empirical Analysis of Economic Strategies for Controlling Air Pollution." *Journal of Environmental Economics and Management* 10(2): 112–124.

Stavins, R., and R. Hahn (1993). *Trading in Greenhouse Permits: A Critical Examination of Design and Implementation Issues.* Cambridge, Mass,: John F. Kennedy School of Government, Harvard University.

Svendsen, G. T. (1999). "U.S. Interest Groups Prefer Emission Trading: A New Perspective." *Public Choice* 101(1–2): 109–128.

Tietenberg, T. H. (1973). "Controlling Pollution by Price and Standard Systems: A General Equilibrium Analysis." *Swedish Journal of Economics* 75: 193–203.

—— (1995). "Tradable Permits for Pollution Control When Emission Location Matters: What Have We Learned?" *Environmental and Resource Economics* 5(2): 95–113.

—— (2006). *Emissions Trading: Principles and Practice.* 2nd ed. Washington, D.C.: Resources for the Future.

COMMENT

Wallace E. Oates

Tietenberg's chapter tells the fascinating story of the evolution of emissions trading as a new and highly innovative policy instrument and provides a careful, insightful assessment of its strengths and limitations. There is no one better positioned than Tietenberg to tell this story. He was a very early proponent and careful analyst of emissions trading. He wrote the first book (1985) on this new approach to environmental regulation, which is now available in a valuable second edition (2006).

This is an important juncture at which to review our experience with emissions trading in view of its current ubiquitous appeal. Emissions-trading systems (ETSs) are in vogue; they are being introduced around the globe as a regulatory instrument for the control of many forms of polluting activities, most notably emissions of greenhouse gases. Moreover, these new measures have widespread support from environmental groups, the business community, and regulators themselves. Here I offer two observations on the evolution of emissions trading and comment briefly on Tietenberg's insightful treatment of the limitations of this policy instrument.

First, the advent of ETSs provides testimony to the power of ideas in the policy arena. Thirty-five years ago the idea of emissions trading was just that–an idea that a small group of economists talked about among themselves and discussed in their classes with diagrams on a blackboard. But emissions trading has now made its way from the ivory towers of academe to the front ranks of environmental management. As Tietenberg points out, a serious confrontation over nonattainment of air-quality standards in the 1970s opened the door to the introduction of so-called pollution offsets. But once this innovative new measure was in place, the existing analysis and empirical work of economists interested in environmental issues provided a solid and persuasive foundation for this approach to environmental management. Economists had been making the general case for the use of economic incentives instead of the more traditional command-and-control techniques, and once they had a foot in the door with pollution offsets, their case was heard with increasing interest and understanding by the policy-making community (including environmentalists and industry interests). My point here is that a well-developed and carefully articulated idea for an alternative to a troubled policy can be a powerful force in a political setting. Ideas matter.[1]

My second observation concerns the role of state and local governments in the evolution of emissions trading. In the literature on fiscal federalism, the point is often made that decentralized policy making in the setting of multilevel government offers an opportunity for the introduction of a variety of new approaches to address policy problems. State and local governments, in short, can provide what Justice Louis Brandeis in 1932 called a "laboratory" in which to "try novel social and economic experiments without risk to the rest of the country" (Osborne 1988, p. 181). This role of encouraging experimentation and promoting "technical progress" in public policy is often described as "laboratory federalism." The evolution of emissions trading provides a nice example of laboratory federalism at work. The 1977 Amendments to the Clean Air Act directed the Environmental Protection Agency (EPA) to establish a general rubric for the transfer of emissions entitlements among sources, and the EPA did just that. But it was left to the individual states to define their programs in more precise terms and to implement specific measures for their own jurisdictions. Thus it was the states (and, in some cases, their local governments) that actually worked out (with some EPA oversight) the form that emissions trading would take in their areas, and it was this experience that over time showed that such systems can actually work: they can achieve their environmental objectives effectively and efficiently. Without this experience, I seriously doubt that policy makers would have been willing to introduce such a new and unfamiliar policy instrument as emissions trading on a national scale, as took place under the 1990 Clean Air Act Amendments to address the problem of acid rain.

Finally, lest we exaggerate the role of emissions trading, it is important, as Tietenberg points out, to understand its limitations. Here I want to focus on two important issues. First, ETSs work best and most simply where there is not a significant spatial dimension to the pollution problems. If exactly where the polluting emissions take place makes a significant difference, things get more complicated, for this means that environmental quality depends on the spatial pattern of permit holdings. We can no longer, in principle, allow one-for-one trading in a permit market because the emissions of some sources will be more damaging than those from other sources. There are ways to address this issue (for example, by establishing "trading zones" or modifying trading rules such that sources' holdings of permits reflect their individual contributions to local levels of pollution), but they make the system significantly more complex and typically reduce the extent (and efficiency) of the permit market.

It is worth noting that an important case where this issue does not arise is global climate change. A ton of CO_2 emissions, for instance, will have the same impact on climate irrespective of whether it takes place in the United States or India. This makes emissions trading especially appealing in that one-for-one trades on a global scale are, in principle, perfectly efficient. However, in certain other settings where the location of emissions matters, the issue becomes more problematic.

Second, as Martin Weitzman (1974) taught us some time ago, in a setting of uncertainty, the use of so-called quantity instruments, such as emissions trading, can involve serious risks. In a setting where regulators are uncertain about the costs of pollution abatement, setting a cap on levels of polluting activities can prove inordinately costly. If regulators underestimate the costs of pollution control and set an excessively stringent cap and if marginal abatement costs tend to rise rapidly over the relevant range, an ETS can impose costs on the economy far above those envisioned and perhaps well in excess of the benefits of the program. This, incidentally, is a distinct danger under global warming, where measures to cut emissions of greenhouse gases on a large scale may be quite expensive and where the precise timing of emissions is not as important. This perspective has led several economists to argue that a primary reliance on taxes on carbon emissions is preferable to a cap-and-trade approach (e.g., Nordhaus 2007).

In sum, emissions trading is an exciting, major innovation in public policy with its roots in economics research. Both theoretical work and careful empirical studies helped make clear the enormous potential of this new policy instrument for effective and efficient environmental management. Much credit must also go to a number of economists who devoted a major effort to careful explanation and support of this new measure in the debate in the policy arena.

Note

1. For a more general treatment of the way in which economic ideas (drawing on both theoretical and empirical research) have come to influence environmental policy, see Oates (2000).

References

Nordhaus, William D. 2007. "To Tax or Not to Tax: Alternative Approaches to Slowing Global Warming." *Review of Environmental Economics and Policy* 1(1): 26–44.

Oates, Wallace E. 2000. "From Research to Policy: The Case of Environmental Economics." *University of Illinois Law Review* 1: 135–153.

Osborne, David. 1988. *Laboratories of Democracy.* Boston: Harvard Business School Press.

Tietenberg, T. H. 1985. *Emissions Trading: An Exercise in Reforming Pollution Policy.* Washington, D.C.: Resources for the Future. 2nd ed., 2006.

Weitzman, M. L. 1974. "Prices vs. Quantities." *Review of Economic Studies* 41: 477–491.

CHAPTER TWO

Better Living through Improved Price Indexes

Michael J. Boskin

Few areas of economics research have produced societal benefits as consequential in recent decades as price-index research. This research has changed how inflation, real gross domestic product (GDP), and productivity are measured, thus providing more accurate information on these key economic indicators for private investors, workers, managers, and public policy makers. These improvements have led to more accurate indexing of government benefit programs and taxes and thus to a lower national debt. And they literally change history, or at least the interpretation of some of it, for example, by revealing that real wages and median income in recent decades have grown (albeit more slowly than previously), not stagnated. Cumulatively the research adds greatly not just to improved measurement of inflation but to economists' general understanding of the dynamics of economic growth. For example, it details the importance of new products, improvement in the quality of existing products, and other innovations in generating rising living standards. Still, there is much more improvement to come in price measurement and in research on it.

Accurately measuring prices and their rate of change is central to almost every public and private economic issue and discussion, including the conduct of monetary policy, the measurement of economic progress over time and across countries, and the cost and structure of indexed government spending programs and taxes. Most of us are familiar with the prices of many things we purchase. We know what we paid recently for a pound of ground beef or a quart of milk. Renters know how much they pay in rent.

Measuring prices, therefore, may seem simple and straightforward, but it is not.

The purpose of a price index is to summarize information on the prices of multiple goods and services over time. Consumer spending accounts for about two-thirds of U.S. GDP. The Consumer Price Index (CPI) and the Personal Consumption Expenditure (PCE) deflator are designed to summarize the prices of goods purchased by consumers over time. In a hypothetical society with only one good, say, one type of food, we would not need a price index; we would just follow the price of that one good. When there are many goods and services, however, we need a method for averaging the price changes or aggregating the information on the many different prices. The rate of change of prices—inflation—is important in both macro- and microeconomics. Estimating inflation and real growth, for example, requires measures of price changes, and in a flexible, dynamic modern market economy, obtaining accurate measures is complicated. A single large superstore may contain 50,000 separately priced items. Within that individual store new items are continually introduced and old items discontinued. The quality of many items improves in some objective way—greater energy efficiency, more durability, or less maintenance, to name a few. Of course, improvements are claimed for many more items. When quality really does improve but the price stays the same, the real price has fallen. How to summarize what happened to prices in just one store over a period as short as one month is complicated, even with modern scanner technology. Doing so for the entire economy is vastly more complex.

To obtain information on the average price change requires us not only to measure the prices but also to weight the various components of the index. Weighting each price change equally would be simple but not very revealing. For example, if the price of Red Delicious apples fell by 5% and rent rose by 5%, an index in which price changes were weighted equally would suggest that there had been no change in the overall price level. But that would be silly. We need to weight goods on which consumers spend more of their income more heavily than those on which they spend less. Hence we also need data on expenditures and quantities purchased.

The United States CPI and the Cost of Living

When economists try to measure the "true" inflation rate—the rate of change of prices—their purpose is to answer the question, "How much more income would consumers need to be just as well off with a new set of prices as the old?" Thus a cost-of-living concept is at the core of proper measures of prices and of changes in prices. This clearly involves tracking how consumers respond to changes in the relative prices of various goods. Their response to such changes is called "substitution." It also requires measuring quality-adjusted prices and the improvement in well-being from new goods. One would not want to count as "inflation" a major improvement in quality that resulted in a trivial price increase.

Most traditional consumer price indexes, including the CPI in the United States, measure prices with a mostly fixed-weight system, holding constant the expenditure weights from some base period. Table 2.1 reports recent weights of very broad categories of goods from 2006; the Bureau of Labor Statistics (BLS) derives these weights from expenditure surveys that report how much consumers spent on different types of goods and services. For example, at a very broad level of aggregation, those weights are 15.0% for food, 6.3% for medical care, 42.7% for housing, and 17.2% for transportation. Within each category, of course, are thousands of specific goods; for example, Red Delicious apples of a certain size and quality are a component of the apples subcategory, which is a component of fresh fruits, which, in turn, is a component of fresh fruits and vegetables, which is a component of food at home, and so on.

Table 2.1   Relative importance of components in the Consumer Price Index (CPI-U)

Component	%
Food and beverages	15.0
At home	7.9
Away from home	6.0
Alcoholic beverages	1.1
Housing (including utilities)	42.7
Apparel and services	3.7
Transportation	17.2
Vehicles	7.6
Gasoline	4.3
Other	5.3
Medical care	6.3
Recreation	5.6
Education and communication	6.0
Education	3.1
Communication	3.0
Other	3.5
Total	100.0

Source: BLS, Relative Importance of Components in the Consumer Price Index, December 2006.
Note: Individual items may not add to totals because of rounding.

With these expenditure weights at hand, or, alternatively, quantities, because expenditures are just price times quantity, a high-quality operation is needed to track the prices accurately. And whose prices? For commodities purchased where, when, and how? In the United States the answer is that there are several closely related consumer price indexes. One measures the change in a weighted average of consumer prices, with the *base year expenditure weights,* for a typical urban family, the so-called CPI-U. A second related but not quite identical construct is the CPI-W, the analogous measure for urban wage and clerical workers. I focus here on the more widely cited CPI-U. Neither of these fixed-weight indexes accounts for substitution, the fact that consumers substitute away from goods whose prices increase more and toward goods whose prices increase less or decline.[1]

The CPI serves, and should serve, many purposes. For example, the CPI is used to measure consumer inflation on a monthly basis; to make cost-of-living adjustments in Social Security, income tax brackets, and other government programs; and to provide price data as inputs to the Commerce Department's National Income and Product Accounts and a third price index, the PCE deflator, which does account for substitution.

Figure 2.1 provides recent data on the U.S. CPI-U. The CPI-U sets the index at 100 for the years 1982–1984. As can be seen, the pace of measured consumer inflation has slowed considerably relative to the 1970s and 1980s, has recently been running in low single digits, and has had considerably less variation than in the high-inflation 1970s and early 1980s.

People change their spending patterns over time, and they do so specifically in response to changes in relative prices. When the price of chicken increases, for example, people may buy more fish, and conversely. Hence the weights change, and a price index such as the fixed-weight base-period CPI that fails to account for those changes overstates the true change in the cost of living.

There are two obvious approaches to weighting the prices. The first uses a fixed-base-period weighting (called a Laspeyres Index after its originator): quantity or expenditure weights remain fixed at their base-period levels, and then we see what happens to the weighted average of prices as prices subsequently change. An alternative possibility, of course, is to use the expenditure weights or quantities in the second period, after the substitution (called a Paasche index after its originator). Economic theory strongly supports the idea of taking an average of these two numbers, a point originally made by the great American economist Irving Fisher.[2] For several years now the BLS has computed a closely related measure called the chained-CPI, or C-CPI-U (Cage, Greenlees, and Jackman 2003); it has

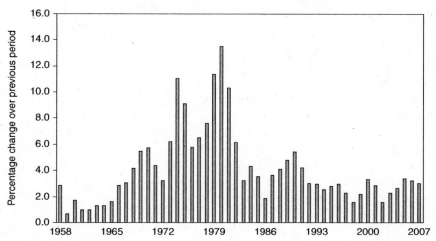

Figure 2.1 Percentage change in U.S. CPI-U, 1958–2007. *Source:* U.S. Bureau of Labor Statistics.

been rising much less rapidly than the traditional CPI-U, suggesting that the failure to account for consumer substitution explicitly is a serious weakness of the official CPI.

Similarly, where people make their purchases changes over time. Discount stores and online sales have become more important and traditional retailers less so. Because price data are collected within outlets, the shift to consumer purchasing from discounters does not show up as a price decline, even though consumers reveal by their purchases that the price decline more than compensates for the potential loss of personal services. Thus in addition to substitution bias among commodities, there is an outlet substitution bias (see discussion in Boskin et al. 1996, 1997, 1998; and Hausman and Leibtag 2004).

Even when purchases are made can become important. We typically measure prices monthly, during a particular week. But if, for example, consumers get wise to post-Christmas discounts and start buying a lot more holiday items after Christmas, surveys that look solely at prices in the second week of December will miss this change in buying patterns and misstate inflation.

Another problem is that price data tend to be collected during the week. In the United States about 1% of price quotes are collected on weekends, despite the fact that the share of purchases made on weekends and holidays is increasing (probably reflecting the increase in prevalence of two-earner couples). Because some outlets emphasize weekend sales, there may be a "when" bias, as well as a "what" and a "where" bias. This phenomenon may explain, in part, recent research suggesting that prices rise less rapidly in data collected by scanners on actual transactions than in data collected by BLS employees from prices on shelves and racks (see Silver and Heravi 2001a,b)

Finally, additional biases result from the difficulty of adjusting fully for quality change and the introduction of new products (Bresnahan and Gordon 1997). In the U.S. CPI, for example, videocassette recorders, microwave ovens, and personal computers were included a decade or more after they had penetrated the market, by which time their prices had already fallen 80% or more. Cellular telephones were not included in the U.S. CPI until 1998, although they were introduced in the United States in 1984 (Hausman 1999).

The CPI currently overstates inflation by about 0.8 percentage point; 0.3 to 0.4 is attributable to failure to account for substitution among goods, 0.1 to failure to account for substitution among retail outlets, and 0.3–0.4 to failure to account adequately for new products and quality improvements (Lebow and Rudd 2003). Thus the first 0.8 percentage point or so of measured CPI inflation is not really inflation at all. This may seem small, but the bias, if left uncorrected for, say, twenty years, would cause the change in the cost of living to be overstated by over 17%.

The U.S. CPI is one of the few economic statistics that are never revised, even if subsequent data reveal that the published statistic is wrong. This has been done historically because many contracts and other government programs are expressly indexed or adjusted to the CPI, and revisions would cause practical and legal complexities.

We know that different sets of consumers have different expenditure weights because they spend different fractions of their income on the various commodities: for example, renters versus homeowners or the middle-aged versus the elderly. Interestingly, most analyses find only modest differences in inflation rates across groups with different expenditure weights, although even modest differences can be consequential when compounded over time.

What about differences across groups in prices and rates of change of prices? For example, do the prices paid by the elderly differ from those paid by the general population, and if they do differ, have the differences changed over time? Economic theory suggests that prices will not differ much for most items, but we do not have sufficient empirical evidence on this score.

Thus inflation—the rate of change of prices—is hard to measure accurately. Government statisticians in all countries, especially those at the U.S.

BLS, have made numerous important improvements over the years (Stewart and Reed 1999). Yet new products are introduced all the time, existing ones are improved, and other products leave the market. Relative prices of various goods and services change frequently, for example, in response to technological and other factors affecting cost and quality, and the changes cause consumers to change their buying patterns. Literally hundreds of thousands of goods and services are available in rich, industrialized economies. As we have become richer, our demands have shifted away from goods to services and to characteristics of goods and services such as enhanced quality, more variety, and greater convenience, which in turn are provided through technology and entrepreneurship. But all these factors mean that a larger fraction of what is produced and consumed in an economy today is harder to measure than decades ago, when a larger fraction of economic activity consisted of easily measured items such as tons of steel and bushels of wheat (although even these items have important quality dimensions). Thus how to obtain information on who is buying what, where, when, why, and how in an economy and then to aggregate it into one or a few measures of price change raises a host of complex analytical and practical problems.

Economics Research and Improving Price Measurement

Once considered very important for practicing economists, price-index research declined for decades in relative importance in academic curricula. Fortunately, important research continued: Erwin Diewert's (1976) and Robert Pollak's (1989) on index number theory; Dale Jorgenson's (with Frank Gollop and Barbara Fraumeni, 1987) theoretically consistent set of production, income, accumulation, and wealth accounts; Zvi Griliches's (with various sets of coauthors, e.g., Carl Kaysen and Franklin Fisher 1962) and Sherwin Rosen's (1974) on hedonics; and Jerry Hausman's research on new products (1997), to name some of the most important contributions that have transformed the way economists think about these issues and, with a lag, how government statisticians measure price.[3]

Important research was also done at the BLS—by Marshall Reinsdorff, Jack Triplett, Brent Moulton, Paul Armknecht and Patrick Jackman, to name a few—and some practical improvements (within the fixed-weight context) were made to the CPI. Related important work occurred at the Bureau of Economic Analysis (BEA) and other statistical agencies worldwide. For example, sampling was introduced to the CPI in 1978, and the treatment of owner-occupied housing was changed to a rental equivalence basis in 1983. Public policy decisions were made to index major programs that constituted large fractions of both sides of the budget: Social Security benefits in the 1970s and income tax brackets in the 1980s. Although I would argue that these were valuable policy improvements, they had the side effect of costing government statisticians their innocence. Not surprisingly, occasional errors were made, by both statisticians and politicians, and then corrected. For example, the introduction of sampling—an enormous improvement—was accompanied by an unexpected upward bias of about 0.2% per year, subsequently discovered and corrected by the BLS. Initially, Social Security benefits were doubly indexed (aside from measurement accuracy issues); this too was corrected after a brief period.

Although my own research and policy interests were in public economics and macroeconomics, exposure to this and related research on these issues piqued my curiosity in economic statistics. From the point of view of cost-benefit analysis, were we not, as a profession and a society, underinvesting in economic statistics? From curricula, training, and professional rewards to the public funds devoted to government statistics, could not some quite valuable improvements be made at rather low cost? But in the 1980s growing pressure on the public fisc led to increasing constraints on financial resources for the statistical agencies.

When I became chairman of the Council of Economic Advisers (CEA) in 1989, I decided to see what could be done to improve economic statistics. Together with representatives of the statistical agencies, I developed an initiative to improve the quality of statistics. We looked at fundamental issues such as whether to centralize the disparate statistical agencies and whether some government activities should be performed in the private sector. But our main product was a list of priority improvements in the generation of the statistics. President George H. W. Bush agreed to make our proposals an initiative in his budget, and we sought funds from Congress. About 70% of the requested funds were appropriated, but different agencies were treated quite disparately because of separate appropriations subcommittees. Funding to improve the National Income and Product Accounts (NIPAs) was increased substantially for the first time in a decade.

My next involvement in economic statistics (other than helping get budgets passed) was in 1995–1996 as chairman of a commission on the CPI (usually, and henceforth in this chapter, called the Boskin Commission, or BC). My colleagues—Ellen Dulberger, Robert Gordon, Zvi Griliches, and Dale Jorgenson—and I were asked both to estimate the likely biases in the CPI and to recommend improvements to the BLS and Congress. We examined everything from data collection (we were each deputized and went on price-collection site visits) to index number theory to practical issues (aided by extensive interaction with BLS personnel and others). On the basis of our evaluations of the research, we made a dozen recommendations to the BLS, some of which have been adopted; four to our elected officials, some of which have been adopted; and one to the economics and statistics profession, which is making some but not enough progress. Remarkably, statistical agencies around the world have been using the Boskin Commission's report as a major input to their own agendas for improvement. The real social value added certainly exceeded our opportunity costs by a large amount.[4]

The BLS, the agency of the Labor Department responsible for producing and disseminating the CPI, has made considerable progress in improving it. Just using today's methods historically would have lowered CPI inflation by 43 basis points per year (reported in the BLS CPI-U-RS research series). Some of these improvements have been ongoing; others were enacted or accelerated after the publication of *Toward a More Accurate Measure of the Cost of Living* (Boskin et al. 1996). In that report my colleagues and I estimated that, taken as a measure of change in a true cost-of-living index,[5] the change in the CPI at that time was overstating inflation by slightly over one percentage point per annum and had been doing so for some time. Of course, there was a range to our estimates; perhaps the overstatement was a little bit smaller or larger. Since that time the BLS has made several important improvements that reduced some measures of the bias, but, as it turns out, our estimates, based in part on Aizcorbe and Jackman (1993), of one important component of the bias appear now to have been substantially underestimated according to the BLS's own subsequent calculations. The new BLS C-CPI-U series implies that the upper-level substitution bias for the last five years was much larger than previously assumed (0.4% or more per year versus 0.2% or less). Over the first ten months of 2007, the C-CPI-U rose 3.0% versus 3.5% (at an annual rate) for the CPI-U. Since its inception in December 1999, the C-CPI-U has risen on average about 0.4% per year less rapidly than the regular CPI-U. Similar differences occur for the core C-CPI and core CPI, which remove volatile food and energy components. The data for 2000–2007 are shown in Figure 2.2.

In the construct of the CPI, data on some 70,000 prices for separate items are collected and aggregated. How that is done is a complex, instructive, and important subject in itself, but I refer the reader to Boskin et al. (1996) for a summary and to Hausman (2003) for important suggestions on improving the process. Upper-level substitution bias refers to the bias in the estimate of the true cost-of-living index created by the use of fixing the weights in the base period, which therefore ignores consumer substitution

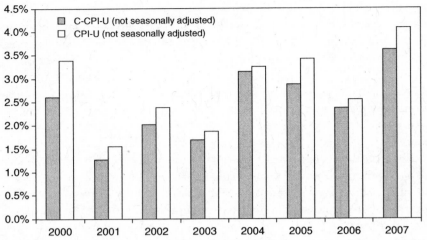

Figure 2.2 Comparison of C-CPI and CPI (annual % change), 2000–2007. *Source:* U.S. Bureau of Labor Statistics.

in response to relative price changes. (There is also a lower-level substitution bias before the CPI is aggregated to the upper level, but the BLS has made a substantial improvement by moving to geometric means for about 60% of the goods and services at the lower level [Dalton, Greenlees, and Stewart 1998].) So, for about 200 broader categories of goods and services, the BLS calculates the fixed-weight Laspeyres index using base-period expenditure weights obtained from consumer expenditure surveys.

That a fixed-weight index misses likely consumer substitution is well known. In part a response to our commission's recommendation to calculate a chained Tornqvist index—a formula that accounts for consumer substitution and falls into a category of indexes called "superlative indexes" because of their desirable properties (Diewert 1976), the BLS now calculates a chained CPI, called the C-CPI-U. This chained Tornqvist index has been published for several years and has risen on annual average a substantial 43 basis points less than the regular CPI-U per year. Our original estimate of substitution bias was 0.2% or less, based on econometric studies at a much higher level of aggregation and some very preliminary BLS unpublished research. A difference of 43 basis points for several years cumulates to a substantively important amount, a total of 3.4% since 2000 (Figure 2.3). Even if the larger estimate of upper-level substitution bias proved to be temporary, the ramifications for overindexing government programs and tax brackets amount to "excess" debt of many billions of dollars annually.

Just in 2007, that bias had implications of many billions of dollars of increased future outlays and decreased revenue for the federal government. The cumulative bias just from 2000–2007 will amount to many hundreds of billions of dollars over the next couple of decades because the overstatement of inflation is built into the baseline amounts of spending and revenue. The likely substantial future bias for years beyond 2007 will make this problem dramatically worse.[6]

It is important to understand how pervasive the use of the CPI is in our economy and, indeed, in academic economics research. As mentioned earlier, other price indexes are available, some of which make important improvements in this dimension relative to the CPI. For example, the BEA's PCE deflator uses a Fisher Ideal Index, an alternative method of adjusting for consumer substitution. Unfortunately, although that effort is important, it is available only quarterly. Therefore, many people, especially people who want to measure things on literally a calendar-year basis and therefore want to measure, for example, real stock returns over the year, need monthly data, especially for December compared with the previous December. Thus many researchers continue to rely on a CPI that is quite faulty in not accurately measuring changes in the cost of living for the purposes they have in mind.

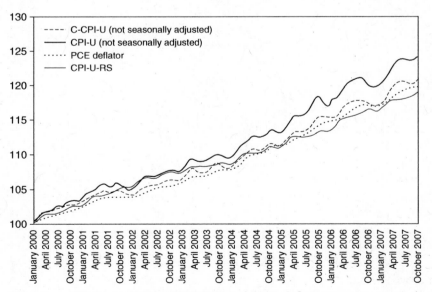

Figure 2.3 CPI-U, C-CPI-U, CPI-U-RS, and PCE deflator, 2000–2007. Index: 1999 = 100 for all indexes. *Source:* U.S. Bureau of Labor Statistics.

Although many aspects of the CPI imply a likely upward bias, it is important to realize that downward biases also can and do occur; for example, it appears that the shelter component of the CPI may well have been overstated historically (Gordon 2003; Gordon and Van Goethem 2007). Likewise, it is important that researchers not look just for upward biases when they are attempting to evaluate and improve the CPI, but for any bias, positive or negative. We want the most accurate price index, not the slowest-growing one.

Understanding Economic Progress

As noted earlier, the Boskin Commission's original 1996 estimate of the bias using changes in the CPI as a measure of the cost of living was about 1.1 percentage points per year. A technical problem called formula bias, introduced into the CPI in 1978 and corrected by the BLS early in 1996, historically had added another 0.2 percentage points per year. Other improvements, net of the larger upper-level substitution bias, reduce the total bias to about 0.8–0.9 percentage points per year. To gain some appreciation of the potential importance and ramifications of the overstatements, suppose that the changes in the CPI have overstated changes in the cost of living by 1.1 percentage points from 1973 to 1995 (ignoring, to be conservative, the 0.2 percentage points attributed to formula bias from 1979 to 1995) and by 0.8 percentage points since. Note that it is not possible that these rates of bias in recent decades have been "permanent" for time spans of centuries, because backcasting such rates would lead to implausibly low standards of living in the distant past.

Table 2.2 presents estimates (updated from Boskin and Jorgenson 1997) of commonly used measures of economic progress: real average hourly and weekly earnings and real median family income, as deflated by the official CPI or CPI-RS, respectively, and by an adjusted cost-of-living index that grows more slowly than the official CPI by the amount of the estimated bias. Instead of falling by about 8% (hourly) or 15% (weekly), real average earnings have risen about 20% or more. Instead of growing a mere 16%, real median family income increased 36%, more than twice as much, from 1973 to 2006. Clearly, the pace of improvement in living standards has slowed relative to the previous quarter century, but it has neither virtually stagnated nor declined, even relative to the early 1970s. These revised estimates accord much more closely with descriptions of living standards in terms of products and services consumed, including consumption by those of modest means.[7]

Table 2.2 Historical implications of upward bias in the CPI measure of the cost of living for selected measures of economic progress

Measure	CPI-U/ CPI-U-RS	Adjusted COLI
Real average earnings (1973–2006)		
Hourly	−8.4%	30.5%
Weekly	−15.9%	23.0%
Real median income (1973–2006)	15.7%	36.3%

Source: Author's estimates.

Bias 1.1%, 1973–1995; 0.8%, 1996–2006, in CPI-U measure. Median income is already deflated by the CPI-U-RS, which grew more slowly than the CPI-U by about 0.43% per year.

Consumption accounts for approximately two-thirds of GDP. Taking 0.4% as a reasonable estimate of the bias flowing into the price data in the NIPAs (after subtracting substitution bias because the NIPA PCE deflator accounts for it) would imply an understatement of the growth of real GDP as a result of understating the growth of real consumption expenditures by perhaps a quarter of a percentage point per year. There undoubtedly are additional and analogous problems in the investment-goods price measures, as well as those for government purchases and net exports. But even if one relied only on the consumption numbers, real GDP growth would be understated by perhaps a quarter of a percentage point per year, equivalent to an understatement of about one-sixth in annual productivity growth. Even a quarter of a percentage point per year compounded over a long span of time accumulates to a sizable number. Real GDP, total and per capita, would be about 8% higher than the official statistics if such a bias held on average since 1973.[8]

Many other conceptual and measurement issues are involved in all the measures of economic progress. For example, fringe benefits and bonus payments become more important over time, rendering nominal average hourly earnings less relevant than a broader measure of compensation. Also, compositional effects change the size, age, and other characteristics of the median family.

Economic progress and economic conditions are compared not just across time but also across countries. It is important to understand that basic index number problems affect the statistics of every country. Although some countries have made progress in ameliorating some of these problems (e.g., Statistics Canada's move to geometric means at the lowest level of aggregation removes some of the substitution bias), in other dimensions the American statistical system is far ahead of most other countries.

For example, the widespread sampling done in the United States to collect price statistics undoubtedly gets some quality-change and new-product bias that is not picked up in other countries. Thus the rates of real GDP growth, inflation, productivity growth, real wage growth, real family-income growth, and analogous measures are all misstated in virtually every country, to varying degrees, and these measurement issues and problems should be borne in mind when cross-country comparisons are made. Fortunately, analogous economics research in many countries in academia and central banks, will over time improve these statistics as well. It should also be borne in mind that there are numerous other important differences between the U.S. NIPAs and those of other countries.

Sometimes the mechanical use of flawed statistics can be inadvertently misleading when they are used as input to other data. For example, Table 2.3 presents historical data on real returns to stocks, bonds, and other financial instruments, as well as measured inflation, over several subperiods for the last two centuries, taken from the invaluable work of Siegel (2002) and Ibbotson (Morningstar 2007).

The long-run average of about 7% real returns to equities is impressively stable over two centuries of economic and demographic change—several depressions, numerous recessions, almost a doubling of life expectancy, world wars, and other events. Of course, these averages suppress the substantial short-run variation in real returns—the standard deviation of real stock returns is more than twice the mean. The real return to government bonds averaged about 2.4% from 1926–2006. These measures are careful estimates of nominal returns; unfortunately, they overstate historical inflation and understate real returns because the change in the official CPI is generally used as the measure of inflation. In contrast to the care in

Table 2.3 Compound annual real returns by type of instrument, 1802–2006

Period	Stock (arithmetic mean)	Stocks	Bonds	Bills	Gold	Inflation[a]	Equity premium
1802–2001*	8.4	6.9	3.5	2.9	0.0	1.4	3.4
1802–1870*		7.0	4.8	5.1	0.2	0.1	2.2
1871–1925*		6.6	3.7	3.2	−0.8	0.6	2.9
1926–2001*		6.9	2.2	0.7	0.4	3.1	4.7
1946–2001*		7.1	1.3	0.6	−0.3	4.1	5.8
1926–2006**		7.4	2.4	0.7	—	3.0	5.0

Sources: *Siegel 2002; **Morningstar 2007.
a. Available from Historical Statistics of the United States, Cambridge University Press, Millenial Edition, online.

measuring nominal returns, the change in the official CPI is simply assumed to measure inflation correctly. In recent decades the change in the CPI has overstated inflation by about 1.0% per year (Boskin et al., 1996, 1997, 1998; Lebow and Rudd 2003) because of the several types of bias discussed earlier. A more accurate inflation measure would thus substantially increase all the measures of real returns for stocks and bonds, by about 100 basis points in recent decades.[9] Just using a CPI series consistent with current, as opposed to mid-1990s, BLS procedures would raise the estimate of real returns for recent decades by 40 to 50 basis points.[10]

Finance theory implies that when investment comes out of retained earnings that produce a rate of return equal to the discount rate, the reciprocal of the price-to-earnings (P/E) ratio equals the rate of return. The historical long-term P/E ratio of just under 15 fits well with the 7% real return estimates. However, if real returns in fact have been perhaps 8% for several decades, this raises several important issues for finance economists.[11]

Priorities in Moving Forward

A useful way to organize one's thoughts on the CPI is to ask the following basic questions: What price and quantity (or, if price and quantity cannot be separated, expenditure) data should be collected? How? Where? How Often? Whose prices and quantities? What methodology should be used to aggregate them? How many indexes? For what purposes? Answering each of these questions involves a series of conceptual, methodological, and practical considerations.[12]

First, the CPI ought to approximate a true cost-of-living index (COLI), a position the BLS has endorsed. For most of the uses of the CPI, from making monetary policy to calculating cost-of-living adjustments in government programs, writing tax rules, and measuring economic progress in many dimensions, it is hard to imagine not at least starting with a cost-of-living concept. Further, my own long interaction with executive- and legislative-branch policy makers in this area suggests that they did indeed have and still have a cost-of-living concept in mind in indexing tax brackets and benefit programs. It would be appropriate to adopt a superlative index such as the chained CPI as the official CPI and to live with the need for revision. This would move the official CPI much closer to a true cost-of-living index. If our elected officials do not like the implications for indexing government programs, the indexing can easily be changed. Government statisticians should not be making policy judgments, and politicians should not be politicizing the production of government statistics.

Better measures of the user cost of housing and consumer durables should be a high priority. Leaving out real capital gains (and losses) in the user cost may avoid some practical oddities, but for a full evaluation of economic well-being, real capital gains and losses need to be included. If my house goes up or down in real value, it will indeed cost me more or less implicitly to rent it to myself, but I may well be better (or worse) off. If we leave real capital gains out of the price index, we ought to think twice about that large component of a cost-of-living adjustment (COLA) to a wealthy home owner financed by payroll taxes on young renters. Bajari, Benkard, and Krainer (2002) suggest that a conceptually proper treatment of housing can be quite consequential, and that the usual methods appear recently to include a substantial upward bias, whereas Gordon and Van Goethem (2007) argue convincingly that over a longer time span, there was likely downward bias in the housing component.

Next, it would be useful to expand the use of hedonics to account for explicit quality change (as in Berndt, Griliches, and Rapport 1995; Berndt, Cockburn, and Griliches 1996; Chwelos, Berndt, and Cockburn 2004; White et al. 2004; and the analyses of Diewert 1998; Triplett 1999, and Pakes 2003). The BLS is in fact making some progress here.

Closely related to quality change is the issue of new goods (e.g., Nordhaus 1997). Historically the BLS has at times entered new products into the index very late, after their prices have fallen appreciably. An important recent example is cellular telephones. Since Hicks (1940) there has been a standard analytical economics treatment of new products in evaluating real income. Hausman (1997) has developed econometric techniques to implement it and has demonstrated that failure to do so can lead to quite large biases. Although more frequent BLS updating of the market basket should help reduce the incidence of major long-lived omissions, it is not sufficient to deal with new products (Griliches and Cockburn 1994; Hausman 1999; Petrin 2002).

Greater use should be made of scanner data (Silver and Heravi, 2001a,b), which, despite their problems, have the advantage not only of sample size but also of actual transaction prices as opposed to prices of goods on shelves, racks, or other displays. For example, the widely reported growing tendency of consumers to shop after rather than before Christmas to take advantage of discounts is difficult to measure accurately with current procedures. Finally, more work on outlets is badly needed. Casual empiricism certainly suggests a growing role of discount outlets, and, for example, Hausman and Leibtag (2004, 2005) estimate that the failure to account just for the emergence of Wal-Mart as the largest retail chain has caused a measurable bias in the CPI. Of course, the rapid growth of online sales also raises new challenges for improving price measurement.

Most important for social welfare, delays in improving our price indexes are enormously consequential. Irving Fisher, perhaps the greatest American economist of the first half of the twentieth century, in his classic *The Making of Index Numbers* in 1922, said that his entire life's work would have been worth while if it but led to the replacement of arithmetic with geometric index number formulas. Three-quarters of a century later, we have finally started using geometric means in about three-fifths of the lower-level data and have an experimental superlative index at the upper level, but we have not yet accounted for upper-level substitution in the official CPI. Although I would be the first to applaud any statistical agency for care in evaluating, experimenting with, and adopting new techniques, the consequences of having adopted such formulas on the fiftieth rather than the seventy-fifth anniversary of Fisher's work would have been enormous: a federal debt over a trillion dollars lower as a result of reduced overindexing of outlays and income taxes from the inaccurate CPI. Explicitly, adopting a superlative index[13] would have immense desirable effects on the accuracy of our data.

These consequences are the most important reason to reiterate the need for economists and statisticians to pay more attention to training in data collection, analysis, and interpretation, with far more attention to these matters in the standard curriculum and more emphasis on measurement and sampling issues in the training of economists and statisticians. The economics research on price indexes, some of which has been described earlier, has made immense contributions to better understanding of price movements. It has, in a very real sense, changed the interpretation of history. If economic research can continue to help the statistical agencies improve our economic statistics, there will be a large social value added: more accurate COLAs, better information for government policy makers and for the private economic decisions of firms, workers, consumers, and investors, and, most important, better assessments of economic conditions and progress by our citizens, not to mention economists.

Perhaps it is just how consequential the (mis)measurement of inflation can be that has sparked the renaissance of research interest in these very practical issues. Economists and statisticians in and out of government will continue to contribute at least as much social value added here as in virtually any other area of economics. Although perhaps regretting their lost innocence, those working on such government statistics hopefully will be more than adequately compensated by their increased relevance.

Notes

This chapter draws heavily from Boskin (2005, 2008). Thanks to Jerry Hausman and John Siegfried for helpful suggestions.

1. A recent improvement by the BLS substitutes geometric for arithmetic mean formulas for aggregating at the lower levels for about 60% of items, thus allowing for some partial substitution.
2. Fisher (1922).
3. See Diewert (1993) for a discussion of the early history of price-index research.
4. Also see the essays in the symposium edited by Triplett (2006).
5. It is widely accepted that a cost-of-living index is the theoretically correct conceptual foundation of measures of inflation for input into monetary policy, making cost-of-living adjustments to government programs and tax rules, and measuring economic progress. Indeed, it is difficult to conceive of any other conceptual basis.
6. Of course, as mentioned earlier, there is no guarantee that the bias will remain this large; it could change in either direction in response to relative price dispersion and the response of expenditures to that dispersion in the future.
7. See the related analysis over a longer period by Nordhaus (1997) and the analysis by Bils and Klenow (2001).
8. There are numerous other conceptual and measurement issues involved in all the measures of economic progress. A full discussion of other measurement issues is beyond the scope of this paper.
9. Of course, it would correspondingly decrease the inflation estimate.
10. See Stewart and Reed (1999).
11. See the discussion of the use of historical data in Shoven (2001) and the other essays in that report.
12. See Boskin et al. (1996) and Schultze and Mackie (2002).
13. Theory and practical alternatives, respectively.

References

Aizcorbe, Ana M., and Patrick C. Jackman (1993). "The Commodity Substitution Effect in CPI Data, 1982–1991." *Monthly Labor Review,* 116(12) (December), 25–33.

Bajari, Patrick, C. Lanier Benkard, and John Krainer (2002). "House Prices and Consumer Welfare". Unpublished mimeo, Stanford University.

Berndt, E. R., Iain Cockburn, and Zvi Griliches (1996). "Pharmaceutical Innovations and Market Dynamics: Tracking Effects of Price Indexes for Antidepressant Drugs." *Brookings Papers on Economic Activity,* 133–199.

Berndt, E. R., Z. Griliches, and N. J. Rapport (1995). "Econometric Estimates of Price Indexes for Personal Computers in the 1990s." *Journal of Econometrics,* 68, 243–268.

Bils, M., and P. Klenow (2001). "Quantifying Quality Growth." *American Economic Review*, 91, 1006–1030.

Boskin, Michael J. (2005). "Causes and Consequences of Bias in the Consumer Price Index as a Measure of the Cost of Living." *Atlantic Economic Journal*, 33(1), 1–13.

——— (2008). "Consumer Price Indexes." In D. Henderson, ed., *Concise Encyclopedia of Economics*. Indianapolis, Ind., Liberty Fund, Library of Economics and Liberty.

Boskin, Michael J., E. Dulberger, R. Gordon, Z. Griliches, and D. Jorgenson (1996). *Toward a More Accurate Measure of the Cost of Living: Final Report of the Advisory Commission on the Consumer Price Index*. Washington, D.C., United States Senate, December.

——— (1997). "The CPI Commission: Findings and Recommendations." *American Economic Review*, 87, 78–83.

——— (1998). "Consumer Prices, the Consumer Price Index, and the Cost of Living." *Journal of Economic Perspectives* 12(1) (Winter), 3–26.

Boskin, Michael J., and D. Jorgenson (1997). "Implications of Overstating Inflation for Indexing Government Programs and Understanding Economic Progress." *American Economic Review*, 87(2), 89–93.

Bresnahan, Timothy F., and R. J. Gordon (1997). *The Economics of New Goods*. Chicago: The University of Chicago Press, for the National Bureau of Economic Research.

Cage, Robert, J. S. Greenlees, and P. Jackman (2003). "Introducing the Chained Consumer Price Indices." In Thierry Lacroix, ed., *International Working Group on Price Indices (Ottawa Group), Proceedings of the Seventh Meeting*. Paris: INSEE, 213–246.

Chwelos, Paul D., Ernst R. Berndt, and Iain M. Cockburn (2004). "Faster, Smaller, Cheaper: An Hedonic Price Analysis of PDAs." *Taylor and Francis Journals*, 40(22), 2839–2856.

Dalton, Kenneth V., John S. Greenlees, and Kenneth J. Stewart (1998). "Incorporating a Geometric Mean Formula into the CPI." *Monthly Labor Review*, 121(10) (October), 3–7.

Diewert, W. E. (1976). "Exact and Superlative Index Numbers." *Journal of Econometrics*, 4, 114–145.

——— (1993). "The Early History of Price Index Research." In W. E. Diewert and A. O. Nakamura, eds., *Essays in Index Number Theory*, vol. 1. Amsterdam: Elsevier: 33–71.

——— (1998). "Index Number Issues in the Consumer Price Index." *Journal of Economic Perspectives* 12, 47–58.

——— (2003). "Hedonic Regressions: A Consumer Theory Approach." In M. Shapiro and R. Feenstra, eds., *Scanner Data and Price Indexes, NBER Studies in Income and Wealth*. Chicago: University of Chicago Press: 317–347.

Fisher, I. (1922). *The Making of Index Numbers*. Boston: Houghton Mifflin.

Gordon, Robert J. (2006). "The Boskin Commission Report: A Retrospective One Decade Later." *International Productivity Monitor* 12, 7–22; also NBER Working Paper 12311.

Gordon, Robert J., and T. Van Goethem.(2007). "Downward Bias in the Biggest CPI Component: The Case of Rental Shelter, 1914–2003." In E. Berndt and C. Hulten, eds., *Hard-to-Measure Goods and Services: Essays in Honor of Zvi Griliches*. Chicago: University of Chicago Press for NBER, 2007; also NBER Working Paper 11776.

Griliches, Zvi, and Iain Cockburn (1994). "Generics and New Goods in Pharmaceutical Price Indexes." *American Economic Review*, 84(5) (December), 1213–1232.

Griliches, Zvi, C. Kaysen, and F. Fisher (1962). "The Cost of Automobile Model Changes Since 1949." *Journal of Political Economy* 70, 433–444.

Hausman, J. (1997). "Valuation of New Goods under Perfect and Imperfect Competition." In T. Bresnahan and Robert J. Gordon, eds., *The Economics of New Goods*. Chicago: University of Chicago Press for NBER, 209–237.

——— (1999). "Cellular Telephone, New Products and the CPI," *Journal of Business and Economic Statistics* 17(2), 188–194.

——— (2003). "Sources of Bias and Solutions to Bias in the CPI." *Journal of Economic Perspectives*, 17(1), 23–44.

Hausman, J., and Ephraim Leibtag (2004). "CPI Bias from Supercenters: Does the BLS Know That Wal-Mart Exists?" NBER Working Paper 10712. Forthcoming in W. E. Diewert, J. P. Greenlees, and C. R. Hulten, eds., *Price Index Concepts and Measurement*.

——— (2007). "Consumer Benefits from Increased Competition in Shopping Outlets: Measuring the Effect of Wal-Mart.", *Journal of Applied Econometrics*, 22, 1157–1177; also NBER Working Paper 11809, 2005.

Hicks, J. (1940). "The Valuation of the Social Income." *Economica* 7 (May), 105–124.

Ibbotson Associates (2002). *Stocks, Bonds, Bills and Inflation—2002 Yearbook*. Chicago: Ibbotson Associates.

Jorgensen, Dale W., F. Gollop, and B. Fraumeni (1987). *Productivity and U.S. Economic Growth*, Cambridge MA: Harvard University Press.

Lebow, D., and J. Rudd (2003). "Measurement Error in the Consumer Price Index: Where Do We Stand?" *Journal of Economic Literature*, 41(1), 159–201.

McClellan, Mark, J. P. Newhouse, and D. Remler (1996). "Are Medical Prices Declining?" NBER Working Paper 5750, September.

Nordhaus, William D. (1997). "Do Real-Output and Real-Wage Measures Capture Reality? The History of Light Suggests Not." In T. Bresnahan and R.J. Gordon, eds., *The Economics of New Goods*. Chicago: University of Chicago Press for NBER, 29–66.

Pakes, A. (2003), "A Reconsideration of Hedonic Price Indices with an Application to PC's." *American Economic Review* 93(5), 1578–1596.

Petrin, A. (2002), "Quantifying the Benefits of New Products: The Case of the Minivan." *Journal of Political Economy*, 110, 705–729.

Pollak, Robert (1989). *The Theory of the Cost-of-Living Index*. New York: Oxford University Press.

Rosen, Sherwin (1974). "Hedonic Prices and Implicit Markets: Product Differentiation in Pure Competition. *Journal of Political Economy* 82(1), 34–55.

Schultze, Charles, and C. Mackie, eds. (2002). "At What Price? Conceptualizing and Measuring Cost-of-Living and Price Indexes." *National Research Council*

Panel on Conceptual, Measurement, and Other Statistical Issues in Developing Cost-of-Living Indexes. Washington, D.C.: National Academy Press.

Shoven, J. (2001). "What Are Reasonable Long-Run Rates of Return to Expect in Equities?" In *Social Security Advisory Board, Estimating the Real Rate of Return on Stocks Over the Long Term.* Washington, D.C.: Social Security Advisory Board.

Siegel, J. (2002). *Stocks for the Long Run.* 2nd ed. New York: McGraw-Hill.

Silver, M. S., and S. Heravi (2001a). "Scanner Data and the Measurement of Inflation." *Economic Journal,* 111, F384–F405.

———— (2001b). "Why the CPI Matched Models Method May Fail Us: Results from an Hedonic and Matched Experiment Using Scanner Data." Mimeo, University of Cardiff.

Stewart, K., and S. Reed (1999). "Consumer Price Index Research Series Using Current Methods, 1978–1998." *Monthly Labor Review,* June. (An update is available on the BLS website.)

Triplett, Jack, ed. (1999). *Measuring the Price of Medical Treatments.* Washington, D.C.: Brookings.

Triplett, Jack (2006). "The Boskin Commission Report after a Decade." *International Productivity Monitor* 12, 42–60.

White, Alan G., Jaison R. Abel, Ernst R. Berndt, and Cory W. Monroe (2004). "Hedonic Price Indexes for Personal Computer Operating Systems and Pro Suites." NBER Working Paper 10427, April.

COMMENT

Jerry Hausman

The Consumer Price Index (CPI) is arguably among the four most important aggregate indexes estimated by the U.S. government each month: real gross domestic product (GDP) growth, the CPI, productivity change, and the unemployment rate. However, real GDP growth and productivity change both depend on the CPI (and the Producer Price Index [PPI]), so three of the four indexes depend on accurate estimation or price indexes, and in an important way because about 67% of GDP is personal consumption expenditure. Thus to answer the question, "How much better off is the average citizen in January 2008 compared with an earlier period, say, January 1978?" CPI-deflated average or median (family) income is compared across the two periods. The crucial role of the CPI in this calculation explains its importance.

Michael Boskin has explained the many important roles of the CPI in economic measurement and policy in the U.S. economy. Although for short-term uses the CPI may be adequate for estimating month-to-month inflation, I find it to be totally inadequate for measuring changes in a cost-of-living index over longer periods of time. Thus it cannot correctly answer the question posed earlier. Consider some changes since 1978 that have affected economic welfare: personal computers, cellular telephones, the Internet, iPods, large-screen televisions, and discount superstores such as Wal-Mart. The effect of these new goods and changes in existing goods are not correctly estimated in the CPI. Indeed, the CPI has a systematic upward bias that becomes increasingly important as the comparison time period increases. Thus although the BLS has improved the CPI over the past decade, much need for improvement remains. I discuss the origins of the bias and approaches for improvement.

A cost-of-living index (COLI) is the correct theoretical tool to measure the effect on consumer welfare of price changes, quality changes, and introduction of new goods, as the academic literature has long noted and as the BLS has recognized. The COLI is based on the expenditure function, which is defined as the minimum income required for a consumer to reach a given utility level:

$$(1.1) \quad y = e(p_1, p_2, \ldots, p_n; \bar{u}) = e(p, \bar{u}) \quad \text{solves} \quad \min \sum_i p_i q_i \ \text{such that} \ u(x) = \bar{u}$$

where there are n goods labeled q_i. The change in the required income when, for instance, prices change between period 1 and period 2 follows from the compensating variation (CV):

$$(1.2) \qquad y^2(p^2, u^1) - y^1 = CV = e(p^2, u^1) - e(p^1, u^1).$$

The exact cost of living index becomes

$$(1.3) \qquad P(p^2, p^1, u^1) = \frac{y_2(p^2, u^1)}{y^1} = \frac{e(p^2, u^1)}{e(p^1, u^1)},$$

which gives the ratio of the required amount of income at period 2 prices for a consumer to be as well off as in period 1.

I now explain the major biases in current CPI estimation in term of equation (1.3).

The Effect of New Goods and Services on a COLI: New-Good Bias

Many new products and services have a significant effect on consumer welfare. For example, in Hausman (2002) I have estimated that the gain in consumer welfare from the introduction of cellular telephones in the United States exceeded $50 billion per year in 1994 and $111 billion per year in 1999. The BLS omits the effect of the introduction of new goods in its calculation of the CPI, thus imparting an upward bias. Exclusion of the effect of new goods creates a first-order bias in a COLI (Hausman 2003).

The Effects of Quality Change on a COLI: Quality-Change Bias

I now consider the effects of quality changes on a COLI. The BLS either does not adjust for quality change (using a "matching procedure" to link in goods with quality change so that quality change is not accounted for) or for some products uses a hedonic adjustment procedure. The economic theory of quality change arises in a way similar to that of the new-good analysis. Similarly, omission of quality change leads to a first-order bias in the estimation of a COLI (Hausman 2003).

The Effect of Lower-Price Stores: Outlet Bias

An important market outcome in retailing over the past thirty years is the growth of discount retail outlets such as Wal-Mart, Best Buy, and Circuit City. Wal-Mart is now the largest supermarket chain in the United States, and for a number of branded goods it now sells 10% to 20% of the output of large branded companies. These outlets offer significantly lower prices than "traditional" outlets such as department stores. These lower prices cause a first-order effect in a COLI when consumers shift their shopping patterns away from traditional outlets to these rapidly growing discount outlets. Hausman and Leibtag (2007, 2009) demonstrate that the bias in the CPI from ignoring this effect is substantial for food purchases. They also find that the BLS procedure that assumes that lower prices at Wal-Mart are completely offset by different service levels is incorrect. Indeed, consumers gain a significant increase in welfare from shopping at Wal-Mart and buying food products at significantly lower prices.

The Effect of Price Change: Substitution Bias

Last, I come to substitution bias, a second-order effect, on which the BLS has spent much of its research attention over the past decade. Using a Taylor approximation around the period 1 price, when only price j changes, I rewrite equation (1.2) as

$$y^2 - y^1 \approx (p_j^2 - p_j^1)h_j(p^1, u^1) + \frac{1}{2}(p_j^2 - p_j^1)^2 \frac{\partial h_j(p^1, u^1)}{\partial p_j}$$

$$(1.4) \qquad = (p_j^2 - p_j^1)q_j(p^1, y^1) + \frac{1}{2}(p_j^2 - p_j^1)^2 \frac{\partial h_j(p^1, y^1)}{\partial p_j}$$

For each given form of expenditure function, or equivalently the demand functions h and q, there exists a given $p_j^\# \in (p^1, p^2)$ that makes equation (1.4) hold with exact equality. The current CPI takes account of the first term (the first-order term), but the substitution bias arises from the second-order term. I would not claim that the second-order terms are not important—because prices change over all n goods, the sum of the second-order substitution effects could be important. However, I do find it a rather strange outcome that the BLS's research attention has concentrated on a partial correction to the substitution-bias effect, which is second order, but the BLS has made limited or no attempted correction to the first-order effects that I discussed earlier.

Improvement in the CPI requires two major changes. First, economics must be incorporated into the analysis rather than an attempt to use arithmetic comparisons of aggregations of prices. To incorporate economics into a COLI requires use of both quantities and prices. Scanner data are now collected in the majority of U.S. retail outlets. The BLS needs to begin to collect these quantity and price data and develop methods to collect quantity data where they do not currently exist (e.g., using consumer panel data). Sending price surveyors out to stores, which is the main approach used by the BLS, will not solve the first-order bias problems that I discussed earlier.

References

Hausman, J. (2002). "Mobile Telephone." In M. Cave et al., eds, *Handbook of Telecommunications Economics*. North-Holland.

——— (2003). "Sources of Bias and Solutions to Bias in the CPI." *Journal of Economic Perspectives, 17*, 23–44.

Hausman, J., and E. Leibtag (2007). "Consumer Benefits from Increased Competition in Shopping Outlets: Measuring the Effect of Wal-Mart." *Journal of Applied Econometrics*.

——— (2009). "CPI Bias from Supercenters: Does the BLS Know that Wal-Mart Exists?" In W. E Diewert, J. S. Greenlees, and C. R. Hulten, eds., *Price Index Concepts and Measurement*. Chicago: University of Chicago Press.

CHAPTER THREE

Economics and the Earned Income Tax Credit

Robert A. Moffitt

The EITC is generally regarded as one of the most successful social policy innovations for low-income families of the past fifty years. It transfers billions of dollars to a needy group regarded as deserving by most people—the working poor—while simultaneously providing significant, nontrivial incentives to work for those at the bottom of the income distribution. It is in the latter characteristic of the program—its work incentives—that the ideas of economists have been most influential. The idea of incentives in general, and work incentives in particular, has long been of particular interest to economists, who have been at pains to emphasize their importance when assessing the merits of different policy measures. In the case of the EITC, economists were heavily involved in public discussions of work incentives in the early 1970s when the EITC was born and had a major influence on its development. Economists were again involved when the EITC was expanded in the late 1980s and early 1990s, when work incentives were becoming an even more forceful component of public policy discussions of programs for the poor.

This chapter discusses the influence of economists and economic ideas on the origin and design of the EITC. The first section lays out the basic economic analysis of work incentives for earnings subsidies in general, and the second section discusses the history of the EITC and the role of this analysis in that history. The third section discusses a few recent issues concerning the program and how economic analysis has informed them.

Economic Analyses of Work Incentives and Assistance
Programs for the Poor

That individual work effort responds to financial incentives to work is a very old idea in economics and is the basis of the standard economic model of welfare reform. Economists' belief in the importance of financial incentives in work decisions is not merely theoretical but has been supported by an extensive body of empirical work. This is particularly true for women in the population, where statistical work has shown that greater financial incentives through a negative income tax lead to nontrivial increases in work effort (Killingsworth 1983). The empirical evidence on the responsiveness of prime-age able-bodied males to financial incentives is more mixed, with some evidence suggesting much lower responsiveness. These empirical patterns have played a role in the development of the EITC and other welfare reform measures, as elaborated later.

The application of the idea of work incentives to welfare reform saw its greatest development in economic analysis in the 1960s and 1970s. Most of that discussion focused on the idea of a negative income tax (NIT), which played a larger role in public discussions and legislative activity at the time than the idea of an earnings subsidy, of which the EITC is an example. Nevertheless, the intellectual and policy origins of the EITC come directly from the discussions of an NIT, and it is therefore necessary to understand the NIT before one can fully understand the EITC.

The economist Milton Friedman is most associated with the idea of an NIT because he introduced the idea in a volume of essays published in 1962 (Friedman 1962; see Moffitt 2003b for a discussion of the evolution of the idea of an NIT). The idea had been formulated in its basic form by discussions between Friedman and the economist George Stigler in the late 1940s (Moynihan 1973). In addition to Milton Friedman, economists Robert Lampman (1965) and James Tobin (1966) were forceful and influential advocates of an NIT. The issue that these economists addressed was the lack of work incentives in the existing U.S. welfare system. In that system increases in work effort by welfare recipients were penalized by dollar-for-dollar reductions in benefits. The welfare benefit for a welfare recipient who began working and earned $400 per month, for example, was reduced by exactly $400. As a result, the recipient's income was no higher after working than before, so she had no financial incentive to work. Friedman termed the benefit reduction a "tax" and stated that the then-existing welfare system imposed a "100 percent tax rate." In contrast, he suggested that work incentives could be improved by reducing welfare benefits by less than dollar-for-dollar when welfare recipients began to work. For example, an NIT with a 50% tax rate would result in only a $200 per month reduction in the welfare benefit if a recipient began earning $400. The recipient would be $200 better off in total income after working and thus would have some degree of work incentive. Although benefits would still be reduced—by definition, they have to be reduced eventually in a welfare program, in one way or another, to prevent high-income families from receiving benefits—they would be reduced by less than in a program with a 100% tax rate.

Although this change would be an improvement in work incentives, a recipient who began working would still lose some of her earnings through benefit reduction. The government would subsidize the income of the family, and the subsidy would fall as earnings rose, so some disincentive to work would remain. The amount of income lost as earnings rose could be greater than what the family would lose if it was off welfare, depending on the tax rate from regular positive tax systems in place. This led economists to consider alternative programs known as earnings subsidies or wage subsidies. In an earnings subsidy program an individual who begins work receives a supplement that increases with earnings instead of falling with earnings. The magnitude of the incentive is again characterized by a rate, in this case a subsidy rate. For example, if the subsidy rate were 20%, an individual who went to work and earned $400 per month would receive from the government a subsidy of $80 per month (.20 × 400), leaving income $480 higher than before. Not surprisingly, economists who analyzed this type of program and compared it with an NIT found that earnings subsidies tended to have greater work incentives (Kesselman 1969; Barth and Greenberg 1971).

The contrast between an NIT and an earnings subsidy is illustrated in Figure 3.1, which plots total take-home income on the vertical axis and earnings from the labor market on the horizontal axis. An NIT is portrayed by line BCD. A family with no earnings or other income receives a payment equal to AB, $1,000 per month in the figure. With a 50% tax rate, increases in earnings reduce benefits by half the earnings, so that earnings of $400 result in a reduction of the benefit by $200, to $800. The line BCD has positive slope, showing that income rises as earnings rise, thus providing some measure of work incentives. An earnings subsidy, by contrast, is portrayed as line AE. No benefit supplement is paid for those who do not work, but the supplement increases with earnings. The figure portrays an earnings subsidy with a 20% subsidy rate, which results in a subsidy of $80 if earnings are $400 and rises to greater levels with higher earnings. The line AE also has positive slope but is steeper than line BCD, thus showing that income rises faster with increased work under an earnings subsidy than under an NIT.

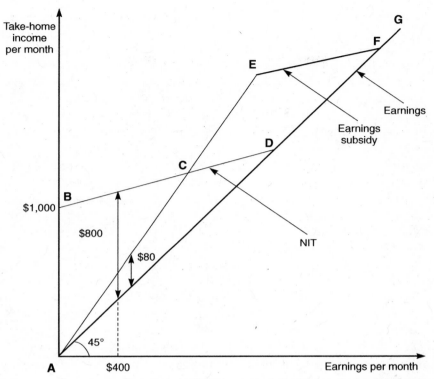

Figure 3.1 Income from earnings, NIT, and earnings subsidy (income from earnings: ADFG; income under an NIT: BCD; income under an earnings subsidy: AEF).

This intuitive result on the superiority of an earnings subsidy has to be qualified in several important respects. The most important is that the earnings subsidy provides no benefits to those with no income. However, the fundamental goal of most welfare programs is to assist families who are at the bottom of the income distribution and who are needy because they have no economic resources of their own. The U.S. public still believes that there are many families whose adults cannot work or have difficulty working because of various health, family, and economic barriers, and that many of these families deserve financial assistance even if they have no earnings. For such families, the replacement of an NIT by an earnings subsidy would not be sensible. This issue goes to the heart of the difference between the two types of programs because Milton Friedman had the explicit goal of designing a program that served twin purposes—to provide some level of support to those with no other income, which he regarded as necessary for humanitarian reasons, but simultaneously to provide some measure of work incentives. The earnings subsidy achieves its greater work incentives only by eliminating the first of these as an objective of the program.

The alternative is to give such families both a welfare payment and an earnings subsidy. The current welfare system in the United States does precisely that for some families, as discussed later. Those who are judged to be needy and to deserve support if they have no income are given a benefit even if they do not work. But the presence of an earnings subsidy means that if they do wish to work, they may be able to receive higher supplements than they would have in the presence of a welfare program with a relatively high tax rate. They can do so if the earnings supplement is sufficiently generous that higher earnings supplements are paid under it than under the welfare program, at least in some ranges of earnings. In Figure 3.1, offering both an NIT-like welfare program and an earnings subsidy would mean offering families either line BCD or line AEF. If one assumes that they would always choose the program that gave them higher income, their "effective" program line can be represented as line BCEF. The earnings subsidy pays more than the welfare program at sufficiently high levels of earnings, namely, at earnings that put the individual to the right of point C. Thus a recipient initially at point B now has a greater incentive to work than was the case under the NIT-like welfare program alone. If the earnings subsidy were much less generous, however, point C and points to the right of it could lie below the welfare program line, and therefore the earnings subsidy would provide lower work incentives.[1]

It is sometimes said that the EITC has simply been a backdoor way of introducing an NIT to the U.S. social support system. This is a correct statement in some ways but not in others, but one way in which it is correct is in the sense I have just discussed. If a welfare program is already in place and available to families, the introduction of an earnings subsidy is the same, in general form, as the reduction of the tax rate in a welfare program. Both raise the potential government benefit at higher levels of earnings. In Figure 3.1 the introduction of the earnings subsidy raises benefits for those in the range of earnings that would put them along line CEF, and this is close to what would happen if the tax rate in a welfare program were lowered, which is what an NIT does.

As discussed later, however, the United States has no significant welfare program (that is, one that pays benefits to families who do not work) for many categories of families. For them, the introduction of an earnings subsidy is nothing like an NIT and has very different incentives to work.

A second qualification to the presumed superiority of an earnings subsidy to an NIT in terms of work incentives is that even an earnings subsidy must eventually be phased out in order to avoid paying benefits to high-income families. The subsidy is generally reduced if earnings reach a certain level. In Figure 3.1, the switch occurs at point E, for after that point the earnings subsidy falls as earnings rise and eventually disappears altogether at point F. In that range there is no difference between an NIT and an earnings subsidy: both phase the subsidy out, and hence the benefit falls as earnings rise, thus reintroducing work disincentives to some degree. An individual who was initially working at such a level to generate earnings between points E and F now faces a positive tax rate on her earnings, for increased work now reduces a subsidy that she is receiving from the government. Although the recipient is still better off than before because she is receiving a benefit that she did not previously have, the implications for work effort are nevertheless negative. The magnitude of this disincentive depends on how wide the EF range is for the particular earnings subsidy—the particular range shown in Figure 3.1 is just an illustration—as well as on the magnitude of the tax rate reduction (i.e., how fast it is phased out along segment EF). The magnitude of this range and the size of the phase-out rate for the EITC program currently in place in the United States will be discussed in the next section.

It is worth noting at this point that the work disincentives introduced by an earnings subsidy may induce an individual who is already working to work somewhat fewer hours (e.g., over a year) but should not cause any individual to quit work entirely. In Figure 3.1 the introduction of the earnings subsidy (line ACEF) where before there was no program (line ADF) will not cause any individual who was working in the EF range to reduce work all the way down to point A, the no-work point, because the subsidy is zero there. Thus although an earnings subsidy introduces some work disincentives, they should affect only the number of hours of work for some of those who were working already and will continue to work. The effect of an earnings subsidy on the employment rate—that is, the fraction of individuals working—is unambiguously positive.[2] This stands in contrast to an NIT, which should be expected to reduce the employment rate. The contrast between an NIT and an earnings subsidy is stronger in terms of their effects on employment rates, which are opposite in sign, than in terms of their effects on hours of work of those who work, which may be less different.

These issues were all completely understood as a result of analyses conducted by economists in the 1960s and 1970s and played a major role in the NIT and EITC developments in that period. But although economists' thinking on programs for the poor focused most heavily on work incentives, they addressed other issues as well. In particular, Milton Friedman proposed four other reforms that would accompany the change in the work-incentive structure (Moffitt 2003b).

First, he proposed that an NIT be administered through the tax system and therefore by the Internal Revenue Service (IRS) rather than by the state welfare bureaucracies that administer traditional welfare programs. Friedman thought that this would be a more efficient system of transferring funds to the poor because the IRS already had had decades of experience in processing and collecting reports of income and paying out refunds. The only difference would be that the IRS would issue more positive payments of funds to families than before. Friedman also thought that administering the program through the tax system would reduce the "stigma" of receiving welfare. In the discussions of welfare reform in the 1960s and 1970s, the presumed stigma of receiving welfare was an often-discussed problem in the existing system, where it appeared that many families did not apply for benefits even though they were eligible because they did not wish to be perceived as dependent on the government. Friedman thought that this stigma and possible invidious distinctions would be reduced if families sent in their tax forms just as everyone else in the population did.

Second, Friedman proposed that eligibility for the NIT be universal and not restricted to any specific type of family. This was in contrast to the welfare system that operated at that time and is still in existence, which provides support primarily to single mothers and their children. Friedman thought that this was partly an issue of fairness, but he also thought that it was an issue of incentives because offering benefits only to single-mother families might encourage the formation of those types of families. It also reflected Friedman's belief, shared by virtually all economists, that benefits should be based only on income and not on any other characteristics of "deservingness" (except possibly the number of children), because these other characteristics are often subjective, as well as being liable to manipulation.

Third, Friedman proposed that the NIT provide the same benefits nationwide, unlike a state-based welfare system in the United States, where states are allowed to pay different levels of benefits. Other economists pointed out that aside from fairness considerations, uniformity of benefits nationwide would reduce incentives for welfare families to migrate to higher-benefit states.

Fourth, Friedman proposed that the NIT replace all other programs and hence be the single welfare program in the country, covering all families in all circumstances. This not only would serve efficiency in administration but also would eliminate the problem of high "cumulative" tax rates on earnings that arise when a family receives benefits from multiple programs, each with its own tax rate on earnings. Even if each program had a low

tax rate, the sum of the tax rates across all programs could result in significant work disincentives for a family receiving support from them all.

Friedman's view that the NIT should replace all other programs, including many that provide in-kind benefits to low-income families (e.g., food
stamps, Medicaid, and housing), was also based on the view held by many
economists that it is always better, from the recipient's point of view, to
provide support in the form of cash instead of specific consumption goods.
With cash, recipients can allocate the new income toward the consumption goods on which they put the highest value (i.e., marginal utility),
whereas giving recipients quantities of specific consumption goods or subsidizing the price of such goods may force recipients to consume goods of
lesser value than those on which they would have spent cash.

The EITC

Initial Design

In the ferment of the late 1960s and early 1970s, when the welfare rolls
were rising at an alarming rate, welfare political advocacy groups were
promoting ideas for a fairer and more equitable system, and riots were occurring in many low-income neighborhoods in the largest cities, the political forces for reform of the welfare system gathered strength. President
Richard Nixon proposed a version of an NIT to Congress, and it passed
the House of Representatives but failed in the Senate in 1969. It was reconsidered in subsequent sessions of Congress through 1972 but never
again came close to passage. Its failure arose from a number of complicated reasons, but one was that conservative legislators focused on the
unrestricted guarantee of benefits for nonworkers that existed in the current system and were not happy with a reform that left that feature in
place (Moynihan 1973). The NIT aimed to lessen the work disincentives
that were in the welfare system but did not eliminate them altogether, and
many in Congress appeared to be unwilling to accept a program that had
any work disincentives. Another source of concern was that the NIT
proposals expanded eligibility for welfare to two-parent families, and there
were concerns that significant work disincentives might arise for able-bodied
males in such families because they would now be given a benefit if they
did not work, whereas they had been eligible for no such benefit before.
Although the prior econometric literature had indicated rather low levels
of work-effort responsiveness to financial incentives for this group, evidence from several randomized field trials testing the work incentives of

an NIT found nontrivial reductions in work effort by men in response to the offer of an unrestricted benefit for nonworkers (Moffitt and Kehrer 1981; Burtless 1987).

After the failure of the NIT, further discussions of welfare reform continued in Congress, and proposals for various forms of earnings subsidies, as well as NIT programs, were introduced. The primary sponsor of earnings subsidy legislation was Senator Russell Long, who introduced several bills for an earnings subsidy, many offered explicitly as an alternative to an NIT (Liebman 1998; Ventry 2000). Long was quite explicit in his desire to introduce work incentives more directly and forcefully than had been proposed in an NIT. Indeed, he had opposed previous legislation for an NIT and had introduced his first earnings subsidy bill in the Senate in 1972 as a direct competitor to President Nixon's NIT bill. Long argued that an earnings subsidy would primarily serve as an offset to payroll taxes for the poor, which were seen as onerous and were rising at the time. His development of the idea of an earnings subsidy was largely influenced by one of his staff members, Michael Stern, who also sought the advice of economic experts.[3] Long's 1972 proposed legislation failed, but he reintroduced his bill every year thereafter and finally won passage in 1975 as part of a general economic stimulus package directed toward the recession occurring at the time. The EITC that passed in 1975 provided for a 10% subsidy up to $4,000 of earnings per year, resulting in a maximum subsidy of $400, and phased out the subsidy at the same 10% rate between $4,000 and $8,000 of earnings.[4] Only families with children were eligible. The initial EITC was enacted on a temporary basis but was made permanent in 1978.

Despite its modesty in work incentives and total expenditure, the EITC captured many of the other characteristics of a desirable welfare reform program that Friedman and other economists had strongly advocated. First, the EITC was to be administered by the IRS through the tax system, and the credit was to be received by taxpayers who filed tax returns just as other taxpayers did. Although there has been some further discussion of the merits of IRS administration and some see the EITC as not part of the traditional IRS mission, this way of administering the program has been judged successful by most observers, and there have been few suggestions to move EITC administration to state-level welfare agencies. As predicted by Friedman, the stigma of EITC receipt has been, to all appearances, remarkably low compared with that of other welfare programs, and participation rates have been high.

Second, eligibility for the EITC, although restricted to families with children, was much broader than in the traditional welfare system. Most important, two-parent families were made eligible for the EITC, a group that received little, if any, assistance from the traditional cash welfare system. Although this was partly a matter of equity and fairness, it also had potential implications for work incentives. An earnings subsidy might be expected to have stronger effects for persons who cannot receive any benefit if they do not work than for persons who have a nonwork benefit available to them. For single-mother families, for example, the EITC represents something close to a reduction of the tax rate in an NIT, which is a quite different programmatic change. However, as we shall see in the discussion of research findings on the relative work incentives of the EITC, its effects on two-parent families have, in fact, been smaller than for single parents.

Third, the EITC was made nationwide, although states were allowed to enact their own supplemental EITC programs if they wished to provide more generous support than that provided by the federal government. As of spring 2009, twenty-four states had done so, adding increased work incentives through their own tax systems that are often substantially greater than those at the federal level (Levitis and Koulish 2007; State EITC Online Research Center, 2009). Nevertheless, there have been no controversies about state-level variations in the level of the EITC in the way there have been for state-level variations in welfare benefits, another interesting contrast. This difference is no doubt because some states set welfare benefits at a level that is considered by many observers to be very low, whereas the federal EITC is already quite generous, so that a state that does not supplement it would not be regarded as allowing too low a level of support.

However, the fourth issue raised by Friedman, consolidation of all major transfer programs into one program, has not occurred. The EITC was layered onto the existing system without much coordination. However, the issue of the cumulative tax rate mentioned earlier does not really arise with the EITC because in the phase-in region the subsidy rate counteracts the effect of high marginal tax rates in state-level welfare programs rather than adding to them. Further, the phase-out region of the EITC is at too high a level for most state-level welfare program receipt, so the new marginal tax rate introduced by the EITC in that range is not added to any other welfare program tax rates (although it is added to the tax rate in income and payroll taxes).

The EITC also did not replace any other welfare program in the United States, including any in-kind programs. Contrary to the view of Friedman and many economists, in-kind programs have been very popular in the United States and have grown dramatically over the years (Moffitt 2003b). The usual interpretation of this popularity is that American voters are "paternalistic," meaning that they think that poor families should be consuming different goods than those families would choose for themselves if they were given cash. In fact, the EITC can be viewed as consistent with this attitude because the EITC is not, like an NIT, an unrestricted transfer of cash—it is a transfer of cash as a reward for specific behavior on the part of the poor, that is, for working. Voters believe that the poor who receive government support "should" work, just as they believe that they "should" spend their government benefits on food, housing, and medical care, the goods most heavily subsidized by in-kind programs (Moffitt 2006).

It is important to note that although work incentives were a major influence on the EITC, they were not the only rationale for the program. Many policy makers and members of the public also wished to provide more support to the "working poor"—those whose adults are working but whose wage rates are sufficiently low that family income is still below the poverty line. Many believed that this group, which receives little support from the existing system—even if they are single-mother families, because benefits in the existing welfare system are very modest—deserved more support. This belief is not inherently related to work incentives and could provide a rationale for the program even if no one changed her work effort as a result of its work incentives. It is primarily a matter of equity and who is thought to deserve support. Economists do not have much to say on this subject, although they allow for these considerations in their analyses of welfare program design through the introduction of what they term "distributional weights"—how much weight the public wishes to place on providing support to families at different points in the income distribution.

Later Developments

The EITC remained at its modest financial level, with only small increases in its size in 1979 and 1985. However, it was indexed to inflation in 1986 (at the same time all tax brackets were indexed), a major step during the Ronald Reagan administration that was enacted with bipartisan support which had little immediate impact on the level of the credit but had important long-run implications. However, the magnitude of the credit was expanded more significantly by President George H. W. Bush, whose proposed expansion passed Congress in 1990 and was phased in over the next few years. Before that expansion was completed, President Bill Clinton oversaw another expansion of the credit in legislation that passed Congress in 1993 and was phased in from 1994 to 1996 (Liebman 1998; Ventry 2000). Subsidy rates were greatly increased, and the subsidy was expanded higher into the earnings distribution, with the result that average levels of benefits expanded enormously. These increases reflected the continued popularity of the EITC as a work-incentive program but also represented its evolution into a major antipoverty program as well. In addition, it coincided with a general movement toward increased work incentives in other welfare programs, especially in traditional cash welfare. Reforms were needed to "make work pay," as the discussions at the time suggested. The landmark federal legislation of 1996 that reformed the U.S. cash welfare program was aimed at this goal, and the EITC expansion was consistent with it (see Blank 2002 and Moffitt 2003a for discussions of those reforms, and see Blank's chapter in this volume for a discussion of the influence of economists on those reforms).

The EITC today offers generous incentives to work. In tax year 2007 annual earnings for families with two or more children were supplemented at a rate of 40% up to $11,790 of earnings, for a maximum subsidy of $4,716. The subsidy was constant for earnings between that level and $15,390 and then was phased out at a rate a bit over 21%, ending at an earnings level of $37,783. For those with one child, the phase-in rate was 34%, the phase-out rate was 16%, and the subsidy ended at $33,241. There is even a modest subsidy now for childless individuals. These rates provide a very strong financial incentive to work, with subsidies often in the thousands of dollars for individuals whose earnings are not that high to begin with. The subsidy also reaches very high up into the earnings distribution compared with any other welfare program in the United States. However, the phase-out region is quite wide, and it is there that there might be some disincentives to work as well.

Expenditures on the EITC dwarf those of most other means-tested transfer programs. In tax year 2005 EITC credits amounted to over $42 billion, more than all other such programs except Medicaid and Supplemental Security Income. Almost 23 million filing units received EITC credits, with an average credit of $1,874. Although this average transfer is rather modest, it should be kept in mind that many families receive credits of over $4,000. Expenditures on the EITC also have been rising rapidly since the 1990s. From 1990 to 2005 EITC expenditures rose by 522%, equal to an average annual rate of increase of about 13% (Tax Policy Center 2007).

A major question is whether the theoretical work incentives that economists' models demonstrate have come to pass. Research suggests stronger evidence of changes in behavior for some groups than for others (see Hotz and Scholz 2003 and Eissa and Hoynes 2006 for reviews which list all studies in the research literature). The strongest evidence of positive effects is for single mothers, whose employment rates have been significantly increased by the EITC. Indeed, employment rates of single mothers have grown dramatically relative to those of other women since the early 1990s, and much of this has been ascribed to the EITC (Meyer and Rosenbaum 2001; Grogger 2003; Fang and Keane 2004). This sizable response may be surprising because single mothers have available to them a nonwork benefit from the traditional cash welfare system, and this may be anticipated to reduce responsiveness to work incentives.[5] However, several other factors work to offset this effect. One is that the tax rate in the traditional cash welfare system before 1996 was approximately 100%, and a reduction in that rate by 40% (the maximum EITC subsidy rate) could have a disproportionate effect. A second is that a large proportion of single mothers were nonworkers before the EITC was introduced, and the work incentives for that group should be expected to be larger than for individuals who are working and possibly close to the phase-out region. A third is that the reforms of the traditional cash welfare system in the 1990s reduced the effective value of the nonwork benefit considerably, and this no doubt increased the receptivity of single mothers to the EITC incentives.

The evidence for married men and women, on the other hand, indicates more modest effects of the EITC on work effort (Hotz and Scholz 2003). The work effort of married men, for example, appears to have been affected relatively little by the EITC. Despite the fact that members of this group are eligible for few benefits if they are not working, their general responsiveness to financial incentives is not large. In addition to possibly lower responsiveness in general for married men compared with, say, single mothers, married men are more likely to be working in the first place and to have earnings that put them close to the phase-out region, where work incentives are muted.

For married women, there is some evidence of some negative effects of the EITC on employment rates and hours of work. This negative effect is usually ascribed to the phase-out region of the EITC, where increases in earnings are taxed (through a reduction in the EITC subsidy) rather than supplemented. In many families wives are essentially secondary earners whose work effort increases family earnings in the phase-out region rather than in the phase-in region, so the effects on them are different from those that might be expected for single mothers, for example, who are more concentrated in the phase-in region. This is one case where the EITC can indeed reduce employment rates and not just hours of work of workers (see earlier discussion).

These results suggest some caution in interpreting the reasons for the continued popularity of the EITC. It may be that the redistributive goal of the program—simply to supplement the incomes of the working poor for equity reasons—is at least as important to policy makers and the general public as the work-incentive goal. For married men and women, it is difficult to see how the large EITC expenditure could be justified on the basis of the effects of the program on work effort alone.

Further Issues with the EITC

As is usually the case with large social reforms, a number of rather messy complications have arisen with the design and implementation of the EITC that the initial models of economists did not anticipate or at least did not initially address. However, economists have been active in addressing these issues after they have arisen.

One important issue is noncompliance with the rules of the EITC. Noncompliance arises from a variety of sources related to incorrectly claiming or not claiming the EITC (Liebman 1998; Hotz and Scholz 2003). The most important are errors related to the residence requirement, which states that a child can be claimed on a tax return only if the child lives for at least six months with the claimant. Fraudulent claims occur, for example, when two parents living apart both claim the child, or when the incorrect parent claims a child, perhaps splitting the number of qualifying children between them, in order to increase the size of the total EITC credit. However, the qualifying rules for the EITC are quite complex, and it has been estimated that the majority of errors, including incorrectly not claiming children, are inadvertent and probably a simple result of the complexity of the tax code. It is fair to say that detecting this type of noncompliance is not an issue with which the IRS has traditionally been concerned.[6] It is also fair to say that state-level welfare agencies have many more years of experience with this issue because methods of detecting true family structure have been central to the eligibility rules of cash transfer programs, and the audit programs, as well as the face-to-face interviews with caseworkers, that exist at the state level would have been better prepared to deal with these problems. A second form of noncompliance occurs when a married couple files separately or as head of household in order to lower income on one or both of the returns to qualify for the EITC. A third, less important form of noncompliance is overreporting of earnings in order to qualify for a greater credit, at least in the phase-in region. Again, the IRS has traditionally been more focused on underreporting of income than overreporting. However, the noncompliance errors of this type have been found to involve both underreporting and overreporting of earnings, as well as errors in reporting other types of income that affect EITC eligibility (e.g., investment income and self-employment income), and are, again, thought largely to involve inadvertent errors. The IRS has been working on improved verification and audit procedures in recent years to address these issues.

A second issue is that the EITC is usually received as a lump-sum tax refund in the spring of every year rather than appearing in the weekly or monthly paychecks received by workers over the course of the previous year. Initially there was some concern that families might not perceive the spring refund as being sufficiently related to their work over the previous year to induce changes in work behavior, but this has clearly not been a problem, at least for single mothers. Nevertheless, a supplement that appears in the paycheck would represent a closer match to most economists' idea of an earnings subsidy than an annual refund. The EITC has an "advance payment" option that allows taxpayers to receive supplements over the course of the year, but there is a nontrivial burden on the worker to fill out the necessary forms for his or her employer, particularly for workers who might change jobs fairly frequently. Partly as a result, very few families have taken up the option. Other countries, like the United Kingdom, have successfully implemented earnings subsidy programs that operate largely through employers. The low take-up rate for intrayear receipt by U.S. families may instead be a result of a positive preference to receive a single large refund that can be used to draw down debt or make purchases of large consumer durables without being forced to save for those items over the year.

A third issue is the effects of the EITC on marriage. The EITC generates a marriage penalty for some individuals in the population not unlike the marriage penalty that is present in the positive income tax. However, the EITC provides marriage bonuses to some families as well. Couples facing penalties are typically those where both spouses are working and have similar earnings, and where the combined earnings if married result in a reduction or elimination of the EITC benefit. The empirical evidence on these effects to date suggests little effect of the EITC on marriage and divorce, however (Hotz and Scholz 2003). Nevertheless, the marriage penalty in the federal income tax, including the EITC, has been the subject of much congressional attention in recent years.

Conclusions

The EITC is been one of the success stories of social policy in the past fifty years. The program has provided important new work incentives for the low-income population in the United States, work incentives that exceed those of any other similar social program. It has provided income support to millions of working poor families. It has had positive effects on the work effort of an important needy group, single mothers with very low skills, and has assisted in the movement of many mothers off welfare and into the labor market. The underlying concept of the EITC can be traced to economists' ideas of the 1960s and 1970s and, hence, economics can be given much of the credit for the EITC.

Despite the work incentives provided by the EITC, levels of work among many low-income families remain low. Many single mothers are still on welfare or are off welfare but not working. Those women need assistance in improving their job skills through education and training. Finding adequate child care is still a barrier to work for many single mothers. Further, many unskilled males in the country are not working and are without government support. Skill improvement through education and training are needed to make these men more attractive to employers. More aggressive and direct intervention in providing employers incentives to hire unskilled individuals and to give them on-the-job training may be needed.

Notes

The author would like to thank Rebecca Blank, Sheldon Danziger, Hilary Hoynes, Jeffrey Liebman, Karl Scholz, and John Siegfried for very helpful comments.

1. This discussion assumes that the family could choose either program but could not receive benefits from both. Equivalently, it assumes that the welfare program includes the earnings subsidy as income and "taxes" it at a 100% rate; that is, it lowers the welfare benefit dollar-for-dollar for any earnings subsidy the family receives. However, if the family could receive both the welfare program and the earnings subsidy, without any taxation of the latter by the former, the incentive to work would increase even at low levels of earnings (earnings less than point C).
2. This prediction does not quite hold for so-called secondary workers in a household. See later discussion.
3. Stern consulted Jodie T. Allen and Heather Ross, who discussed the economic issues with him and informed Stern of the research literature on earnings subsidies, including the work of economist Robert Haveman (Haveman 1972).
4. The payroll tax in 1975 was about 5%, assessed on both employee and employer, for a total of 10%.
5. Formally speaking, traditional economic labor-supply models imply that individuals with higher nonwork income have higher reservation wages, that is, require a higher wage rate in order to be induced to go to work.
6. However, the IRS does have some other residence rules in the tax code and has a traditional support test for claiming dependents, so it is not completely unfamiliar with the issues. The EITC used a support test before 1990, but this was replaced by the currently used residency requirement.

References

Barth, M., and D. Greenberg. 1971. "Incentive Effects of Some Pure and Mixed Transfer Systems." *Journal of Human Resources* 6 (Spring): 149–170.

Blank, R. 2002. "Evaluating Welfare Reform in the United States." *Journal of Economic Literature* 40 (December): 1105–1166.

Burtless, G. 1987. "The Work Response to a Guaranteed Income: A Survey of Experimental Evidence." In *Lessons from the Income Maintenance Experiments,* ed. A. Munnell. Boston: Federal Reserve Bank of Boston: 22–52.

Eissa, N., and H. Hoynes. 2006. "Behavioral Responses to Taxes: Lessons from the EITC and Labor Supply." In *Tax Policy and the Economy,* vol. 20, ed. J. M. Poterba. Cambridge, Mass: MIT Press: 74–110.

Fang, H., and M. Keane. 2004. "Assessing the Impact of Welfare Reform on Single Mothers." *Brookings Papers on Economic Activity* 1: 1–116.

Friedman, M. 1962. *Capitalism and Freedom.* Chicago: University of Chicago Press.

Grogger, J. 2003. "The Effects of Time Limits, the EITC, and Other Policy Changes on Welfare Use, Work, and Income among Female-Headed Families." *Review of Economics and Statistics* 85 (May): 394–408.

Haveman, R. 1972. "Work-Conditioned Subsidies as an Income Maintenance Strategy: Issues of Program Structure and Integration." Discussion Paper 141–72, Institute for Research on Poverty, Madison, Wis.

Hotz, V. J., and J. K. Scholz. 2003. "The Earned Income Tax Credit." In *Means-Tested Transfer Programs in the United States,* ed. R. Moffitt. Chicago: University of Chicago Press: 141–197.

Kesselman, J. R. 1969. "Labor-Supply Effects of Income, Income-Work, and Wage Subsidies." *Journal of Human Resources* 4 (Summer): 275–292.

Killingsworth, M. 1983. *Labor Supply.* Cambridge: Cambridge University Press.

Lampman, R. 1965. "Approaches to the Reduction of Poverty." *American Economic Review* 55 (May): 521–529.

Levitis, J., and J. Koulish. 2007. "A Majority of States with Income Taxes Have Enacted State Earned Income Tax Credits." Washington: Center on Budget and Policy Priorities.

Liebman, J. 1998. "The Impact of the Earned Income Tax Credit on Incentives and Income Distribution." In *Tax Policy and the Economy,* ed. J. Poterba. Cambridge, Mass.: MIT Press: 83–119.

Meyer, B., and D. Rosenbaum. 2001. "Welfare, the Earned Income Tax Credit, and the Labor Supply of Single Mothers." *Quarterly Journal of Economics* 116 (August): 1063–1114.

Moffitt, R. 2003a. "The Temporary Assistance for Needy Families Program." In *Means-Tested Transfer Programs in the United States,* ed. R. Moffitt. Chicago: University of Chicago Press: 291–363.

———. 2003b. "The Negative Income Tax and the Evolution of U.S. Welfare Policy." *Journal of Economic Perspectives* 17 (Summer): 119–140.

———. 2006. "Welfare Work Requirements with Paternalistic Government Preferences." *Economic Journal* 116 (November): F441–F458.

Moffitt, R., and K. Kehrer. 1981. "The Effect of Tax and Transfer Programs on Labor Supply: The Evidence from the Income Maintenance Experiments." In *Research in Labor Economics,* ed. R. Ehrenberg. Greenwich, Conn: JAI Press: 103–150.

Moynihan, D. 1973. *The Politics of a Guaranteed Annual Income: The Nixon Administration and the Family Assistance Plan.* New York: Random House.

State EITC Online Research Center. Available at www.stateeitc.com, accessed May 5, 2009.

Tax Policy Center. 2007. "Tax Facts: Low Income." www.taxpolicycenter.org/TaxFacts/listdocs.cfm?topic2id=40.

Tobin, J. 1966. "On the Economic Status of the Negro." *Daedalus* 94 (Fall): 878–899.

Ventry, D. 2000. "The Collision of Tax and Welfare Politics: The Political History of the Earned Income Tax Credit, 1969–99." *National Tax Journal* 53, pt. 2 (December): 983–1026.

COMMENT

V. Joseph Hotz

Robert Moffitt has provided an excellent, concise discussion of the economics of the Earned Income Tax Credit (EITC) and the contributions that economists have made to both conceptualizing and analyzing the effects of this important social program for the working poor. As Moffitt notes, the apparent support for the EITC among policy makers, from the political Left and the Right, may reflect a desire by policy makers out of a sense of fairness to do something for a disadvantaged group thought to be largely neglected during the 1960s and 1970s, namely, the working poor. But, as Moffitt makes clear by contrasting the design of the EITC with that of the negative income tax (NIT), the former more clearly incentivizes work for the poor than does the latter. And economists—notably Moffitt himself—have clearly played an important role not only in pointing out these incentive effects but also in developing empirical evidence on the effects of these two social policies on work, especially employment.

I have little to quibble with in Moffitt's excellent discussion. Rather, I shall use my comments to consider a potential consequence of the pro-work-incentive effects of the EITC for low-skilled workers. As Moffitt has noted, the theoretical effect of the EITC on employment rates among those eligible for the credit is unambiguously positive. Moreover, a number of studies have documented that these predictions are borne out in the data, finding that the increases in the EITC have resulted in higher rates of employment among single mothers (see Hotz and Scholz 2003, and Eissa and

Hoynes 2006 for reviews). These effects are sizable and substantively important. For example, Meyer and Rosenbaum (2001) estimate that the EITC increased the annual employment rate of single mothers by 7.2 percentage points from 1984 to 1992, accounting for over 60% of the overall employment increase experienced by this group. These findings suggest that the EITC has been a public policy success in "making work pay" for a group in society for whom work had not been the norm. But, as is often the case, policies can potentially have unexpected consequences. In what follows, I consider one of them, namely, that this sizable EITC-induced increase in the employment of single mothers may have had the unintended consequence of lowering the wages of less skilled workers, including those who are either ineligible for or only marginally benefit from the EITC.

Simple economic models of labor markets suggest that exogenously induced increases in the supply of labor tend to lower the equilibrium wage rate unless the demand for labor in these markets is perfectly elastic. More generally, how increases in the supply of a factor of production affect the equilibrium factor price depends on the substitutability between that factor and the other factors in the production of aggregate output and the extent to which technological change affects the factor's relative productivity. Moreover, these features of production determine how and to what extent such supply shifts will affect the equilibrium prices of these other factors. With respect to the expansions in the generosity of the EITC, it follows that the sizable EITC-induced increases in the labor supply (employment) of single mothers noted earlier may have depressed the wages of this group, thereby reducing the poverty-reducing benefits of the expansions of these tax credits. Moreover, to the extent that the EITC expansions did depress the equilibrium wages in such markets, workers who are close or perfect substitutes for this group in production—including those who are not eligible for the credit (i.e., workers with incomes above the phase-out range of the credit) or are eligible for a much lower credit (i.e., childless workers)—would have been unintentionally harmed by these expansions through lower wages and no or small offsetting EITC payments.

Two recent studies by economists have looked at these potential wage effects of the EITC. Leigh (2007) estimated the effects of changes in the generosity of the EITC on the pretax wages of various demographic groups in the United States, using intertemporal variation in the federal EITC and across-state and intertemporal variations in state EITCs. Leigh's findings confirm the findings noted earlier that increases in the generosity of the EITC had positive effects on the employment rates of various groups of low-skilled workers (e.g., high-school dropouts and those with only

high-school diplomas), but no effects on the labor supply of college graduates, a group typically not eligible for the EITC. More important for my
discussion here, Leigh estimated that a 10% increase in the generosity of
the EITC results in a 4% drop in the wages of high-school dropouts, a 2%
drop for high-school graduates—with negative effects that typically are
even larger for those with children—and no effect on the wages of college
graduates. Using these estimates, Leigh found an elasticity of labor demand
of around −0.3, an estimate close to the one found by Borjas (2003) in his
analysis of the effects of immigration on the wages of native-born workers
in the United States.

Rothstein (2007) also estimates the effects of the EITC-induced increase
in employment on wages in less skilled labor markets. In his analysis Rothstein exploits the fact that women, who differ in their marital and child-
bearing statuses but are in the same skill group (and, therefore, are assumed
to be perfect substitutes in production) face different average tax rates
because of their differential treatment under the EITC. He uses this variation in tax rates as an instrumental variable to obtain estimates of the effects of exogenous changes in women's labor supply on wages of workers
across the skill distribution. Rothstein's initial estimates of this effect were
positive, suggesting that labor-demand functions are upward sloping.
Rothstein argues that this wrong-signed effect is likely the result of either
a cyclical increase in the demand for low-skilled labor or a skill-biased
technical change that favored low-skilled workers. After attempts to adjust for these potential shifts in labor demand, Rothstein obtains estimates
of the demand for labor between −0.28 and −0.37, which is a range of estimates that are consistent with those found by Leigh and by Borjas in his
2003 study of the labor-market effects of immigration.

As suggested earlier, this recent analysis of the effects of EITC-induced
increases in the labor supply of a low-skilled group on market wage rates
is closely related to the more developed literature in economics on the effects of immigration-induced increases in the supply of (foreign) low-
skilled workers on the wages of low-skilled, native-born workers. This
latter literature has been highly contentious, with evidence ranging from
sizable and negative effects of the influx of low-skilled, foreign workers to
the United States over the last twenty to thirty years on the wages of low-
skilled, native-born workers (Borjas 2003) to small and insignificant ones
(Card 2001). As noted in several studies (Borjas 2003; Ottaviano and Peri
2007; Borjas, Grogger, and Hanson 2008), the effect of immigration on the
wages of less skilled workers hinges on the substitutability in production
of different types of workers (e.g., foreign-born versus native-born workers
and single mothers versus childless single women) and how technological

change may have affected the productivity of such workers, and, most notably, how one deals with these two features of aggregate production when estimating the elasticities of demand for low-skilled workers in the United States over the past fifteen to twenty years. Progress on ways to account for these features in estimation is essential not only to improve our understanding of the effects of immigration on low-wage labor markets but also to determine the extent to which the EITC has had unintended consequences for the wages of low-skilled workers in the United States.

References

Borjas, George. 2003. "The Labor Demand Curve Is Downward Sloping: Reexamining the Impact of Immigration on the Labor Market." *Quarterly Journal of Economics* 118(4): 1335–1374.

Borjas, George, Jeffrey Grogger, and Gordon Hanson. 2008. "Imperfect Substitution between Immigrants and Natives: A Reappraisal." NBER Working Paper 13887, March.

Card, David. 2001. "Immigrant Inflows, Native Outflows, and the Local Labor Market Impacts of Higher Immigration." *Journal of Labor Economics* 19(1): 22–64.

Eissa, Nada, and Hillary Hoynes. 2006. "Behavioral Responses to Taxes: Lessons from the EITC and Labor Supply." In *Tax Policy and the Economy*, vol. 20, ed. J. M. Poterba. Cambridge, Mass: MIT Press, 74–110.

Hotz, V. Joseph, and John Karl Scholz. 2003. "The Earned Income Tax Credit." In *Means-Tested Transfer Programs in the United States*, ed. R. A. Moffitt. Chicago: University of Chicago Press, 141–198.

Leigh, Andrew. 2007. "Who Benefits from the Earned Income Tax Credit? Incidence among Recipients, Coworkers and Firms." Unpublished manuscript, Australian National University, July.

Meyer, Bruce, and Daniel Rosenbaum. 2001. "Welfare, the Earned Income Tax Credit, and the Labor Supply of Single Mothers." *Quarterly Journal of Economics* 116(3): 1063–1114.

Ottaviano, Gianmarco, and Giovanni Peri. 2007. "Rethinking the Effects of Immigration on Wages." Unpublished manuscript, University of California at Davis, November.

Rothstein, J. 2007. "The Unintended Consequences of Encouraging Work: Is the EITC as Good as an NIT?" Unpublished manuscript, Princeton University, November.

CHAPTER FOUR

Trade Liberalization and Growth in Developing Countries

Anne O. Krueger

A half century ago the non-Communist world was regarded as consisting of two blocs: the industrial countries and the "underdeveloped" countries, as they were then called. The economies of the industrial part of the world were growing at an unprecedented pace. In developing countries (as I shall call them), by contrast, growth was generally at lower rates than in the rich countries. In addition, most developing countries were experiencing rates of population growth that were very high and often rising.

Most assessments of the prospects of the developing countries were therefore pessimistic: with rates of growth of per capita income in industrial countries above those of all but the highest-income group of developing countries, it appeared that not only the absolute gap between living standards but also the relative gap would continue increasing.[1] There was great pessimism about the possibility of declining rates of population growth, which seemed to exacerbate the outlook.

This can easily be seen from numbers given in the early 1960s. Although there was considerable variation from country to country, only two countries (both in Africa) were estimated to have grown at rates per capita above 6%, while only nine countries were in the 4%–6% range. Forty-three countries had experienced growth rates less than 2%, and twenty-six were in the 2%–4% range.[2] From 1950 to 1960, low-income countries (then defined as having a per capita income of $265 or less) had experienced falling per capita incomes at an average annual rate of 1.4%, and middle-income (per capita incomes of $266 to $520) and upper-middle-income (per capita incomes of $521 to $1,075) countries had grown at average annual rates of 2.2 and 2.4%, respectively, while higher-income developing countries had experienced per capita income growth of 3.2% annually during the decade. These numbers contrasted with an average annual 3.0% growth rate among the industrial countries. Moreover, in the 1960s per capita incomes in the industrial countries accelerated to an average annual growth rate of 4%, while the developing countries did little better, and some groups did worse, than they had in the preceding decade.[3]

To be sure, there were some signs of progress in important dimensions in many countries. Life expectancies, which had been abysmally low— thirty-two years in India, for example—had increased significantly. Health and nutrition indicators also suggested at least modest improvement in most countries. School enrollments, although still low, had risen.

But overall, living standards were unimaginably low by Western standards. Infant mortality rates were over 100 per 1,000 in many developing countries and over 200 per 1,000 in some. Malnutrition was pervasive, especially in rural areas, and waterborne and other diseases were prevalent. Safe drinking water was available only in major cities, albeit often erratically, and it was generally unavailable in rural areas and urban slums.

During the quarter century to 1975, there had been a remarkable similarity of policies in the developing countries. Almost all developing countries had large rural populations, and a large fraction—typically 60% to 70%—was engaged in agriculture, which usually accounted for half or more of gross domestic product (GDP). There was a widespread view, if not total consensus, that developing countries had to develop their industry and would not, at least initially, be able to compete with manufacturing industries in the industrial countries. It was also thought that without the development of industry, developing countries would remain poor. Industrialization was equated with development and modernization.

It was generally believed that economic development and rising living standards should be a major, if not the primary, objective of government policy. Given the consensus on that belief and the need for industrialization, policies were adopted to foster the growth of new industrial activities. Although the details varied, the overall thrust of these policies was similar in all countries: they in effect prohibited imports of goods that might compete with newly established industries. Sometimes prohibitive tariffs were imposed. In other instances import licensing was required, and licenses were granted only when it was determined that there was no domestic source of supply available. Often these (very strong) incentives for establishing new industries were supplemented by domestic-content requirements (so that a producer of, say, automobiles would be required to obtain a certain percentage of his parts and components from domestic sources), thus requiring the development of suppliers to manufacturing industries.

These import-substitution policies were consistent with, and part of, a development strategy that assumed government ownership or regulation of most modern economic activities. Foreign-trade and exchange controls were a necessary background against which these other interventions could be effective, and they contributed to the difficulties that followed. Space limitations prevent elaboration of the myriad regulations and controls that surrounded economic activity in the "formal economy" of most countries. The interested reader can consult the World Bank's *Doing Business* (2008) or a similar source to glean some idea of the extent of these regulations. Bureaucratic delays of many months could shut down a factory or factories for want of an import license for a particular spare part or replacement machine. Smuggling became widespread, and corruption in the issuance of licenses was the rule rather than the exception. Administrative efforts to thwart smuggling and misrepresentation on licenses often resulted in reduced production because of delays in receiving raw materials and other needed inputs.

The effects of import-substitution regimes did not immediately become evident, but over time would-be entrepreneurs knew that their start-ups would be protected. Accordingly, they paid little heed to cost controls. Resources available for investment were channeled into new industries, sometimes in state economic enterprises and sometimes by rationing scarce credit to private-sector firms that would develop the desired products. Producers inevitably found new monopoly positions more attractive than expanding capacity in their existing lines of activity. It was also more profitable for an entrant to establish its own monopoly position than to compete with rivals in an already-existing import-substitution industry. The result was that industries were established that sold their products on the domestic market at prices often far above those of competing imports; meanwhile, the monopoly positions held by producers often meant that quality was poor and costs very high.

At first, many of these activities appeared sensible: assembly of radios and bicycles, production of garments and later of textiles and footwear, and similar activities. They were intensive in the use of unskilled labor, had relatively large domestic markets, at least in the more populous countries, and did not place excessive burdens on scarce engineering and technical skills or limited capital resources. But as the drive for "import substitution" continued, because of the small size of the domestic market, lack of skilled workers, and other difficulties, it was generally necessary to move into activities where costs were intrinsically higher in tiny domestic markets than those prevailing internationally, and there could be either one firm that met market demand with a monopoly position or several small firms, each of which was so small that it had high costs. New industries were often increasingly capital intensive, despite the fact that developing countries had very little capital per person relative to industrial countries. The fact that sheltered producers had little incentive to seek productivity improvements compounded the inefficiencies.

All these factors contributed to very low productivity growth in developing countries; in some countries it was even negative. Artificially cheap capital goods imports (for those fortunate enough to receive import licenses) encouraged the use of capital-intensive means of production. That, in turn, led to very low rates of growth of employment in the very industries in which growth was to be concentrated. Moreover, in most countries "informal sectors" emerged and grew rapidly; these were economic activities that avoided the bureaucratic controls and regulations that governed economic activity in the new import-substitution industries. They were labor intensive, but generally had very low productivity, lacked access to imported machinery or equipment, and were generally very small in scale.

Moreover, export earnings grew at much lower rates than the demand for imports. This was in significant part because incentives were so highly directed toward producing goods that would compete with imports that few investments were made in exportable production. Even if there were potentially exportable lines of activity, the requirement that producers use domestic inputs (usually of inferior quality and high cost) and the great attractiveness of investing in import-competing sectors generally discouraged export growth.

In consequence, balance-of-payments crises were frequent among the developing countries. Almost all these countries (just like the industrial countries) adhered to fixed nominal exchange rates and were reluctant to change them, even though inflation rates were generally higher, and often much higher, than in industrial countries. As inflation proceeded, exporting became less and less profitable at constant nominal exchange rates, while imports of permitted items—the machinery, equipment, raw materials, and intermediate goods used in production of import-competing goods—were becoming relatively cheaper. The authorities usually at first resorted to tighter quantitative restrictions on imports, permitting entry only for those goods deemed "essential" for domestic production. But even with those restrictions, the day came when it was clear that there was no way to finance even essential imports.

As that time approached and imports became increasingly scarce, domestic production—which was by then heavily dependent on imports for inputs of raw materials and intermediate goods—leveled off and began to fall. Concurrently, of course, the rate of economic growth fell, if real output did not decline absolutely. Investment was greatly reduced because much machinery and equipment needed for investment could not be produced domestically and the inability to provide foreign exchange precluded importing it.

To alleviate the foreign-exchange crisis, the authorities generally had to take several measures, tightening domestic monetary and fiscal policy to reduce inflation and domestic aggregate demand and devaluing the currency in order to curb import demand and to make exporting more attractive. That tightening, of course, resulted in a further slowdown of economic activity in the short run, although often foreign financial support from the International Monetary Fund, the World Bank, and others enabled importing to resume and consequently production to increase relatively rapidly.

At first, policy makers and analysts blamed "foreign-exchange crises" for a slowdown in growth, but slowly they recognized that the upswing in each successive "stop-go" cycle was generally shorter than the last and had a lower overall growth rate, while the downturns were longer lasting and deeper. In consequence, growth rates in developing countries generally tended to slow down, while at the same time the overall foreign-trade and exchange-rate regime became more and more restrictive, with increasingly adverse effects on economic growth and living standards.

Although many economists accepted the infant-industry argument—the supposed need for an initial period of "protection" for industries while they developed—many questioned the ways in which protection was provided almost indiscriminately across the board, extended to virtually anyone who decided to produce import-competing goods, and retained indefinitely. But the appeal, especially to the modernizing elite, of the argument that in order to have rapid growth and achieve high living standards, one had to have domestic industrial development through import substitution was hardly dented in most developing countries.

Economists had long argued that there were enormous advantages to trade, including the ability to use comparative advantage (for example, in producing very unskilled-labor-intensive products), the removal of domestic monopoly positions and provision of competition for producers, and learning from activities abroad. But in most countries and for a considerable period of time, the arguments fell on deaf ears,[4] in large part because decision makers in developing countries believed that their industries were so weak that they would not be able to compete at all with competitors in the developed world. A commitment to import substitution was a central tenet of most governments' stated strategies for economic development.

In each individual country it was difficult, if not impossible, to determine the extent to which domestic policies, weather vagaries, or external conditions were contributing to poor economic performance. That enabled analysts to believe that the low growth performance in their country was attributable to factors other than the import-substitution strategy itself. Adverse movements in the terms of trade, bureaucratic failures in administering licensing and other regulations, particulars of the import-substitution strategy, inadequacy of infrastructure, corruption and smuggling, and a host of other reasons were given. In most countries the policy reaction to the perceived deceleration of growth was to impose even further regulations in an attempt to thwart the undesired behavior, to increase spending on infrastructure, or otherwise to intensify efforts, leaving the underlying import-substitution strategy unchanged.

By the late 1960s evidence was beginning to accumulate across countries that the strategy was a failure. A major research project to analyze the difficulties developing countries were having, involving leading economic development and trade researchers, was mounted through the National Bureau of Economic Research. Each researcher was to investigate the trade restrictions, the trade and payments regime, and their effects in a particular country. Common questions were set to be addressed in each study. The outcome was a series of ten country studies plus two summary volumes. All but one of the country studies were published, and each of the ten delineated the regulations governing trade and their effects on incentives in the country in question.

The researchers quantified the effects of the trade and payments regime: the variability of the real exchange rate, the protection actually accorded to imports, the differentials in incentives for producing exportables and import-competing goods, and other factors. They also reported the inefficiencies associated with the import-substitution strategies in the individual countries.

Individual researchers' findings were each suggestive of, but not conclusive about, the detrimental effects of these import-substitution regimes. But when the results of the individual studies were compared, what was striking was the similarity of the overall effects of these regimes. Infant industries had become "senescent" without any period of adulthood and competitiveness in between. Few, if any, of the encouraged industries had become able to compete on world markets, and protection had seldom been reduced, much less removed; indeed, levels of protection for many new industries had often increased over time.

The economic inefficiencies encouraged by import-substitution regimes were glaringly evident. For example, a policy to ration scarce foreign exchange to producers in proportion to their productive capacities had resulted in expansion of each firm in the industry, in an effort to increase market share, when there were already insufficient imports to enable existing capacity to be reasonably fully used. The same policy also gave each producer a guaranteed share of the market because the amounts that each could produce were broadly determined by their imports of intermediate goods and raw materials.

These and related findings were met initially with considerable skepticism, so entrenched were the beliefs in import substitution.[5] But during the 1960s South Korea and Taiwan began to follow an alternative approach in which they dramatically altered their economic policies. I shall recount the broad outlines of the South Korean story here, partly because it is one of the most dramatic, and partly for lack of space to do more. That story well illustrates the benefits of the alternative strategy and the enormous advances in economic (and political) well-being of the South Korean people that resulted.

As of 1960 South Korea was one of the poorest countries in Asia (which was then still the continent—except Japan—with the lowest per capita income). Its per capita income is estimated to have been very close to that of India. A Japanese colony until 1946, South Korea had then experienced a bout of hyperinflation, followed by the Korean War from 1950 to 1953, during which battles were fought up and down the peninsula with widespread destruction.

During the rest of the 1950s after the end of the war, South Korean economic growth, even during the reconstruction period, when it should have been rapid, never exceeded 5%, which meant that per capita income was increasing at less than 2.5% annually, even after its big drop during the Korean War. And that was despite large foreign aid inflows that averaged close to 10% of GDP.

In the 1950s South Korean economic policies were directed toward import substitution. Exports, of which 88% were primary commodities, grew very slowly. The country had the then-highest rate of inflation in the world (officially 25% annually, but judged by many observers to be much higher because price controls were in effect) and large government budget deficits. The nominal exchange rate was held constant for long periods despite the high rate of inflation, and import surcharges were often imposed on top of highly restrictive import licensing. Even with the surcharges, import licenses were very valuable commodities, and favoritism and corruption surrounded the administration of the licensing regime.[6]

South Korea seemed economically disadvantaged. It had the highest rate of population density in agriculture in the world, despite a mountainous and inhospitable terrain. There were few natural resources. Population growth was rapid. The domestic savings rate was close to zero, and virtually all investment was financed by foreign aid receipts.

Even several years after the Korean War, economic prospects did not seem to have improved significantly. Growth rates were still in the 3–5% range, very low given reconstruction, while inflation was high, and prospects for improvement seemed dim. The American Congress, in debating foreign aid in the mid-1950s, concluded that there was little or no hope for sustained growth in South Korea, that henceforth the volume of aid should start declining, and that aid should be limited to goods for "sustaining" the population rather than attempting to support more rapid growth.[7]

The prospects of declining aid and other factors were quite clearly a shock to the Korean people. Recounting all the considerations that went into policy reform would take us too far afield—books have been written on the subject.[8]

But economics helped enormously. A Chinese American economist, S. C. Tsiang, had been a major advisor to the Taiwanese government since the early 1950s. Taiwan had rejected the highly biased import-substitution strategy and had followed economists' precepts. The economy's exports began growing rapidly, and, with that, economic growth accelerated dramatically.[9] South Korean economists were well aware of Taiwan's success and also of economists' arguments for open trade regimes and against high levels of protection. The first step in policy reform was taken in 1958, shortly after Congress's decision.

With the support of the International Monetary Fund, a stabilization program was undertaken that removed many of the inefficiencies of the multiple-exchange-rate regime. It led to a reduction in the rate of inflation and to a more realistic exchange rate.

That, however, was only the first step. By 1960 measures were taken so that exporters could obtain needed imports at world prices and without the delays that had accompanied import licensing. They were also entitled to, and given priority in, allocations of domestic credit (which was still rationed at very low interest rates). The authorities began offsetting the effects of domestic inflation by altering the exchange rate in line with inflation. That measure assured exporters that their foreign-exchange earnings would not be eroded between the time they accepted an order and receipt of payment after delivery. All these measures were aimed at encouraging exporting activities. It did not matter what was exported; entitlements to credit, tax provisions, and receipts of won for dollars earned were the same for all. This meant that incentives were fairly uniform across export activities.

Except for the provision that exporters could get their needed imports duty-free, little was done initially to dismantle the high rates of protection extended to import-competing producers. But the export incentives, which were available to all exporters without discrimination regarding the nature of the product being sold, were sufficient to offset almost all the bias that had existed against exporting in the prior trade and payments regime.[10]

By 1963 the authorities began addressing problems of macroeconomic stability, reforming their tax and public expenditure policies so that inflationary pressures were greatly diminished. By the mid-1960s inflation had fallen to single digits, and simultaneously, interest rates were increased so that they exceeded the rate of inflation. Duties on imports were greatly reduced by the late 1960s (and even further in later years). Over the next several decades additional policy reforms were undertaken to support economic growth. All these reforms—positive real interest rates, the reduction in protection of domestic industries, and fiscal reforms—were undertaken by an economics team and were in line with economic policy precepts.

For present purposes there are two important points. First, the sea change in economic policy undertaken by the Koreans was largely in line with the economic policies of open trade advocated by economists since Adam Smith and David Ricardo and was very different from the sorts of policies that were still being pursued in most developing countries. Second, the results were spectacular: peoples' lives were transformed.

It is hard to convey the magnitude and extent of the Korean transformation. In 1960 Korea's per capita income, in 1990 prices, is estimated to have been $1,302. By 1970 it had almost doubled, to $2,208; by 1990 it was $8,977, or almost seven times the 1960 level. Over the period from 1963 to 1995, real national income is estimated to have grown at an average annual rate of 7.89%.[11] To put that figure in comparative perspective, in 1960 Korea's per capita income was about 12% of U.S. per capita income and less than three-quarters of that of Ghana. By 1990 Korea's per capita income was over 40% of that of the United States and nine times that of Ghana.[12] Korea was no longer a developing country; it was a "newly industrialized country" or "emerging market."

During the first decade of Korea's remarkable growth story, export value (in U.S. dollars) grew at a phenomenal and unheard-of average annual rate of 40%. In 1985 prices, exports rose from 2.4% of GDP in 1961 to 11.1% of GDP in 1970, 32% of GDP by 1980, and 39.0% of GDP by 1992. Of these exports, 15% were manufactured goods in 1960, 77% in

1970, and 93.8% by 1990.[13] This growth, of course, completely undermined the arguments of those who had said that manufacturing industries in developing countries could never be started and become internationally competitive without protection from international competitors.

But the improvement in people's lives went well beyond improved living standards and release from poverty. It is estimated that in 1964 about 16% of the urban labor force was unemployed. That figure fell to about 7% by the late 1960s and to less than 3% by 1988. Simultaneously, average real wages in manufacturing grew at a breathtaking rate of 8% annually over the subsequent three decades, and the Korean income distribution remained more equal than that of most developing countries and relatively unchanged until the 1980s.

The rate of population growth decreased sharply: whereas population growth had been 2.4% in the 1963–1970 period, it fell to 0.5% by the first few years of the twenty-first century. Life expectancies increased dramatically, from 54 and 58 years for men and women, respectively, in 1960 to 63 and 67 by 1970 and to 74 and 81 in 2005.[14] The infant mortality rate, which had been 85 per 1,000 in 1960, had fallen to 21 per 1,000 by 1991 (data from Mason et al. 1980, 90).

There was also a major shift from rural to urban areas and employment. In 1961, 48.8% of GDP had originated in agriculture and mining; by 1993 the figure had fallen to 7.4% (Cha, Kim, and Perkins 1977, 61), while that of the industrial sector had risen from 12.3% to 43%. Educational attainments of the population also rose sharply. In 1960, 43% of the population over the age of fifteen had had no formal education, and only 10.2% had had more than a primary-school education. By 1995 only 6.5% of the population over the age of fifteen had had no formal education, and 80% had had more than a primary education.

One could continue. The savings rate rose dramatically, from virtually 0% to over 30%; the rate of productivity growth increased remarkably; and other indicators showed improvements. Overall, the quality of life for the vast majority of the Korean people was transformed. From an uneducated, rural, poor, and short-lived population, the people became much more highly educated, urban, reasonably well off, and with life expectancies matching those in other industrial countries.

Discussion of the Asian crisis and Korea's crisis of the late 1990s would take us too far afield. Two things should be noted, however. First, even at the depth of the crisis in 1998, Korean per capita income was well above that of countries such as India and Ghana; Koreans were still better off than in the 1960s by a much wider margin than people in most developing countries. Second, after the onset of the crisis, growth resumed in less than a year and a half, and Korean economic growth has continued since that time at around 5% a year.

The more general point is that although it took many policy reforms to enable the Korean economy to achieve such a spectacular transformation, trade liberalization was hugely important, and probably a sine qua non, for it to happen. People's lives in Korea were transformed in terms of health and nutrition, education, and all indicators of well-being. The policy changes that brought this about were undertaken by an economics team using the standard tools of economics. The team was reinforced in its commitment by the Taiwanese success and by research findings that related that success to policy reforms.

After the Korean experience (and that of Taiwan, Hong Kong, and Singapore), other countries began altering their economic policies and their trade and payments regime in the late 1970s. In Asia the next countries to change policies were in Southeast Asia, with China abandoning inner-looking policies in the early 1980s. The rapid rate of growth of the Chinese economy is well known to all; living standards have risen, and millions have been lifted out of poverty as a consequence.

Indian economic reforms began a decade later than the Chinese, but in recent years Indian economic growth has accelerated sharply. All estimates of the improvement in living standards suggest great strides forward in what was an extremely poor country, and that the percentage of people in poverty has fallen dramatically. It was earlier mentioned that Indian average life expectancy in the 1950s was thirty-two years; it is now well above sixty.

There have been substantial reforms and significant improvements in other countries too. The Chilean economy was transformed by policy reforms that began in the mid-1970s. Mexico liberalized significantly in the late 1980s and cemented that liberalization by joining the North American Free Trade Agreement (NAFTA). Among developing countries as a group, trade barriers have dropped sharply. Even in Africa, which has arguably been the slowest to reform, tariff rates began falling and quantitative restrictions began diminishing in importance by the turn of the twenty-first century.

Economic growth is generally faster in countries with more open trade regimes.[15] In part, this is because of the gains that accrue through openness itself. But in significant part, openness is a "forcing variable"—that is, there are many counterproductive policies that may tempt policy makers in countries with inner-oriented policies but that they either cannot adopt or are quickly led to abandon in countries with outer-oriented trade regimes. An easy illustration is import licensing itself: once an outer-oriented trade strategy is adopted, licensing must quickly be abandoned for exporters. Once that happens, the overall restrictiveness of the regime is greatly diminished. And once exports have begun growing rapidly, further relaxation of the regime, and finally abandonment, follow. But there are other policies that are affected. Establishing state-owned enterprises, or even prohibiting imports to establish a new industry, is no longer a feasible policy. Government controls over expansion plans and other aspects of firm behavior must be relaxed rapidly. As exports grow, policy in general becomes more exporter and, therefore, more market friendly, and policies tend to rely more on incentives and less on direct controls.

Other policy reforms that have made a difference have been those in fiscal and monetary policy. In earlier years most developing countries had double-digit and sometimes triple-digit rates of inflation. One lesson that has been learned from research into expenditure patterns and behavior of different income groups in developing countries is the extent to which the poor are harmed by inflation and to which the rich can protect themselves and even profit. Today there are very few countries in the world with double-digit inflation, and the average inflation rate in developing countries is in the single digits. From the viewpoint of encouraging better economic performance and more rapid economic growth, changes in inflation rates and fiscal policy have had a significant and positive impact both through the effects on overall economic growth and through the positive impact on the poor.

As a consequence of trade liberalization and other economic policy reforms, economic growth has accelerated in most of the developing world, with the most rapid growth in the countries whose reforms have gone furthest. The world economy as a whole experienced very high growth rates over the five years to 2007, and that growth enabled developing countries to grow more rapidly. But the most rapid growth has generally been in countries whose reforms have been most pronounced or that were already outer oriented. The Chinese experience is certainly the most dramatic example, but progress has accelerated in many other countries.

Even in sub-Saharan Africa, where the terrible effects of AIDS have been a major drag on growth, and where policy reforms are at an earlier stage, the average rate of economic growth has been above 5% for the past three years, contrasted with zero or negative growth of per capita incomes in many of those same countries in the 1980s and 1990s. The rate of population growth is still high, and poverty is still pervasive, but signals are much more hopeful than was earlier the case.

Life expectancies in most developing countries are much higher than they were in the early 1950s, the exception being those African countries where AIDS has taken a huge toll. Life expectancy depends to some extent on health-care delivery, but also importantly on nutrition and other aspects of living standards and higher per capita incomes. Overall, not only has life expectancy risen to an average of about sixty-four years from its earlier forty years, but the gap between the industrial countries' average life expectancy (which was above sixty years in 1950 and is now above seventy) is much smaller.

Similarly, literacy rates have increased sharply, as have average levels of educational attainment. Although there is considerable variation in the extent of improvement among countries—with some countries reaching almost 100% literacy of those fifteen and older[16]—the overall achievements represent major progress in most countries.

In a nutshell, whereas in the 1960s and 1970s there were ample grounds for fearing that the divide between the rich and the poor countries would widen, there is now a basis for expecting that many, if not most, can be lifted out of poverty. Improvements in understanding economic policies and their impact have played a key role in permitting this change.

This is not to assert that all is well. There are still more than a billion people living on less than a dollar a day, many of them in sub-Saharan Africa, but also in south central Asia and a few other countries.[17] Learning more about ways to address the very severe problems of some of these countries remains challenging, and there is still much to be learned about economic policies and their impact in emerging markets and in industrial countries as well. One of the lessons of the past fifty years is that economic growth and change require policy improvements and reforms if growth is to be sustained; policies that can support an initial acceleration of growth, such as in Korea in the early 1960s, must be further amended to sustain growth.

But the accrued understanding of what is needed from research and analyses of the past half century's experience has enabled a major transformation in the world economy and in many people's lives. Even in countries where policies are not yet sufficiently conducive to rapid growth, some of the changes that have been made, such as reduced inflation, mean that when other policies are altered, their positive effects can be larger and more immediately felt. If policies in developed and developing countries alike continue to sustain growth and use the knowledge that has been acquired,[18] there is every reason to believe that further progress can take place and even accelerate relative to the past.

Notes

1. See Morawetz (1977).
2. Ibid., Appendix, Table 4.
3. Data are from Morawetz (1977), Appendix, Tables 1 and 2. Morawetz's estimates for China are much higher than current estimates for the period before 1975, so that a modern estimate of growth rates would place developing countries' average growth rates over the period somewhat lower. But his data were the basis for thinking at the time, which led to pessimism about prospects for catch-up even with the overestimate for China.
4. See, for example, Bhagwati and Srinivasan (1975) on India, Hansen and Nashashibi (1975) on Egypt, and Krueger (1974) on Turkey.
5. Perhaps the most important earlier research project had been led by Little, Scitovsky, and Scott (1970) under the auspices of the Organization for Economic Cooperation and Development (OECD). Their findings focused on industrialization rather than the trade regime itself and were entirely consistent with the results of the later study by the NBER. The cumulative impact of these systematic comparisons, along with individual studies of circumstances in particular countries, was highly significant, and it was probably necessary to have several studies before those adhering to the import-substitution philosophy and strategy were willing to reconsider. Even with all the evidence, the authorities in some countries adjusted their policies much more rapidly than those in other countries.
6. Growing corruption and generally unsatisfactory economic performance were major factors in bringing about the overthrow of the Syngman Rhee regime in 1960. Analysts of the early 1960s suggest that the Park Chung Hee government was generally supported at that time because of the improved economic performance. See Mason et al. (1980) for a discussion.
7. In the early 1960s World Bank analyses of the Korean economy reported that the resource base and other initial conditions were such that industrial growth in Korea was not feasible.
8. See, for example, Cole and Lyman (1971) and Mason et al. (1980).
9. The reader interested in Taiwan's early success can consult S. C. Tsiang, "Foreign Trade and Investment as Boosters for Take-off: The Experience of Taiwan," in Vittorio Corbo, Anne O. Krueger, and Fernando Ossa, eds., *Export-Oriented Development Strategies* (Boulder, Colo.: Westview Press, 1980).
10. See the estimates in Frank, Kim, and Westphal (1975) and reported in Krueger (1978).
11. Data are from Kim and Hong (1997).
12. Estimates for 2006 put Korean per capita income at $23,800, the United States at $44,260, and Ghana at $2,640. See World Bank (2007), Appendix, Table 1.
13. Cha, Kim, and Perkins (1997), 61–62.
14. Data for 1960 and 1970 are from Mason et al. (1980), 398, Table 107. Data for 2005 are from World Bank (2007).
15. See, for example, Sachs and Warner (1995), as well as Krueger and Berg (2003) and the references cited there.

16. See World Bank (2007), Table 1, for recent numbers.
17. See Collier (2007) for an account.
18. One key issue is the future of the international trading system. As this was written in the fall of 2007, the outcome of the Doha Round of trade negotiations under the World Trade Organization (WTO) was still in doubt, and as of early 2009, still is. A successful conclusion would augur well for future economic gains; failure would be dangerous for all but would probably be most harmful for developing countries.

References

Bhagwati, Jagdish N., and T. N. Srinivasan. 1975. *Foreign Trade Regimes and Economic Development: India.* New York: National Bureau of Economic Research.

Cha, Dong-Se, Kwang Suk Kim, and Dwight H. Perkins, eds. 1977. *The Korean Economy, 1945–1995: Performance and Vision for the Twenty-First Century.* Seoul: Korea Development Institute.

Cole, David, and Princeton Lyman. 1971. *Korean Development: The Interplay of Politics and Economics.* Cambridge, Mass.: Harvard University Press.

Collier, Paul. 2007. *The Bottom Billion.* Oxford and New York: Oxford University Press.

Frank, Charles R., Kwang Suk Kim, and Larry E. Westphal. 1975. *Foreign Trade Regimes and Economic Development: South Korea.* New York: National Bureau of Economic Research.

Hansen, Bent, and Karim Nashashibi. 1975. *Foreign Trade Regimes and Economic Development: Egypt.* New York: National Bureau of Economic Research.

Kim, Kwang Suk, and Sung Duk Hong. 1997. *Accounting for Rapid Economic Growth In Korea, 1963–1995.* Seoul: Korea Development Institute.

Krueger, Anne O. 1974. *Foreign Trade Regimes and Economic Development: Turkey.* New York: National Bureau of Economic Research.

———. 1978. *Foreign Trade Regimes and Economic Development: Liberalization Attempts and Consequences.* Cambridge, Mass.: Ballinger Press for the National Bureau of Economic Research.

Krueger, Anne O., and Andrew Berg. 2003. "Trade, Growth and Poverty—a Selective Survey." 2002 Annual Bank Conference on Development Economics, World Bank, Washington, D.C.

Little, Ian, Tibor Scitovsky, and Maurice Scott. 1970. *Industry and Trade in Some Developing Countries.* Oxford: Oxford University Press.

Mason, Edward S., Mahn Je Kim, Dwight H. Perkins, Kwang Suk Kim, and David C. Cole. 1980. *The Economic and Social Modernization of the Republic of Korea.* Cambridge, Mass.: Harvard University Press.

Morawetz, David. 1977. *Twenty-Five Years of Economic Development, 1950 to 1975.* Washington, D.C.: International Bank for Reconstruction and Development.

Sachs, Jeffrey, and Andrew Warner. 1995. "Economic Reform and the Process of Global Integration." *Brookings Papers on Economic Activity* 1: 1–117.
World Bank. 2007. *World Development Report, 2008.* Washington, D.C.: World Bank.
———. 2008. *Doing Business.* Washington, D.C.: World Bank.

COMMENT

Douglas A. Irwin

In her presidential address before the American Economic Association, Anne Krueger (1997) gave a tour de force review of how the economics profession's views on trade and development have changed over the decades. In the 1950s and 1960s, as she pointed out, there were great doubts about the benefits of open trade for developing countries. Instead, import-substitution industrialization involving high levels of protection was commonly viewed as the more effective way of promoting development. However, partly as a result of economic studies and partly as a result of the success of several East Asian countries in export-led growth, more and more economists began to appreciate the benefits of trade liberalization. Today most economists would argue that trade openness in the developing world has been an important part of the economic policy changes that have reduced poverty and improved economic performance in many countries, notably China and India.

Anne Krueger's chapter in this book is a valuable follow-up description of how the people of many countries, such as South Korea, have benefited from opening up to the world market. Countries can only participate in, and benefit from, the expansion of world trade by reducing government barriers to that trade. The rise of a middle class in China and India, which involves improvement in the lives of hundreds of millions of people, is a testimony to the tremendous opportunity that economic reforms and world markets present.

Krueger and I approach this issue very much in the same way (see Irwin 2009 for my views), so I do not take any issue with the main point of her chapter, with which I very much agree. Instead of offering a critique, in this comment I will offer one extension, one qualification, and one concluding observation.

My one extension is that we know a lot more about the channels by which trade liberalization leads to better economic performance than Krueger is able to discuss in her chapter. The static gains from trade and the benefit of allocating resources along the lines of comparative advantage are just a small part of the gains from openness. Instead, the main advantage of openness is productivity gains. These large and valuable productivity gains from trade are the major reason that trade openness is advantageous to countries that are behind the technological frontier. There are many studies of this issue. Frankel and Romer (1999) show that the geographic component of trade leads to greater income mainly through higher productivity, with a smaller portion due to greater capital accumulation. Rodríguez-Clare (2007) finds that the gains from the diffusion of technology could be an order of magnitude larger than the static gains from trade. A large literature also finds that trade increases competition, which has selection effects: less productive firms shut down, and resources are allocated to more efficient firms within an industry (Bernard et al. 2007).

Thus trade liberalization can raise incomes not simply by reallocating capital and labor between industries or between agriculture and industry but by raising productivity across all sectors. For Korea, as Krueger points out, as well as for many other countries, such as China and Vietnam, the productivity gains are clearly identifiable. Thus the welfare gains from openness to trade in goods are not just small Harberger "deadweight loss" triangles but large productivity rectangles. The larger are the gains, the less important are political economy conflicts due to any redistributive effects trade might have on income.

My one qualification is that trade reform is not a magic bullet that will solve all the problems of economic development or even guarantee large gains unless other, complementary policies are also instituted. One reason that Mexico's economic performance has been disappointing since NAFTA is that the financial system has functioned poorly (Tornell, Westermann, and Martínez 2004). If capital markets do not allocate capital very effectively or efficiently, then the payoff from trade liberalization will be much lower. One reason that India and New Zealand have not been able to reap the full advantages of open trade is that labor markets have not been liberalized; many remaining policy barriers inhibit the mobility of labor across firms and industries. Because trade reform affects relative prices, and factors must adapt to new conditions, any policies that prevent those factors from adjusting in response to economic changes diminish the value of trade reform. (For example, I recall from a visit to New Zealand a number of years ago that when the major economic liberalization reforms of the 1980s were taking place, the government decided for political reasons to postpone labor-market reforms until after all the other trade and macroeconomic reforms took place. The problem with this approach was that it exposed the economy to large and disruptive shocks while not allowing resources to adjust and hence reduced the value of the reforms.) As Krueger notes in the case of South Korea, strong macroeconomic performance helps reinforce the value of, and the political support for, trade reforms.

My final observation is to reiterate the spirit of this book. Economists have a bad reputation in many quarters because of their advocacy of open trade. As Martin Wolf (2004, 23) has pointed out, "If the critics were right, supporters of the global market economy would be in favor of mass poverty, grotesque inequality, destruction of state-provided welfare, infringement of national sovereignty, subversion of democracy, unbridled corporate power, environmental degradation, human rights abuses, and much more."

Of course, these critics are wrong. Economists do not advocate trade liberalization for crass materialistic reasons but because it can demonstrably improve people's lives. Economists are focused on a higher goal than simply raising income. The higher income that comes with more trade is not an end in itself. Rather, it is what higher incomes can purchase that is important: better nutrition, better health care, longer life expectancy, higher literacy and better education, lower infant mortality, and less child labor. The reduction of poverty and the tangible improvements in the quality of people's lives in China and India over the past two decades have been simply awe inspiring. Trade liberalization has played a key role in making that reduction in poverty and those improvements possible.

There are additional, unquantifiable benefits of freedom to trade. Amartya Sen's (1999) *Development as Freedom* argues that freedom is equally as important a component of development as material welfare, if not more so. Trade creates opportunities that can powerfully change people's lives. The sociologist Ching Kwan Lee (1998) investigated sweatshops in China and asked young women why they wanted to work there. Aside from the enormous economic benefits (their incomes were seven to eight times greater than their parents' income in their rural village), there was one consistent response: the young women wanted to get away from their fathers, who would otherwise run their lives, telling them whom to marry and what they could do. These young women valued the independence, the autonomy, and the sense that they could create their own destinies and shape their own lives by working in the factory. Those sweatshops would not have existed had China not embraced the world market. The ability of such opportunities to change people's lives for the better cannot be underestimated.

References

Bernard, Andrew, J. Bradford Jensen, Stephen Redding, and Peter Schott. 2007. "Firms in International Trade." *Journal of Economic Perspectives* 21, 105–130.

Frankel, Jeffrey A., and David Romer. 1999. "Does Trade Cause Growth?" *American Economic Review,* 89, 379–399.

Irwin, Douglas A. 2009. *Free Trade under Fire.* 3rd ed. Princeton, N.J.: Princeton University Press.

Krueger, Anne O. 1997. "Trade Policy and Economic Development: How We Learn." *American Economic Review,* 87, 1–22.

Lee, Ching Kwan. 1998. *Gender and the South China Miracle: Two Worlds of Factory Women.* Berkeley: University of California Press.

Rodríguez-Clare, Andres. 2007. "Trade, Diffusion, and the Gains from Openness." NBER Working Paper 13662, December.

Sen, Amartya. 1999. Development as Freedom. New York: Knopf.

Tornell, Aaron, Frank Westermann, and Lorenzo Martínez. 2004. "NAFTA and Mexico's Less-Than-Stellar Performance." NBER Working Paper 10289, February.

Wolf, Martin. 2004. *Why Globalization Works.* New Haven, Conn.: Yale University Press.

CHAPTER FIVE

The Role of Economics in the Welfare-to-Work Reforms of the 1990s

Rebecca M. Blank

In August 1996 Congress passed one of the most comprehensive reforms of public assistance programs in U.S. history. At the core of these reforms was an effort to reduce reliance on cash assistance for nonworkers and to provide greater incentives for welfare recipients to move into work. In the years since then, the share of families collecting cash welfare and not working has plummeted, while there has been a steep increase in those who work and simultaneously receive subsidies. Although many factors led to these changes, what I will call the economists' "efficiency critique" of traditional cash welfare programs was influential in a variety of ways. The first section of this chapter discusses the economic analysis of traditional welfare programs and the research analyzing these programs in the United States. The second section summarizes the events leading to the 1990s reforms and the changes in behavior that followed these reforms. The third section assesses the ways in which economic reasoning affected these political and program changes.

An Economic Analysis of Welfare Programs

Public assistance programs are typically designed to assist families that experience economic need. Their intent is to prevent extreme poverty and avoid outcomes that are harmful to families and their children, such as homelessness or malnutrition. Although such programs can take many forms, we focus here on cash public assistance, often called welfare. It is worth noting that the United States provides substantial noncash public assistance by subsidizing access to key commodities. These programs include food stamps, which subsidize food purchases; housing assistance, which subsidizes rent payments; and Medicaid, which provides public health insurance for some low-income families.

Since the passage of the 1936 Social Security Act, the federal government has helped states fund cash assistance to needy families. The federal-state program created in 1936, Aid to Families with Dependent Children (AFDC), was particularly aimed at single mothers, who in the 1930s were primarily widows. Because it was viewed as unsuitable for (white) women to work and because jobs were scarce, a goal of the program was to allow mothers to stay home with their children and not compete with men in the labor market. I will assume throughout this chapter that welfare recipients are single mothers. In the United States more than 90% of cash welfare recipients fall into this category, although assistance to married couples is also available. In other countries cash assistance is often received by a much broader group in the population.

Use of the AFDC program expanded in the late 1960s when the War on Poverty created a strong push for AFDC to serve as many eligible women as possible.[1] The federal government created national eligibility rules in the 1960s, at least partly in response to concerns that black women were systematically excluded from benefits in many southern states. This increased the size of the AFDC program; further increases in enrollment occurred in the following decades as the share of single mothers in the population grew. Benefit levels were set by states and varied substantially across states. Offsetting the increased numbers of women potentially eligible for welfare, states typically did not raise benefit levels to keep up with inflation, and AFDC benefits eroded in real value for more than two decades before 1996.

The AFDC program was set up like most cash welfare programs. Figure 5.1 graphically describes the income constraint that a welfare program creates for its recipients. A woman who does not work at all can receive cash assistance of level G (the so-called guarantee level at zero hours of work). If she were to go to work at hourly wage w, her earnings would increase at rate w per hour of work. Her cash benefits would be taxed at rate t, the benefit-reduction rate, as her earnings rose. In Figure 5.1 this is shown by line $G–BE$, which has the slope $w(1 - t)$, the effective wage that the woman receives. Her income increases by less than her wage rate because she loses benefits (at rate t) for each additional dollar earned. As her

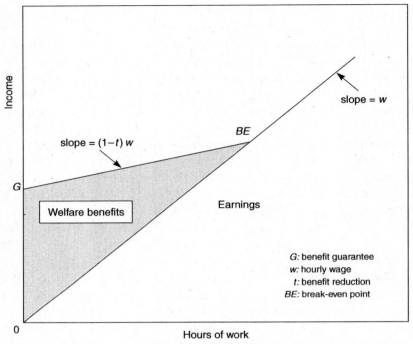

Figure 5.1 Income constraint resulting from a typical welfare program

earnings increase, at some point she reaches the break-even point *(BE)* at which benefits go to zero. Beyond this point she is off welfare entirely.

The standard economic analysis of welfare focuses on its work disincentives. A typical assignment in undergraduate labor economics classes is to analyze work incentives with and without a welfare program. (For a more formal analysis, see Rosen 2005, chap. 8.) The benefit guarantee makes nonwork far more attractive than it would be in a world without welfare. Furthermore, the reduction in benefits once a woman goes to work means that working a little bit pays very little—the gain in earnings is partially offset by the loss of benefits. This analysis of the work disincentives within a standard welfare program is what I will refer to as the "efficiency critique" within economics.

It is worth noting that any full evaluation of the impact of welfare programs must be concerned with far more than its work disincentives. Cash assistance raises the well-being of low-income families, particularly families with adults who are ill, disabled, elderly, or caring for small children or ill relatives. Indeed, if many of those on welfare are unable to work, the work-disincentive effect might be quite low and the increased well-being from welfare might be quite large. One criticism of economists' discussions of welfare is that they have often focused narrowly on the efficiency critique without attention to the broader set of issues that would be part of a full cost-benefit analysis of welfare's effects.

At least four factors determine the size of the work disincentive for single mothers. First, the higher G is set, the fewer single mothers one would expect to work. If the benefit guarantee is so low that no family can live on it, then single mothers will have to work even with a welfare program in place. Second, the higher t is set, the less attractive entering work will be unless a woman can work so many hours that she leaves welfare entirely. When t approaches 100%, welfare benefits are taxed away dollar-for-dollar as earnings increase. In this case the incentive to work at any level of hours below the break-even point is zero for a woman on welfare. In the AFDC program the benefit-reduction rate was raised to 100% for many recipients in the early 1980s, a move that economists greatly criticized. One of the motivations behind welfare reform was to create a program with greater work incentives.

Third, the work incentive is affected by the wage w the woman can earn. If single mothers are low skilled and can work only in low-wage jobs, their gains from earnings will be low, and they will be more likely to stay out of work and receive benefit dollars G. Finally, the value of women's time outside work is also important. If women have valuable things to do when they are not working—such as caring for small children—then this also makes work less attractive. Realize that if a woman had to pay hourly child care (say C dollars per hour) in order to work, this would reduce her wages to $w - C$ and further decrease her gains from work.

This analysis suggests that welfare programs might create significant work disincentives. Once in place, these programs can change women's behavior. If only 20% of single mothers do not work or work little before the implementation of a welfare program, it would be inaccurate to assume that the cost of the program is just the payments that will be made to this group of women. The availability of benefits could lead many more women to decide to stay home with their children, greatly increasing program costs.

A substantial amount of economics research focused on measuring these efficiency costs in the decades before welfare reform. An early set of experiments tested a so-called negative income tax (NIT), which was a welfare program similar to that described in Figure 5.1 but available to the entire population, including childless couples and adults. NIT programs were tested in several cities in the early 1970s, and these tests generated a substantial early literature on the labor-market effects of transfer programs.[2] Other work attempted to estimate the effects of AFDC parameters (such as the size of *G* or of *t*) on labor supply by comparing behavior across states with different AFDC programs.

Depending on how the effects were estimated and on the data used, estimates of reduced labor supply ranged from 10% to 50% relative to a world without AFDC.[3] This seems quite large, but one must realize that most of these studies estimated that many of these women were likely to work only part-time even in the absence of AFDC, so this was a big percentage change in a small number. The general conclusion should be that economics research found significant work disincentives in the AFDC program and similar transfer programs, as expected. The size of these disincentives was much debated, however, as was the question of how these disincentives should be viewed relative to the well-being gains provided by welfare programs.

These concerns about efficiency were less important in a world where women were not expected to work or even were actively discouraged from work. But by the last decade of the twentieth century women's role in the labor market had changed markedly. Between 1950 and 1990 the share of nonelderly adult women (ages twenty-five to fifty-four) who worked in the labor force increased from 35.0% to 70.6%. Although women continued to take time out of work at a much higher rate than men, primarily to care for children, women worked for pay in the labor market for a growing share of their adult lives. In fact, by 1990, 54.1% of women with preschool children were working, although many of them were working part-time.

As women were increasingly viewed as labor-market participants, the work disincentives in welfare programs became more salient. In fact, because we know that wages increase with experience, a program that encourages single mothers to stay out of the labor market may reduce not only today's earnings but also their wages over time and make them less able to support themselves and their children in the long run. This point of view was controversial, however, because welfare programs also increase economic well-being among single mothers. The alternative point of view was that the welfare gains from these subsidies were worth the efficiency costs because low-wage work could leave families both in economic need and without time for parenting.

The Welfare Reforms of the 1990s

The debate over work disincentives was only one factor leading to national welfare reform in the mid-1990s.[4] For instance, disincentives to marry were also much discussed. The rising number of women who were unmarried mothers and who received welfare led many to worry that welfare made it easier for women to have children outside marriage. Charles Murray's (1984) famous analysis of Phyllis and Harold suggested that Phyllis was economically better off not marrying Harold, the father of her children, in a state with generous welfare benefits.

These concerns also overlapped with ongoing debates about the role of race and ethnicity in public support for welfare programs. Although the majority of women on welfare were white in 1990, African American women were more likely to be poor and were disproportionately represented on the welfare rolls, compared with their overall population share. Growing immigration led to greater concerns that welfare was supporting immigrant women. All these concerns have traditionally been larger among more conservative legislators, and the turnover in 1994 to a Republican Congress greatly affected the exact legislation that was written and approved in 1996.

Other political factors also mattered. President Bill Clinton was a former governor who had worked hard to implement welfare-to-work programs in Arkansas. He campaigned in 1992 on a promise to "end welfare as we know it." This concern resonated with other state governors, who faced serious financial problems in the early 1990s and saw reductions in welfare spending as a way to help balance their budgets.

One other important strand feeding into welfare reform was the evidence from a variety of experimental welfare-to-work programs. As concerns rose about encouraging more single mothers to acquire work experience, a growing number of states began to experiment with welfare-to-work programs in the late 1980s. These experiments were greatly encouraged by federal legislation that allowed states to request waivers from federal program rules in order to run alternative programs to AFDC. Economists were closely involved in the design and, even more important, in the evaluation of these experiments.

An organization known as MDRC pioneered efforts to evaluate social programs with randomized assignment in the early 1980s. MDRC was the primary evaluator of many of the welfare-to-work experiments, in part because the federal agency overseeing these waiver programs wanted random-assignment evaluations. The result was a series of program evaluations in which persons were randomly assigned to welfare-to-work programs or to traditional AFDC. (Many of these programs had other elements in addition to strong welfare-to-work efforts, as discussed in Hamilton 2002.) This made evaluation of the results straightforward, without the need to argue over econometric specifications. One could simply compare the outcomes in the group receiving the new program with the outcomes in the (randomly assigned and hence observationally identical) group that remained on AFDC. Many of the key people involved in designing these evaluations and in analyzing the resulting data were economists, using the analytical tools of the profession.

As a result of these evaluations, a growing base of persuasive evidence by the mid-1990s suggested that welfare-to-work programs significantly reduced welfare use and increased work participation (Michalopoulos and Berlin 2001). Although the earnings gains were modest in many places, they were quite large in a few locations. This evidence was particularly credible because of the randomized evaluations that underlay the results. This evidence only increased the concern about work disincentives. It suggested that many welfare recipients could successfully move to work.

Welfare reform legislation (the Personal Responsibility and Work Opportunities Reconciliation Act) that made major changes to U.S. social programs passed in August 1996. This legislation affected many programs beyond cash welfare, but I focus here on its impact on that program. Further discussion of the act and its provisions is available in Blank (2002) and Moffitt (2003). Here I briefly describe the key changes relating to welfare recipients.

The AFDC program was abolished and replaced with a block-grant funding stream known as Temporary Assistance for Needy Families (TANF). This action turned responsibility for cash welfare program design back to the states. The federal government shared funding but abolished the federal rules in the AFDC program that constrained states to operate their cash welfare programs in particular ways. In order to put teeth into the "Temporary" part of the TANF title, the legislation imposed a sixty-month (five-year) time limit on the receipt of TANF funds. States could continue to fund recipients after sixty months but had to use their own money.

The federal government imposed new regulations on work requirements for state TANF programs. States had to run welfare-to-work programs and were expected to move a significant share of their welfare recipient population into work over a specified period of time. As a result of this legislation, all states launched major welfare-to-work initiatives.

With their newfound discretion, states made many changes in creating TANF programs out of their old AFDC programs. Two program changes were particularly important and were enacted by many states. First, states imposed sanctions on those who did not participate in the welfare-to-work programs as expected. In many cases this meant reduced benefits or (in the face of multiple violations) permanent loss of eligibility for welfare. During the following decade a growing share of women left welfare because they were hit with sanctions.

Second, states lowered their benefit-reduction rates (*t* in Figure 5.1), hoping to increase work incentives. This was in direct response to the criticism that 100% benefit-reduction rates created zero work incentives. Of course, a lower benefit-reduction rate meant that families could work and still receive benefits at relatively low levels of earnings. This provided additional subsidies to earnings.

The result of these changes was to increase greatly the pressure on welfare recipients to enter work. On the one hand, there were serious "sticks" in these changes, particularly the mandate that women who were declared "work eligible" must participate in welfare-to-work programs or face sanctions for nonparticipation. Those not immediately work eligible could face potential future time limits on welfare receipt. On the other hand, the lower benefit-reduction rate also created a "carrot" by subsidizing women in low-wage work with ongoing (albeit reduced) benefits.

The implementation of TANF programs was not the only policy change that occurred in the mid-1990s. Other major changes coincided with welfare reform and also helped improved work incentives. Robert Moffitt (this volume) discusses changes in the Earned Income Tax Credit (EITC) that substantially increased subsidies to low-wage workers through the tax system. Big increases in the EITC were enacted at exactly the same time as welfare reform legislation. Increases in the minimum wage also were passed in the mid-1990s. The combination of a higher EITC and a higher minimum wage meant that the earnings available to even very low-skilled women working minimum-wage jobs were substantially higher in the late 1990s than just a decade before. The real earnings plus wage subsidy (in 2000 dollars) received by a single mother working full-time at the minimum wage rose from $10,568 in 1989 to $12,653 (with one child) or $14,188 (with two children) by 2000 (Blank 2002). These changes were proposed and passed with many explicit references to the standard economic analysis of work incentives.

Furthermore, the economy entered a period of extended and strong growth in the late 1990s as well. Unemployment rates, even among very low-skilled workers, were the lowest in decades. In the years when states were designing and implementing their new TANF programs, they did not have to worry about job availability. Virtually any welfare recipient who searched could find employment, even if it did not last long or pay very well.

The result of these reforms in welfare, combined with other policy changes and with the macroeconomic expansion, was dramatic.[5] Figure 5.2 shows two of the more dramatic changes following welfare reform. The solid line in Figure 5.2 indicates the decline in welfare caseloads during the 1990s. They plummeted over the decade so that by the early 2000s fewer than

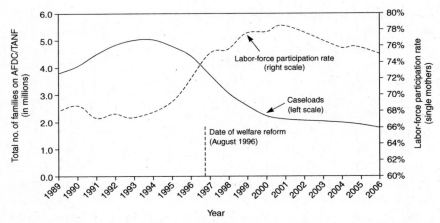

Figure 5.2 Total welfare caseloads and labor-force participation rates for single women, 1989–2006. *Sources:* Total caseload data are from the Agency for Children and Families, Department of Health and Human Services, www.acf.hhs.gov/ programs/ofa/caseloadindex.htm#afdc. Labor-force participation data come from the author's tabulations of the March Current Population Survey for single mothers aged twenty to sixty-five.

half as many families were receiving TANF benefits as had received AFDC benefits in the early 1990s. The dotted line in Figure 5.2 indicates the labor-force participation rate among single mothers. This rate increased substantially, although the gains eroded somewhat in the period of slower economic growth of the early 2000s.

Of course, reduced benefits offset increased earnings from work. For less skilled single mothers, however, total family income increased. Among single mothers with less than a high-school education, family income (in 2005 dollars) rose from $23,891 to $25,023 between 1995 and 2005 (Blank and Kovak 2009). Poverty among single-mother families fell in the late 1990s as well, and in 2006 their poverty rate was well below its level in the early 1990s. Poverty did not fall as fast as caseloads, however. By the end of the 1990s the number of working poor single mothers was growing, and the share of nonworking poor mothers was shrinking.

On the basis of these data, welfare reform has been judged a success. If the goal was to decrease the use of welfare, increase work, and even improve the economic position of less skilled single mothers, these policy changes (along with the EITC and a relatively strong economy) appear to have achieved that goal. As one might expect, not everyone has benefited from these changes, however. Some mothers seem to be no longer receiving welfare but are not working steadily. There is evidence that welfare reform has had more negative effects for this group (Blank and Kovak 2009). But for the average less skilled single mother, who might have been out of the workforce and on welfare full-time in the early 1990s, these changes have produced a substantial behavioral change that seems to be linked to slightly higher levels of family income, as well as greater labor-market experience.

Welfare Reform and Economics: What Have We Learned?

The efficiency critique of welfare, concerned with work disincentives, became increasingly important over time as welfare recipients were viewed more and more as persons who could and should be expected to participate in the labor market. Although many factors led to the 1996 welfare reforms, certainly a concern with work disincentives was a primary and frequently cited reason for abolishing AFDC and replacing it with a work-oriented system of public assistance. Ten years after it occurred, most of the evidence suggests that the impact of this policy change has been positive for many women.

The specific design of the new state TANF programs at least partially reflected economists' views about creating incentives in public assistance programs. On the one hand, many economists are uncomfortable with behavioral mandates, which are an important part of current state welfare-to-work programs, with strong sanctions for not participating when one is assigned to a mandatory welfare-to-work program. Economists often want to suggest that one should "get the incentives right" for good behavior rather than impose mandates. The problem, in the case of welfare, is that there are mixed incentives. For adults (and particularly parents) who hit difficult economic times and cannot work or cannot find a job that fully supports them and their children, one wants to provide reasonable benefits. But it is difficult to distinguish those who can work from those who cannot and create a nuanced program of incentives for one and support for another. Hence the new rules allowed caseworkers to decide who was work ready and to mandate assistance in moving toward jobs among this population.

On the other hand, these mandates came with strong incentives that helped make work more economically rewarding and more attractive. This surely made women far more willing to move toward work and kept them at work after they located an initial job. Some of these incentives were punitive, such as sanctions, but some provided expanded support for low-wage workers. Lower benefit-reduction rates or tax subsidies to low-wage workers are exactly the sorts of policies that economists typically propose and support as ways to encourage work while still providing subsidies to disadvantaged populations.

Of course, the efficiency critique of welfare focuses on one aspect of what welfare programs are designed to accomplish, namely, work disincentives, without paying attention to the well-being gains of welfare. Critics of welfare reform tend to argue that the reduced home time available to single mothers through greater labor-market participation might make them worse off, even with slightly higher earnings. This might be particularly true if working means a substantial increase in child-care expenses. Furthermore, the effects of reduced home time on child development and the long-term outcomes of children are also important. We have relatively few studies of these effects, although they tend to suggest that preschoolers were not harmed by welfare-to-work programs when they included enough child-care funding to place the children in adequate day-care programs.[6] Both of these points provide strong policy guidance by suggesting that child-care subsidies are a key part of effective welfare-to-work programs.

What should be clear from this discussion is that economists were at the front and center of virtually all these debates. Economic research and economic theory helped build dissatisfaction with the old AFDC program and were used in the design of new state TANF programs. Economists were heavily involved in evaluating these reforms as well; I have cited economists in this article not because they are my friends, but because much of the policy evaluation and research around welfare reform was done by economists. Ultimately, the language of the entire debate about welfare has been couched in the language of economics, which has been the language used to discuss disincentive effects, program design, and cost-benefit analysis of the new programs.

These reforms were part of a movement to a work-oriented public assistance system in which single mothers and other less skilled adults receive assistance conditioned on work. If they are working, they can receive the EITC or child-care subsidies or continue to receive partial TANF benefits. For this system to remain viable in the long run, there must be adequate labor-market demand for less skilled mothers. If jobs are not available, demanding work from single mothers is less feasible. It will be interesting to see how (if) these programs change as we enter a deep recession in the late 2000s. In the long run the effectiveness of welfare reforms will depend on another group of economists, those who work to assure a stable, high-employment, and growing economy.

Notes

The opinions expressed in this chapter are the author's and do not reflect the position of the U.S. Department of Commerce.

1. Patterson (2000) provides a good history of the AFDC program.
2. See Burtless (1986) or Ashenfelter and Plant (1990) for a summary of these results.
3. Moffit (2003) discusses these numbers. See also Hoynes (1997) and Moffitt (1992).
4. Weaver (2000) provides an extended discussion of the politics and debate over welfare reform.
5. See Blank (2002) or Grogger and Karoly (2005) for much more detailed discussion of this research. Blank (2007) summarizes the most recent research. It is quite difficult to separate the effects of the welfare reform changes from these other policy and economic changes.
6. See Morris et al. (2001). The results for adolescents are more negative.

References

Ashenfelter, Orley, and Mark W. Plant. 1990. "Nonparametric Estimates of the Labor Supply Effects of Negative income Tax Programs." *Journal of Labor Economics* 8(1, pt. 2): S396–S415.

Blank, Rebecca M. 2002. "Evaluating Welfare Reform in the United States." *Journal of Economic Literature* 40(4): 1105–1166.

———. 2007. "What We Know, What We Don't Know, and What We Need to Know about Welfare Reform." National Poverty Center Working Paper 2007-19, University of Michigan.

Blank, Rebecca M., and Brian Kovak. 2009. "The Growing Problem of Disconnected Single Mothers." In *Making the Work-Based Safety Net Work Better*, Carolyn J. Heinrich and John Karl Scholz, eds. New York: Russell Sage Press.

Burtless, Gary. 1986. "The Work Response to a Guaranteed Income: A Survey of Experimental Evidence." In *Lessons from the Income Maintenance Experiments*, Alicia H. Munnell, ed. Boston: Federal Reserve Bank of Boston: 22–59.

Grogger, Jeffrey, and Lynn A. Karoly. 2005. *Welfare Reform: Effects of a Decade of Change*. Cambridge, Mass.: Harvard University Press.

Hamilton, Gayle. 2002. *Moving People from Welfare to Work: Lessons from the National Evaluation of Welfare-to-Work Strategies*. Prepared by MDRC for the U.S. Department of Health and Human Services and the U.S. Department of Education. www.mdrc.org/publications/52/summary.html.

Hoynes, Hilary. 1997. "Work, Welfare, and Family Structure: What Have We Learned?" In *Fiscal Policy: Lessons from Economic Research*, Alan Auerbach, ed. Cambridge, Mass.: MIT Press: 101–146.

Michalopoulos, Charles, and Gordon Berlin. 2001. "Financial Work Incentives for Low-Wage Workers." In *The New World of Welfare,* Rebecca Blank and Ron Haskins, eds. Washington, D.C.: Brookings Press: 270–286.

Moffitt, Robert. 1992. "Incentive Effects of the U.S. Welfare System: A Review." *Journal of Economic Literature* 30(1): 1–61.

———. 2003. "The Temporary Assistance for Needy Families Program." In *Means-Tested Transfer Programs in the United States,* Robert A. Moffitt, ed. Chicago: University of Chicago Press: 291–364.

Morris, Pamela A., Aletha C. Huston, Greg J. Duncan, Danielle A. Crosby, and Johannes M. Box. 2001. *How Welfare and Work Policies Affect Children: A Synthesis of Research.* New York: MDRC.

Murray, Charles. 1984. *Losing Ground.* New York: Basic Books.

Patterson, James T. 2000. *America's Struggle against Poverty in the 20th Century.* Cambridge, Mass.: Harvard University Press.

Rosen, Harvey S. 2005. *Public Finance.* 7th ed. New York: McGraw-Hill Irwin.

Weaver, R. Kent. 2000. *Ending Welfare as We Know It.* Washington, D.C.: Brookings.

COMMENT

Nancy Folbre

I agree with much of what Rebecca Blank argues in her chapter. I agree that Aid to Families with Dependent Children was a flawed program. I agree that it provides a great opportunity to teach undergraduates how to illustrate graphically disincentives to paid employment. I agree that it was a good idea to encourage single parents living in poverty to increase their labor-force participation. I also agree with what seems to be the premise behind Better Living through Economics: economists are smart and well-intentioned people who could make the world a better place. I believe that Rebecca Blank is an especially smart and well-intentioned economist.

I do not agree that the welfare reform of 1996 was a success. Yes, it cut the welfare rolls. It is not difficult to cut welfare rolls and increase labor-force participation by reducing eligibility for assistance. One does not need a graph to illustrate this point. This reform did little to reduce child poverty rates, which remain very high in the United States by international standards, especially among blacks and Latinos. We know relatively little about the reform's actual impact on child poverty because our methods of defining and measuring poverty are so bad.

Why should child poverty itself be a major concern? Because it is both unfair and inefficient. A growing body of evidence shows that growing up in poor families and poor communities and attending poor schools limit the development of children's capabilities. Inequality itself has disincentive effects. Why try hard if you have little chance of succeeding? (Folbre 2008a.)

The Labour Party in the United Kingdom made a commitment to eliminate child poverty by 2020 and, on the basis of rather strict benchmarks, has demonstrated progress toward reaching that goal. This is especially remarkable given that it defines poverty in relative terms as a family income below 50% of the median. It is using the same basic policy tools that Blank describes. Its policy is a welfare reform that I could be proud of (Folbre 2008b).

But economists there, here, and elsewhere should face up to the fact that market income is not an adequate measure of family living standards. As economic theorists have pointed out for a very long time, nonmarket work contributes significantly to the basket of goods and services that families consume. Like most other affluent countries and many developing ones, the United States now conducts an annual survey of time use that makes it possible to measure the amount of time devoted to nonmarket work. The results show that about one-half of all work activity takes place outside paid employment, even in affluent countries.

Economists should stop pretending that market income is an adequate measure of family living standards. True, we do not have time-use surveys that allow us to go back and track the effect of welfare reform. But we have ample opportunity to ask what an additional hour of market work "costs" a household in terms of reduced production for its own consumption, and we can use such estimates to adjust measures of family income that have almost certainly been artificially inflated. To her credit, Blank mentions that out-of-pocket child-care costs should be subtracted. But the distortions run much deeper, from substitution of fast food for home-produced meals to more fundamental issues like the importance of shared family time and the stresses of combining forty hours of work with sixty hours of family care.

The historic rise in women's labor-force participation rates in the United States has leveled out since about 1996. I think that no one completely understands why yet, but the evidence certainly suggests that we are approaching some kind of cultural or perhaps even technical limit to the substitution of market for nonmarket work. That is another reason that economists should stop assuming that higher levels of labor-force participation are good in and of themselves.

This brings me to my final disagreement with the perspective outlined in this chapter. It does not pay enough attention to incentives. It seems to assume that incentives apply only to paid employment. What about disincentives to home production and family care? Many economists continue to treat these as though these are merely forms of consumption—like what people decide to do in their leisure time. But home production and family care are fundamental aspects of production—the production of the next generation of workers and taxpayers. Is the supply of labor to these activities completely inelastic? No, and nothing illustrates their responsiveness to economic trends more profoundly than the decline in fertility, which has now dipped below replacement levels in many of the advanced industrial countries (Folbre 2008a). The quantity of children that we raise, however, is far less important than the quality—which brings me full circle to the problem of child poverty.

Blank's chapter notes that "In the long run the effectiveness of these reforms will depend on another group of economists as well, those who work to assure a stable, high-employment, and growing economy." I believe that it will also depend on another group of economists, those who recognize that the market represents only a small part of our economic system, and that reliance on market income and gross domestic product as measures of progress threatens the well-being of our families and communities, as well as the ecological health of our planet.

References

Folbre, Nancy. 2008a. *Valuing Children: Rethinking the Economics of the Family.* Cambridge, Mass.: Harvard University Press.

———. 2008b. "Taxes Help Support Children." In *Ten Excellent Reasons Not to Hate Taxes*, ed. Stephanie Greenwood, pp. 52–62. New York: New Press.

CHAPTER SIX

Better Living through Monetary Economics

John B. Taylor

In the mid-1990s macroeconomists began noticing and studying a remarkable change in the performance of the U.S. economy. The economy had become much more stable than in the past. The change appeared to have occurred some fifteen years earlier, in the early 1980s. Not only had inflation and interest rates and their volatilities diminished compared with the experience of the 1970s, but the volatility of real gross domestic product (GDP) had reached lows never seen before. Economic expansions had become longer and stronger, while recessions had become rarer and shorter.

At the time I called this phenomenon the Long Boom (Taylor 1998). It was as if there was one long growth expansion starting with the end of the deep recession in 1982 and continuing right through its fifteenth anniversary in 1997, with the mild 1990–1991 recession seeming like a small interruption compared with recessions of the past. Others called the phenomenon the Great Moderation (Blanchard and Simon 2001) because of the general decline in volatility of output growth and the inflation rate.

I conjectured that the improved macroeconomic performance could be explained by a regime shift in monetary policy, which also occurred in the early 1980s. I argued that this shift in monetary policy could be explained by a major change in monetary theory (Taylor 1997), which also occurred at about the same time. In other words, there was a Great Moderation in economic performance, which could be explained by a Great Regime Shift in monetary policy, which in turn could be explained by a Great Awakening in monetary theory.

Neither the Great Moderation, the Great Regime Shift, nor the Great Awakening turned out to be a flash in the pan. Each lasted for another ten years. The Long Boom reached its twenty-fifth anniversary in 2007, with the mild 2001 recession turning out to be an even smaller interruption than the 1990–1991 recession. The monetary policy that characterized the Great Regime Shift continued, and the Great Awakening of monetary theory blossomed into a more fully developed theory that some called New Keynesian economics. Great moderations were seen in many other economies around the world with associated monetary policy regime shifts and an apparent spread of these monetary ideas. Indeed, at the start of the twenty-first century we had a Long Boom on a global scale.

All these events have been researched thoroughly to the point where I think that it is possible to go beyond conjecture and to present evidence of the influence of theory on policy and outcomes. The purpose of this chapter is to review and present that evidence. There is no question that these improvements in economic performance during this period—the shorter, milder recessions and the lower, more stable inflation rates—in the United States and around the world improved people's lives. If we can establish that the ultimate cause of this improvement was economics—and, in particular, monetary economics—then this is an excellent example of "better living through economics."

As we look into the future, it is of course an open question whether the good economic performance seen during the Great Moderation will last. Will future researchers conclude that its twenty-fifth anniversary in 2007 turned out to be its end? If so, will they find that the end was caused by yet another monetary policy shift, this time away from the policy followed during the Great Moderation? As I write in 2009, there is clear evidence of a large recession along with a financial crisis more serious than any other in the previous twenty-five years, perhaps since the Great Depression. But there is also evidence of another shift in monetary policy—a reversal. During the period leading up to this crisis, especially in 2002–2005, interest rates were held far below what historical experience during the Great Moderation would have predicted. Thus the connection between monetary policy and macroeconomic performance may indeed hold up when future economic researchers examine this period. Whether this policy reversal was caused by some underlying change in monetary theory or by something else will determine whether monetary economics is again chosen to be a chapter in a future "better living through economics" volume.

Documenting the Great Moderation

Many research studies have documented the improved cyclical performance of the U.S. economy and pinpointed the date as starting in the early
1980s, including Kim and Nelson (1999), McConnell and Pérez-Quirós
(2000), Blanchard and Simon (2001), and Koenig and Ball (2007). No
matter what metric one uses—the variance in the real GDP growth rate,
the variance in the real GDP gap, the average length of expansions, the
frequency of recessions, or the duration of recessions—there was a huge
improvement in economic performance. There was also an improvement
in price stability, with the inflation rate much lower and less volatile than
in the period from the late 1960s to the early 1980s.

Figures 6.1 and 6.2 present a simple summary of the facts. Figure 6.1,
which is based on Koenig and Ball (2007), shows the quarterly growth
rate of real GDP from the 1950s to the present. It is clear that the volatility
of the growth rate declined sharply starting in the early 1980s. Figure 6.2,
which is based on Rosenblum (2007), measures the improvement in terms
of the reduction in the time that the economy spends in recession. This is a
remarkable change and clearly an improvement in people's lives.

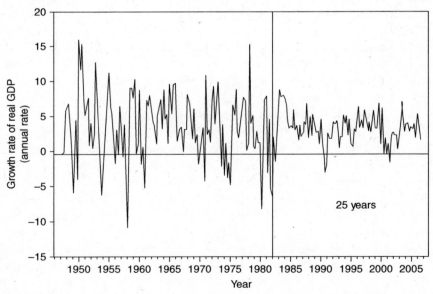

Figure 6.1 Decline in the volatility of the growth rate of real GDP. *Source:* Koenig
and Ball 2007.

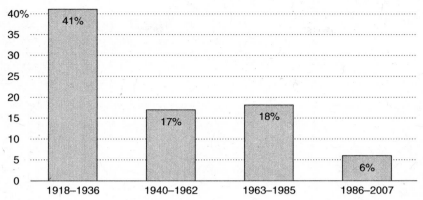

Figure 6.2 Percentage of time spent in recession in the United States. *Source:* Rosenblum 2007.

Much of the research on the Great Moderation in the United States focused on the decline in variability in the 1980s compared with the earlier post–World War II period as exemplified by Figure 6.2. However, as shown in Figure 6.1, the decline appears to be part of a longer-term trend. Of course, a large component of the high proportion of time the economy spent in recession in the pre–World War II period was due to the Great Depression. If one excludes the Great Depression, looks at the earlier pre–World War II period, and makes adjustments in the data as recommended by Romer (1986), then one finds that there was not much of a reduction in the post–World War II period until the early 1980s. In this analysis the shift in the 1980s is unique and not part of a longer-term trend.

Table 6.1, which is drawn from Cecchetti et al. (2007), shows that this same type of improved performance occurred in other developed countries. Related work by Cecchetti, Flores-Lagunes, and Krause (2006) shows that the same is true of an even broader group of countries, including most developing countries.

Finally, it has been widely documented that the rate of inflation and the volatility of the inflation rate came down dramatically in the United States in the 1980s and stayed low compared with the period of high and rising inflation of the late 1960s and 1970s. Researchers have also documented that the inflation rate and the volatility of inflation declined dramatically for many other economies around the world. For the industrial countries as a whole, the timing is similar to that in the United States; for the developing countries the decline in inflation and volatility occurred later. Figure 6.3, which is based on International Monetary Fund (IMF) staff research, reported in the April 2006 *World Economic Outlook*, shows that

Table 6.1   Standard deviation of real GDP growth in the G7 economies (median)

Country	Full sample	1970– 1979	1980– 1989	1990– 1999	2000– 2006
Canada	2.30	2.32	2.56	1.58	1.32
France	1.41	2.69	2.00	1.12	0.66
Germany	2.18	2.70	2.08	2.33	2.23
Italy	1.64	3.55	1.89	1.52	1.33
Japan	2.34	1.69	1.41	1.31	1.25
United Kingdom	1.95	2.50	2.20	1.60	1.20
United States	2.11	2.78	1.81	1.43	1.32
Median	2.11	2.69	2.00	1.52	1.32

Source: Cecchetti et al. 2007.

the decline in inflation was more recent in the developing countries. Figure 6.4 shows that the volatility also decreased in the developing countries.

The Great Regime Shift in Monetary Policy

Just as there are several ways to document the Great Moderation, there are several ways to document a regime shift in monetary policy. I will consider four here. By all these measures a shift appears to have occurred in the early to mid-1980s and to have continued at least through the 1990s and perhaps longer. The shift is thereby closely temporally correlated with the Great Moderation in output volatility.

First, consistent with the view that inflation is ultimately a monetary phenomenon, the decline in the inflation rate, as shown in Figure 6.3, must be included as part of the evidence of a regime change. Over long periods of time inflation and money growth, suitably measured, are strongly correlated. Hence, in effect, a shift in monetary policy from consistently inflationary levels of money growth to consistently noninflationary levels of money growth represents a regime change. However, as monetary policy is currently practiced, money growth does not play a central role in day-to-day decisions, which are focused on the appropriate settings for short-term interest rates. Fortunately, as I describe later, there is evidence of a regime shift that is based on measures of how central banks set interest rates.

A second piece of evidence is the greater focus on inflation targets, either informally, as has been the case at the Federal Reserve, or more formally, as at the Reserve Bank of New Zealand, the Central Bank of Chile, the

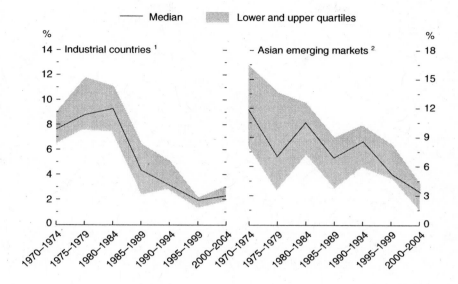

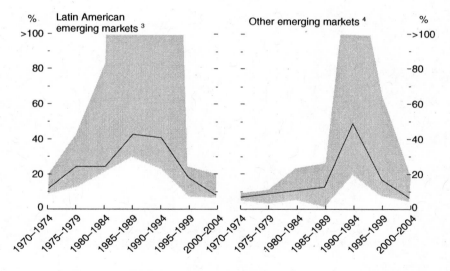

¹ Australia, Austria, Belgium, Canada, Denmark, Finland, France, Germany, Greece, Iceland, Ireland, Italy, Japan, Luxembourg, the Netherlands, Norway, Portugal, Spain, Sweden, Switzerland, the United Kingdom, and the United States.

² China, India, Indonesia, Korea, Malaysia, the Philippines, and Thailand.

³ Argentina, Brazil, Chile, Colombia, Dominican Republic, Ecuador, Mexico, Peru, and Venezuela.

⁴ Czech Republic, Egypt, Hungary, Poland, Romania, Russia, South Africa, and Turkey.

Figure 6.3 CPI inflation rates: five-year moving averages. *Source:* IMF, *World Economic Outlook*, April 2006, Figure 3.1.

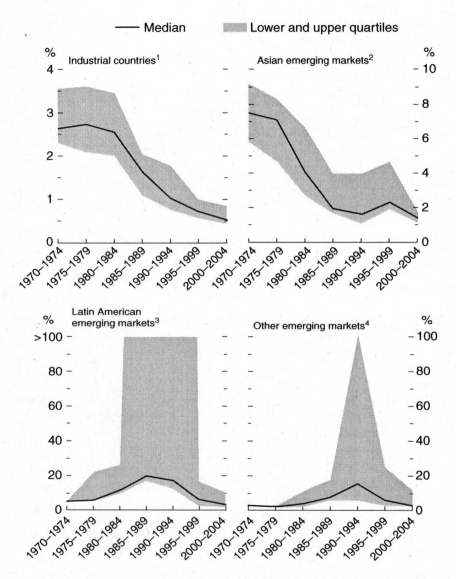

—— Median ▨ Lower and upper quartiles

[1] Australia, Austria, Belgium, Canada, Denmark, Finland, France, Germany, Greece, Iceland, Ireland, Italy, Japan, Luxembourg, the Netherlands, Norway, Portugal, Spain, Sweden, Switzerland, the United Kingdom, and the United States.
[2] China, India, Indonesia, Korea, Malaysia, the Philippines, and Thailand.
[3] Argentina, Brazil, Chile, Colombia, Dominican Republic, Ecuadar, Mexico, Peru, and Venezuela.
[4] Czech Republic, Egypt, Hungary, Poland, Romania, Russia, South Africa, and Turkey

Figure 6.4 Standard deviations of CPI inflation: five-year moving averages. *Source:* IMF, *World Economic Outlook*, April 2006, Figure 3.2.

Bank of England, the Riksbank, and now many other central banks. The shift to a regime that focused much more on price stability than in the 1970s under the leadership of Paul Volcker was the most dramatic and obvious. Volcker, his colleagues, and his successors were clear about the goal of price stability, arguing that at least, inflation should be low enough not to interfere with the decision making of firms and investors. The use of more formal inflation targets at other central banks was also a dramatic and obvious change; it has helped spread the idea of price stability as the primary goal of monetary policy around the world. A closely related development was the shift, for example, in the United Kingdom, to more independent central banks, although there was no similar formal change in the United States.

Third, in the new regime central banks focused much more on predictable or rulelike decision making, including a focus on transparency and expectations of future policy actions. The increase in transparency in the process of making decisions can be seen in many different ways. For example, at the Federal Reserve, before the 1980s decisions about an interest-rate change were tied in vague ways to decisions about borrowed reserves and were usually left to the market to figure out. A far different and clearer communications method was used after the 1980s, in which the Fed announced its interest-rate decision immediately after making it and explained to the markets what it was thinking about the future. This change enhanced the central bank's credibility to stick to its predictable operations and inflation targets.

Other central banks have also been clearer about their policy process, sometimes by publishing inflation reports with their own inflation and output forecasts and their analyses of the current situation. The intent has been to be as predictable and systematic as possible and to aim the instruments of policy convincingly and consistently at the inflation target or price-stability goal. This was a huge change from the days when central bankers tried to preserve their mystique and thought that they had to surprise markets from time to time in order for monetary policy to be effective.

Fourth, central banks became markedly more responsive to developments in the economy when they adjusted their policy interest rate. In my view this is the most important part of the regime change. It refers specifically to the actual actions of central banks rather than to their words, and it can be measured and investigated empirically to determine whether the change in policy has affected economic performance, as discussed later. Indeed, this is a policy regime change in the classic sense in that one can observe it by estimating, during different periods, the coefficients of the central bank's policy rule—in particular by using a rule that describes how the central bank sets its interest rate in response to inflation and real GDP.

A number of researchers have used this technique to detect a regime shift (see, for example, Stock and Watson, 2003). Such studies have shown that the Fed's interest-rate moves were less responsive to changes in inflation and to real GDP in the old regime, before the 1980s. After the mid-1980s the reaction coefficients increased significantly. The reaction coefficient to inflation nearly doubled. The estimated reaction of the interest rate to a one percentage point increase in inflation rose from about three-quarters to about one and one-half. The reaction to real output also rose. In general, the coefficients are much closer to the parameters of a Taylor rule in the period after the mid-1980s than they were before. I found similar results over longer sample periods for the United States: the implied reaction coefficients were also low in the highly volatile pre–World War II period (Taylor 1999).

Cecchetti et al. (2007) and others have shown that this same type of shift occurred in other countries. Figure 6.5, which is drawn from Cecchetti et al. (2007), pinpoints the regime shift as having occurred in a number of countries in the early 1980s. It presents the deviations from a Taylor rule, which indicate that monetary policy reactions were much different in the earlier period in these countries.

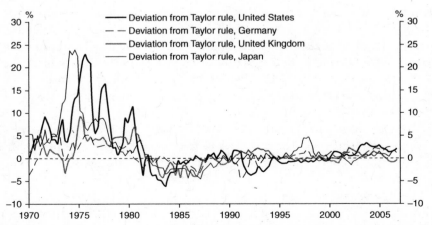

Figure 6.5 Evidence of a regime shift in the early 1980s. *Source:* Cecchetti et al. (2007).

The Causal Connection between Policy Regime Change and Improved Performance

So far we have established that there was a Great Moderation that has lasted for about twenty-five years and a Great Regime Shift that has lasted for about the same twenty-five years. This coincidence of timing suggests, of course, that the two were related and that the regime shift may have led to the improved performance, but it does not prove this. For this reason researchers have endeavored to use formal statistical techniques or macroeconomic models to help assess causality and help us understand what aspects of the regime shift led to the improvement in performance. Beyond causality, it is important for the future to know what parts of the regime change were essential and what may have been incidental.

For example, Stock and Watson (2003) used a statistical time-series decomposition technique to assess causality. They found that the change in monetary policy did have an effect on performance, although they also found that other factors—mainly a reduction in other sources of shocks to the economy (inventories, supply factors)—were responsible for a larger part of the reduction in volatility. In particular, they showed that the shift in the monetary policy rule (the fourth piece of evidence listed in the previous section) led to a more efficient point on the trade-off between variance in inflation and variance in output.

With the same goals in mind, Cecchetti, Flores-Lagunes, and Krause (2006) used a more structural model and empirically studied many different countries. For twenty of the twenty-one countries that had experienced moderation in the variance of inflation and output, they found that better monetary policy accounted for over 80% of the moderation. They used the same type of output-inflation variability trade-off that Stock and Watson (2003) used.

At a fundamental level I think that there is a more straightforward way to make the case that the change in regime improved performance. First, simply making policy more predictable, which has been a key part of the regime change, reduces uncertainty by making it easier for the private sector to plan and thereby reduces volatility. In his last academic paper Milton Friedman (2006), for example, argued that it was the reduction in the fluctuations and uncertainty relating to money growth that led to the reduction in output volatility.

Moreover, as I show in the next section, the change in regime was precisely in the direction recommended by new monetary models of the economy. The recommendations from simulations and analyses with these monetary models were policy prescriptions with an inflation target and rules for the instruments to achieve this target. The models predicted that the variance of inflation and output (or at least a weighted sum of the variance of inflation and output) would decline if monetary policy was conducted in the recommended way rather than in the way it was conducted in the 1970s and earlier. In other words, the policy rules that were recommended were derived from an empirically based monetary theory that showed that such policy rules would bring about a great moderation. So it should not be surprising that when actual policy was conducted in this way, such a moderation was realized.

A Great Awakening in Monetary Theory

I now turn to developments in monetary economics and their role in helping bring about a change in monetary policy and the resulting improvement in performance. It was during the mid- to late 1970s that monetary economists began to focus intently on finding policies that would reduce the volatility of real GDP and inflation. Some evidence of this is found in the very explicit and frequent use of an objective function that captured that goal. It was usually written in the form of a loss function $lVar(y)+(1-l)Var(p)$, which was to be minimized, where y represented real GDP relative to normal levels and p represented the inflation rate relative to the target. The weight l described the relative importance of each variable, and for most of the models there was a trade-off between these two variances (see, for example, Sargent and Wallace 1975; Kydland and Prescott 1977; and Taylor 1979).

In this research the form of the policy to accomplish this objective was usually a policy rule for the monetary instruments. One reason for the focus on policy rules was the idea of rational expectations, which required that contingency plans for policy be part of the analysis, as laid out by Lucas (1976).

The monetary theory that was developed to address this policy objective had at its center a description of the inflation process that included both rational expectations—the importance of which was clear from Lucas's critique—*and* sticky prices, which were the source of monetary nonneutrality. Also included was a description of how the real economy was affected by the policy interest rate and a description of how the policy interest rate is set, again usually through a policy rule.

Before the advent of rational expectations in monetary economics, Milton Friedman and Edmund Phelps proposed, in the late 1960s, the expectations-

augmented Phillips curve, which showed that if inflation rose above expected inflation, then output and employment would rise above normal. It
also showed that if inflation were to be reduced below its currently expected
level, then real output and employment would have to fall below normal
levels for a time. As long as expectations were adaptive, the expectations-
augmented Phillips curve gave a reasonably accurate description of the time-
series pattern of inflation and real GDP. But rational expectations changed
this. If expectations were rational, then monetary policy—if it was anticipated or followed a known rule—could not create a difference between
the actual and expected inflation rate; thus there was no way for monetary
policy to affect real GDP. It could achieve any inflation rate it wanted with
any degree of accuracy without any adverse impact on the real economy.

Although this result attracted much attention at the time, it was not very
useful for monetary policy analysis. For this reason a new theory was developed with a defining characteristic: the combination of sticky prices
and rational expectations (Clarida, Gali, and Gertler, 2000). The basic idea
was that firms would not change their prices instantaneously. There would
be a period during which the firm's prices would be fixed, and the pricing
decisions of different firms would not all be made at the same time. Rather,
they would be staggered and unsynchronized.

With this new pricing assumption, the usual equilibrium theory in which
price was given by the intersection of the supply and demand curves would
not work, and a number of important issues arose that were not part of
the classic supply-and-demand framework. Some firms' prices will be out-
standing when another firm is deciding on a price to set. Thus this firm
needs to look back at the price decisions of other firms. Also, each firm's
prices will last for a period; hence firms must forecast the future, including
the prices of other firms.

One of the ways this theoretical problem was first handled in the 1970s
was to make the simplifying assumption that the price is set at a fixed
level for a fixed period (Taylor 1980), similar to the simplifying assumption in the original overlapping-generation model that all people live for
exactly two periods. This was the staggered-pricing assumption, and like
the overlapping-generations model, the simplifying aspects of the assumption were dropped in practical empirical work.

Despite the simplicity of staggered pricing with rational expectations,
the theory yielded a set of results with implications for monetary policy.
The first result was that expectations of future inflation matter for pricing
decisions today. The reason is that because the current price decision is
expected to last into the future, some prices set in the future will be relevant for today's decision. This is very important for monetary policy.

For the first time, expectations of future inflation come into play in determining the current inflation rate. This gave a rationale for central-bank credibility in its commitment to price stability and for setting an inflation target.

Second, inertia in the inflation process is more complex than in the expectations-augmented Phillips curve and other earlier models without the combination of rational expectations and staggered pricing. Past prices matter because they are relevant for present price decisions, but inertia lasts longer than the period during which prices are fixed. Price shocks take a long time to run through the market because last period's price decisions depend on price decisions in the period before that, and so on into the distant past. The theory also predicted that the degree of inertia or persistence depends on monetary policy. The more aggressively the central bank responds to inflation, the less persistent are inflation shocks. That this prediction was later shown to be true is part of the evidence that the theory and the policy were related. Indeed, over time, inflation persistence has come down as the monetary responses have gone up.

Third, the newer theory implied a trade-off curve between price stability and output stability, and monetary policy could achieve better results in both dimensions by moving the economy toward the curve. In other words, inefficient monetary policies would be off the curve, while efficient monetary policies would be on the curve. Moreover, changes in policy could actually move the trade-off curve in a favorable direction because of expectations effects that would change the price-setting process. For example, a policy that resulted in a movement along the curve toward more price stability and less output stability could shift the curve, bringing about more output stability. Bernanke (2004) used this trade-off curve to explain the role of monetary policy in the Great Moderation. This is the type of framework that led to the recommendations for particular policy rules.

Fourth, the optimal monetary policy rule to minimize the variability of output and inflation could be calculated numerically either by simulating the new monetary models or by using optimal control theory with these models. The optimal monetary policy involved reacting to both inflation and real GDP. If the policy instrument was the money supply, as it was in the earliest research, then it was optimal to react to real GDP, unlike a fixed growth rate of the money supply. If the policy instrument was the interest rate, as it was coming to be in the early 1980s, then it would involve moving the interest rate more aggressively to control inflation and real GDP.

Fifth, the costs of disinflation were less than in the expectations-augmented Phillips curve. This prediction proved accurate when people later examined the disinflation of the early 1980s. It is relevant for the current discussion because it may have been one of the factors tipping the balance in favor of undertaking the disinflation that occurred from 1980 to 1983.

Over time the underlying monetary theory that yielded these results and principles has evolved and improved greatly. An important improvement is that the price-adjustment equations have now been derived formally from an individual-firm optimization problem (see Woodford 2003 for this and other examples of how the theory has developed). In general, the original principles and results, at least the five listed here, have proved robust to these changes. For example, simulations of policy rules derived in the early models perform well in the more recent models with optimally derived equations (Taylor 1999). The defining characteristic of the theory as it first developed—the combination of rational expectations and staggered unsynchronized price setting—remains the same.

More recently, researchers have relaxed the simplifying assumption that prices are set for an exogenous interval of time. Rather, firms' pricing decisions depend on the state of the market, which has given rise to the name "state-dependent" pricing models and has created the need to give the original models a new name, "time-dependent" (Dotsey, King, and Wolman 1999; Gertler and Leahy 2006; Golosov and Lucas 2006). Klenow and Kryvtsov (2007) consider some of the pros and cons of the newer models by looking at how they compare with actual pricing decisions obtained from Bureau of Labor Statistics (BLS) microdata.

The Causal Connection between Theory and Policy

There is a close connection in time between what I am calling the Great Regime Shift in monetary policy and the Great Awakening in monetary economics. Moreover, as the summaries of the theory and the policy make clear, there are close connections between the principles and recommendations and the actual policy, including the importance for expectations of setting an inflation target, the importance of more predictable policy, and the importance of responding aggressively to inflation and real output. That policy changed in the directions of the recommendations is certainly some evidence that there was a causal connection.

But can we go further in establishing a connection? Or must we settle for Keynes's famous generalization that policy makers are the slaves of some defunct economists no matter what the policy makers say? Although it is difficult, I believe that we can go further. For example, Asso, Kahn, and Leeson (2007) have documented many references to policy rules and related developments in the transcripts of the Federal Open Market Committee (FOMC). Meyer (2004), who is one of the policy makers referred to in their paper, makes it clear in his insider's story that there was a framework underlying the policy and that this framework is similar to the theory that I have outlined earlier. If one compares Meyer's (2004) account during the period after the regime shift with the account of an insider such as Maisel (1973) before the regime shift, one finds a huge difference in the framework underlying policy decisions. There is a section on policy rules in chapter 2 of the most recent editions of the Fed's official *Purposes and Functions* (Board of Governors of the Federal Reserve System, 2005). Other evidence comes from the increased interaction between researchers at central banks and monetary economists more generally. Indeed, much of the research that has formed this Great Awakening has been conducted by the staffs at the central banks.

In assessing causation it is essential to distinguish between the role of the Great Awakening in (1) ending the old regime and opening the way to a new regime versus (2) shaping and sustaining a new regime. There is more evidence of the latter than of the former. The dramatic moves of the Fed in the 1980s to reduce inflation under Volcker's leadership were in part a reaction to the harm caused by high inflation during the 1970s, and one suspects that this was more of a factor than the Great Awakening in monetary theory. In contrast, we have more evidence that the policy followed during the 1990s has been influenced by the Great Awakening, as my examples in the previous paragraph illustrate.

To put this another way, like most regime changes, the Great Regime Shift in monetary policy consisted of two interconnected phases: (1) the end of the old inflationary regime of the late 1960s and 1970s, which was largely accomplished through a sharp increase in interest rates until inflation was broken, and (2) the effort to put in place and maintain a new regime in which interest rates rise and fall according to some monetary principles. I think the Great Awakening was very important to the second phase even if it was not important to the first phase.

Conclusion

I began this chapter by summarizing the key characteristics of the Great Moderation of the past twenty-five years. I then reviewed developments in monetary policy and monetary economics that took place during the same period, and I drew attention to a Great Regime Shift in monetary policy and a Great Awakening in monetary economics. This review, as well as more direct evidence of causality, suggests that all three of these developments were closely related and that monetary theory had a constructive influence on monetary policy and thereby on the favorable macroeconomic outcomes.

Of course, monetary economics was not all that mattered. Factors other than monetary theory were certainly part of the influence on monetary policy, and factors other than monetary policy were certainly partly responsible for the improved cyclical performance. Nonetheless, monetary economics mattered significantly and is thus an excellent example of better living through economics.

As I mentioned in the introduction to this chapter, it is possible that the financial crisis that began in 2007 will mark the end of the Great Moderation. But consistent with the theme of this chapter, there is evidence that another monetary policy shift may have been a cause of this crisis. In particular, in remarks prepared for the annual conference of central bankers in Jackson Hole, Wyoming, in August 2007 (see Taylor 2007), I showed that interest rates were set too low in 2002–2005 (compared with levels that would have been expected from the experience since the early 1980s), and this led, at least in part, to the housing boom and the subsequent housing bust that was at the heart of the financial crisis.

In thinking about future research on this topic, however, it is important to recall that the Great Moderation and the Long Boom were already nearly fifteen years old before economists started noticing and documenting them and determining the date of their beginning. Unless the Great Moderation has a dramatic and tumultuous death with a massive decline in real GDP and an unemployment rate higher than the peaks in the 1970s, I believe that it will take as long to document and establish its end.

References

Asso, Pier Francesco, George Kahn, and Robert Leeson (2007). "Monetary Policy Rules: from Adam Smith to John Taylor," Paper presented at the Dallas Federal Reserve Bank conference, October.

Bernanke, Ben (2004), "The Great Moderation." Paper presented to the Eastern Economic Association, Washington, D.C. February 20.

Blanchard, Olivier, and John Simon (2001). "The Long and Large Decline in U.S. Output Volatility." *Brookings Papers on Economic Activity*, 2001, no. 1, 135–164.

Board of Governors of the Federal Reserve System (2005). *Purposes and Functions.* 9th ed., June, Washington, D.C.: Federal Reserve System.

Cecchetti, Stephen G., Alfonso Flores-Lagunes, and Stefan Krause (2006). "Has Monetary Policy Become More Efficient? A Cross-Country Analysis." *Economic Journal* 116, no. 4, 408–433.

Cecchetti, Stephen G., Peter Hooper, Bruce C. Kasman, Kermit L. Schoenholtz, and Mark W. Watson (2007). "Understanding the Evolving Inflation Process." Paper presented at the U.S. Monetary Policy Forum 2007, Washington D.C.

Clarida, Richard, Jordi Gali, and Mark Gertler (2000). "Monetary Policy Rules and Macroeconomic Stability: Evidence and Some Theory." *Quarterly Journal of Economics*, 115, no. 1 (February), 147–180.

Dotsey, Michael, Robert G. King, and Alex Wolman (1999). "State-Dependent Pricing and the General Equilibrium Dynamics of Money and Output." *Quarterly Journal of Economics*, 114, no. 3, 655–690.

Friedman, Milton (2006). "Tradeoffs in Monetary Policy." Paper prepared for David Laidler Festschrift, Hoover Institution.

Gertler, Mark, and John Leahy (2006). "A Phillips Curve with an (S,s) Foundation." NBER Working Paper 11971.

Golosov, Mikhail, and Robert E. Lucas, Jr. (2006). "Menu Costs and the Phillips Curve." *Journal of Political Economy*, 115, no. 2, 171–199.

Judd, John, and Glenn D. Rudebusch (1998). "Taylor's Rule and the Fed: 1970–1997." Federal Reserve Bank of San Francisco, *Economic Review*, 3, 1–16.

Kim, Chang-Jin, and Charles R. Nelson (1999). "Has the U.S. Economy Become More Stable? A Bayesian Approach Based on a Markov Switching Model." *Review of Economics and Statistics*, 81, no. 4, 608–616.

Klenow, Peter J., and Oleksiy Kryvtsov (2007). "State-Dependent or Time-Dependent Pricing: Does It Matter for Recent U.S. Inflation?" Stanford University.

Koenig, Evan F., and Nicole Ball (2007). "The Great Moderation in Output and Employment Volatility," Federal Reserve Bank of Dallas, *Economic Letter*, 2, no. 9 (September).

Kydland, Finn E., and Edward C. Prescott (1977). "Rules Rather than Discretion: The Inconsistency of Optimal Policy." *Journal of Political Economy*, 85, no. 3, 473–492.

Lucas, Robert E. (1976). "Econometric Policy Evaluation: A Critique." *Carnegie-Rochester Conference Series on Public Policy*, 1, 19–46.

Maisel, Sherman J. (1973), *Managing the Dollar*. New York: W. W. Norton.

McConnell. Margaret M., and Gabriel Pérez-Quirós (2000). "Output Fluctuations in the United States: What Has Changed since the Early 1990s?" *American Economic Review*, 90, no. 5, 314–334.

Meyer, Laurence (2004). *A Term at the Fed: An Insider's View*. New York: Harper-Collins.

Romer, Christina (1986). "Is the Stabilization of the Postwar Economy a Figment of the Data?" *American Economic Review*, 76, 314–334.

Rosenblum, Harvey (2007). "Fed Policy and Moral Hazard." *Wall Street Journal*, October 18.

Sargent, Thomas J., and Neil Wallace (1975). "'Rational' Expectations, the Optimal Monetary Instrument, and the Optimal Money Supply Rule." *Journal of Political Economy*, 83, no. 2, 241–255.

Stock, James, and Mark Watson (2003). "Has the Business Cycle Changed?" In *Monetary Policy and Uncertainty: Adapting to a Changing Economy*, Kansas City: Federal Reserve Bank of Kansas City, 9–56.

Taylor. John B. (1979). "Estimation and Control of an Econometric Model with Rational Expectations." *Econometrica*, 47, no. 5 (September), 1267–86.

——— (1980). "Aggregate Dynamics and Staggered Contracts." *Journal of Political Economy*, 88, no. 1, 1–23.

——— (1997). "A Core of Practical Macroeconomics." *American Economic Review, Papers and Proceedings*, 87, no. 2 (May), 233–235.

——— (1998). "Monetary Policy and the Long Boom." Federal Reserve Bank of St. Louis, *Review*, November/December.

——— (1999). *Monetary Policy Rules*. Chicago: University of Chicago Press.

——— (2007). "Housing and Monetary Policy." Remarks at the Policy Panel at the Federal Reserve Bank of Kansas City Jackson Hole Symposium, August.

Woodford, Michael (2003). *Interest and Prices: Foundations of a Theory of Monetary Policy*. Princeton, N.J.: Princeton University Press.

COMMENT

Laurence H. Meyer

It is a real pleasure to have the opportunity to comment on John Taylor's chapter. I will start by summarizing the chapter to set up my comments. Taylor's basic thesis is that advances in monetary theory were principally responsible for a shift to a more disciplined monetary policy that, in turn, importantly contributed to improved macroeconomic performance. Or, in Taylor's language, the Great Awakening produced the Great Regime Shift, which, in turn, caused the Great Moderation. Perhaps a more precise way of saying this is that as monetary policy makers came to appreciate the Taylor principle embedded in the Taylor rule, the economy first moved to the Taylor curve,[1] and the effectiveness of monetary policy in anchoring inflation expectations then shifted the Taylor curve inward, resulting in a reduction in both inflation and output variability.

I have gotten quickly to the first of my two critiques of Taylor's chapter. He fails to do justice to his own contributions to monetary theory and macroeconomic modeling, to our understanding of the effective conduct of monetary policy, and to the interaction between the conduct of monetary policy and the nature of inflation dynamics.

Taylor's thesis has two causal links. The first link—from the Great Awakening to the Great Regime Shift—is about the history of thought. There is no empirical verification possible, just a question of plausibility. The second link—from the Great Regime Shift to the Great Moderation— is one for which theory can provide some support and that is subject to empirical verification. Taylor provides much evidence for the Great Moderation, and although I also believe that there is a link from the shift to a more disciplined monetary policy to the Great Moderation, there is not much focus on either the theoretical case for this link or the empirical verification of such a link.

I will focus the remainder of my comments on the first link. Personally, I do not find this link very plausible. Indeed, my second and more important criticism is that Taylor gives too much credit to his contemporary macroeconomic colleagues for the advances in monetary theory that "caused" the shift in monetary policy. The work that dominated the research agenda from the mid-1970s through the mid-1990s—specifically the New Classical Macroeconomics and Real Business Cycle models—on the whole set back the macroeconomic modeling that would have further advanced our understanding of the effective role of monetary policy. Taylor was both building on the rational-expectations revolution of that period and running upstream with how that revolution was being implemented in macro modeling.

The shift in monetary policy was, in my view, due more to the rediscovery of classical monetary theory than to advances in modern macroeconomics. With all due respect to the key players in the advances in modern macroeconomic theory—including Sargent and Wallace (1975), Lucas (1976), and Kydland and Prescott (1977), among others—the heavy lifting on how to control inflation was done by classical monetary theorists and later by Milton Friedman (1960) and his monetarist colleagues and by Don Patinkin (1965). True, the logic of classical monetary theory had to be rediscovered—and that rediscovery was facilitated in part by the "new classical macroeconomic" models—but classical monetary theorists had the story basically right. There was no mystery about what caused inflation and therefore what it would take to control inflation.

So if modern macroeconomics research did not cause the shift in the conduct of monetary policy, what did? The foundations were laid by Milton Friedman and his monetarist colleagues, reemphasizing the link between money growth and inflation, the appreciation of a vertical long-run Phillips curve and the role of slack in bringing inflation down, realistic estimates of the natural rate of unemployment, and recognition of the role of forward-looking expectations about inflation. But the timing was very much due to inflation itself, the so-called Great Inflation. Indeed, I will argue that the Great Inflation had more to do with the Great Regime Shift than the Great Awakening. Ironically, the Great Inflation helped redirect monetary policy in a direction that contributed to the Great Moderation.

The best story about the timing of the shift in monetary policy is that it was not caused by advances in modern macroeconomics but rather resulted from an unpleasant experiment. We tried the policies that led to higher inflation and decided that we did not like the results; this displeasure in turn both empowered central banks to do whatever was necessary to bring inflation under control and led central banks to return to the solid ground of classical macroeconomics and the link between money growth and inflation. Along the journey, John Taylor and his sensible and pragmatic macroeconomic colleagues working on policy regimes advanced the understanding of what was required for disciplined and effective conduct of policy under an interest-rate-setting regime, one that effectively duplicated the policy discipline of the monetarist approach with respect to inflation but was more consistent with the spirit of the dual mandate.

Note

1. The Taylor principle refers to the requirement that the coefficient of inflation in the Taylor rule must be greater than 1 to ensure that policy will be stabilizing and return inflation to its objective following shocks that open a gap between inflation and the objective. The Taylor rule is a policy rule that describes how policy makers have adjusted (or should adjust) the policy rate to departures of output and inflation from their respective objectives. The Taylor curve describes the efficient trade-off frontier between output and inflation variability.

References

Bernanke, Ben S. "The Great Moderation." Speech, Federal Reserve Board, February 20, 2004.

Friedman, Milton. *A Program for Monetary Stability.* New York: Fordham University Press, 1960.

Kydland, Finn E., and Edward C. Prescott. "Rules Rather than Discretion: The Inconsistency of Optimal Policy." *Journal of Political Economy,* 85 (1977), 473–491.

Lucas, Robert. "Econometric Policy Evaluation: A Critique." *Carnegie-Rochester Conference Series on Public Policy,* 1 (1976), 19–46.

Patinkin, Don. *Money, Interest, and Prices.* New York: Harper and Row, 1965.

Sargent, Tom J., and Neil Wallace. "'Rational' Expectations, the Optimal Monetary Instrument, and the Optimal Money Supply Rule." *Journal of Political Economy,* 83 (1975), 241–254.

Taylor, John B. "Aggregate Dynamics and Staggered Contracts." *Journal of Political Economy*, 88 (1980), 1–23.

———. "A Core of Practical Macroeconomics." *American Economic Review, Papers and Proceedings*, 87, no. 2 (May 1997), 233–235.

———. "Discretion vs Policy Rules in Practice." *Carnegie- Rochester Conference Series on Public Policy*, 1993, 195–214.

———. "Monetary Policy and the Long Boom." 1998 Homer Jones Lecture. *Federal Reserve Bank of St. Louis Review*, November/December 1998, 2–12.

CHAPTER SEVEN

The Greatest Auction in History

R. Preston McAfee, John McMillan, Simon Wilkie

In August 1993 President Bill Clinton signed a historic law granting the U.S. Federal Communications Commission (FCC) the authority to auction spectrum licenses.[1] The origin of this law dates back to Ronald Coase's 1959 proposal to sell the radio spectrum. Congress gave the FCC until August 1994 to begin the first auction. To someone inexperienced in the activities of large bureaucracies, a year sounds adequate to design and operate an auction, but it is remarkable that the FCC was able to meet this requirement and commence its first auction on July 25, 1994. In order to run an auction, the FCC needed to choose an auction design, and in order to do that, it was required by law to provide adequate time for persons to file formal comments and reply comments on its proposed procedures. These comments, along with staff recommendations, were used by the FCC commissioners to determine an auction form that would survive judicial challenge. Finally, the FCC staff then implemented the commission's decision, relying on outside contractors to develop auction software. Timely implementation was particularly challenging given that the commission decided on a novel auction method, the electronic simultaneous multiple-round bidding auction, based on economic advice.

Congress and many economists underestimated the number of choices in designing an auction. In modern business parlance, auctions have many "dials and levers" that can be used to tweak performance and outcomes, but the presence of these choices creates an enormous economic and political challenge. This chapter describes how that challenge was met using modern game theory. The efforts of economists led to what William Safire (1995) called "the greatest auction in history," using methods that have been copied around the world to sell over U.S. $100 billion in radio spectrum.

Auctions were not seriously considered for awarding spectrum licenses until two other methods ran into difficulty. The bureaucratic mainstay, administrative allocation by comparative hearing, began to break down as the value of the items to be allocated increased. Hearings and court challenges take years and incur large costs for both participants and the government. Congress replaced these cumbersome administrative procedures with lotteries in 1982. The potential for a windfall gain from winning a license resulted in nearly 400,000 applications for cellular licenses. With so many applications, the magnitude of the total private expenditures in obtaining licenses (rent seeking) was large for a process that only by accident assigns licenses to parties that value them most highly.

When Congress mandated the use of auctions, expert academic economists became involved primarily because neither the potential bidders nor the FCC had experience in auctions. The FCC hired John McMillan as a consultant to advise it on auction design; he supplemented FCC economist Evan Kwerel, the driving force behind the auctions. The major bidders hired economists, including Paul Milgrom, Robert Wilson, Preston McAfee, Barry Nalebuff, Peter Cramton, David Salant, and Rob Gertner, to write comments to file with the FCC on auction design and to advise on bidding strategy during the auctions.

The absence of a history of auctions at the FCC was a significant advantage to the commission in developing a novel and appropriate design based on recent advances in auction theory. It is incredibly difficult for a bureaucracy to change an existing methodology that works moderately well, even if an alternative is clearly superior. Change involves career-destroying risks and opens lobbying doors that might result in worse choices. In the design of the Personal Communication Services (PCS) auctions, the absence of an existing default meant that all designs were on the table. Moreover, the use of academic economists helped focus the debate on the public interest rather than on the firms who in most cases paid their bills. Academic economists were generally unwilling to defend their clients' goals when these goals conflicted with the social interest. In addition, the determination of FCC chairman Reed Hundt to "do the right thing" helped prevent the agency capture all too common in Washington, a determination strongly aided by Kwerel's analyses.

FCC Auction Issues

Congress mandated that the FCC auctions should

- promote efficient and intensive use of the electromagnetic spectrum;
- promote rapid deployment of new technologies;
- promote economic opportunity and competition by dissemination of licenses to a wide variety of applicants;
- recover for the public a portion of the value of the public spectrum resource.[2]

Economists emphasized four goals: simplicity, efficiency, revenue, and diversity. Although simplicity was not a goal specified by Congress nor found in economics texts, economists recognized immediately that because the spectrum auctions would be conducted for the first time with inexperienced bidders, the auction design needed to be simple to understand. A complex design was likely to be misunderstood, leading to unintended choices and inefficient outcomes.

A second aspect of simplicity, and one harder to implement, requires that a simple strategy be optimal or nearly optimal behavior in the auction. For example, "bid your estimated value" is a reasonable strategy in a Vickrey auction[3] but a terrible strategy in a first-price (winners pay their bid prices) sealed-bid auction. A first-price sealed-bid auction has the property that bidding sensibly requires assessing the bidding strategies of rivals, a hard thing to do in a static game. Thus the first-price sealed-bid auction, although simple to understand, has no sensible simple strategy for participants. Economists were very much concerned to articulate simple bidding strategies for bidders that would perform well. It was expected that novice bidders would probably adopt such strategies.

Congress mandated some form of efficiency, which economists generally interpreted to mean that the bidders with the highest value should obtain the license. If there had been only one license, efficiency would not have been a significant challenge. However, thousands of licenses were available, spanning different geographic regions and distinct spectrum bands. Efficiency therefore meant both figuring out which aggregations of licenses made sense and doing so without substantial delay, because delay itself is a cost. With the exception of some work on bundling, economic analysis provided little guidance. Efficiency requires appropriately defining licenses both geographically and across spectrum bands and designing the auction mechanism to award those licenses. In defining the geographic scope of licenses, one must consider the ability of the auction mechanism and secondary markets efficiently to aggregate small licenses into larger coverage areas versus the ability of secondary markets to efficiently disaggregate large licenses into smaller areas.

Before the broadband PCS auctions, some economists argued for dividing the country into large regions (or even the entire nation). The problem with this band plan was that most of the potential bidders owned some portion of the existing cellular spectrum and generally would be seeking to buy a complement of their existing holdings. Indeed, limits on ownership precluded them from buying in areas where they already had holdings. Large regions would not permit purchase of complementary holdings in the auction and would lead to few bidders or requiring divestiture of existing holdings by participants.[4]

Other economists argued for dividing the nation into many small geographic areas without proposing an auction that would be likely to facilitate efficient aggregation. These economists relied on secondary markets to achieve efficiency. On the basis of experience with administrative assignment and lotteries, we know that high transaction costs in secondary markets can delay and in some cases prevent altogether the efficient aggregation of spectrum. The cellular spectrum allocated earlier remained a patchwork of ownership, with incomplete roaming agreements, even twelve years later. History suggests that getting the initial allocation substantially right was very important for the speed of comprehensive deployment of wireless services.

A major challenge to efficient allocation is the presence of local synergies in value. Local synergies generally arise from three distinct motivations— creation of seamless roaming, elimination of boundary interference, and advertising or scale economies in management. Ausubel et al. (1997) find evidence of such synergies in the bidding. The history of spectrum license aggregations suggested that it was difficult to forecast the shape of efficient assignments. GTE created an aggregation of licenses in the Southwest along interstate highways; McCaw had a similar aggregation in the Northeast. Both resulted in a spidery allocation, strange in appearance until it was compared with an interstate highway map. Moreover, new services might require spectrum in unanticipated geographic concentrations. It seemed important to let the market choose the allocation in the process of bidding.

Most of the academic economists involved in the design considered revenue an important goal. With the United States' substantial government debt and prevailing deficit, revenue had value beyond the strict dollar amount raised because increased revenue permitted a reduction in distorting taxation. Revenue has an additional importance, however. Revenue is evidence that high-value bidders are being selected; that is, revenue is itself evidence that the price system is working. In principle, of course, higher revenue need not signal allocative efficiency, as is easily seen by noting that the monopoly quantity has higher revenue than the efficient competitive price.

The 1993 legislation authorizing auctions directed the FCC to "disseminate licenses to a wide variety of applicants, including small businesses, rural telephone companies, and businesses owned by members of minority groups and women." Collectively these groups came to be known as "designated entities." Historically, the U.S. government has favored such groups by set-asides. In a set-aside a portion of the items for sale (or contracts to buy) is reserved for the designated entities. This is a potentially costly means of meeting the congressional requirement; McAfee and McMillan (1989) have argued that price preferences, in which the designated entity obtains a bidding credit or can submit a given bid at less cost than other bidders, are a more effective and less costly means of achieving the same ends. The FCC has used bidding credits, spectrum set-asides, and installment payments to promote participation by designated entities. It discontinued use of installment payments in 1997.

Most of the auction-design discussions among the economists, FCC staff, and participating companies came down to eight basic choices discussed in the subsequent sections.

Ascending versus Sealed Bids

The most fundamental choice in auction design is whether to use a once-and-for-all bid or to permit revision of bids over time. Governments generally choose sealed bids over ascending bids; corporations are more likely to prefer ascending bids.

The usual view is that a simultaneous sealed bid is more difficult to rig than an ascending auction. A member of a conspiracy to rig the bids can cheat on the conspiracy by submitting a bid secretly; thus sealed bids encourage breakdown of cartels. In contrast, a cartel can punish a deviation in an oral auction immediately. On the other hand, sealed bids open the door to collusion with a government official, who secretly reports on others' bids to one of the bidders. Sealed bids are less susceptible to collusion among the bidders but more susceptible to malfeasance by government officials. In any case, organized conspiracy was not anticipated to be a problem.

Ascending auctions differ from sealed bids in the release of information: in an ascending auction bidders can respond to the behavior of others during the course of the auction. This ability to revise bids in light of the behavior of others has consequences developed by Paul Milgrom and Robert Weber (1982) and on average increases the revenue in the auction in a symmetric environment. An ascending auction reveals information about the bidders to the bidders. Revealing information reduces the size of the information rents obtained by bidders and increases prices on average. This positive relationship between revenues and information transmission during the auction has been labeled "the linkage principle" in, for example, Milgrom (1989, p. 16).

In addition, when bidders are asymmetric, sealed-bid auctions tend to select inefficiently, while ascending auctions tend to be more efficient. Intuitively, the reason is that in a sealed-bid auction a strong bidder faces less competition than a weak bidder. The strong bidder faces the field minus itself, while the weak bidder faces a field that includes the strong bidder. Thus a strong bidder will seek a higher profit, while a weak bidder, facing stronger competition, will bid closer to actual value. The strong bidder will sometimes lose in circumstances when it has the higher value. In an ascending auction the strong bidder would revise its bid upward to win if it were actually the high-value bidder.

Ascending auctions have the virtue of reducing regret: bidders need not "leave money on the table," the euphemism for a bid substantially higher than the second-highest bid. Such bids make the bidder appear to pay too much, which could harm the bidder's career even if the bid was in fact ex ante optimal. In an ascending auction actual competition, rather than an expectation about competition, forces bids to the level achieved, and this feature reduces regret.

Although the weight of the economic literature favored ascending auctions, the case was far from transparent, primarily because of the history of government auctions using sealed bids, including the Department of the Interior's offshore oil auctions, which use a simultaneous sealed-bid auction of as many as 150 distinct tracts. That the Department of the Interior continues to use such a flawed mechanism demonstrates the difficulty of changing the status quo.

Simultaneous versus Sequential

Auctioneers Christie's and Sotheby's have sold billions of dollars of goods by sequential oral auctions, and there was a strong sense that what is good enough for antiques sellers is good enough for the U.S. government. Several economists persisted in the view that the simultaneous designs were unnecessarily complicated, both for the government to implement and for bidders to participate. This view still prevails in some circles. As will become clear, the nature of spectrum auctions renders this view naïve.

In a sequential design, licenses are ordered and then sold in a series of auctions. When the amount a bidder is willing to pay for an item depends on the other items it acquires, sequential auctions deny the bidder crucial information. Consider a bidder who values two items separately at $1 each, but collectively at $3. This bidder on the first item would be willing to pay up to $2, provided it expected the third item to sell for no more than $1. On the other hand, having bought the first item for $2, the bidder would now be willing to pay up to $2 for the second item, even though this creates a $1 loss on the pair. This problem for the bidder is known as the exposure problem: holding one item exposes one to a loss created by the complementarities in values. The bidder has to forecast the price of future items to bid sensibly on the earlier items. This need to forecast creates a dilemma for the bidder, whether to bid safely and probably lose, or bid aggressively and wind up stuck with an incomplete aggregation. Only a combinatorial design avoids the exposure problem, but at the expense of creating other problems.

Sequential auctions are problematic when items are substitutes, as well as complements. Suppose that two identical items are auctioned sequentially and a bidder wants only one. In bidding on the first item, the bidder must guess the selling price of the second item. There is no reason to expect that the selling price will be the same for both items, and bad guesses may result in the items not being awarded to the parties who value them the most. Empirical auction data have shown that this inefficiency is a problem. In particular, Gandal (1997) demonstrated that use of sequential auctions for cable television franchises in Israel affected revenues and arguably affected efficiency. Similarly, it has been argued that sequential auctioning by country of licenses intended for third generation (3G) cellular technology in Europe led to the inflation of early prices and collapse of prices in countries later in the sequence, although many economists view this as implausible.

A major problem for sequential designs is the order in which licenses are to be sold, especially when different orders advantage different firms. The orders of sequential sales of broadband PCS licenses proposed by different parties included largest to smallest, smallest to largest, east to west, and west to east. Ordering induces a bias; particular firms care more about some markets than others and will prefer learning from the markets they care less about first. In addition, sorting out the most important markets before less important complementary markets is advantageous. No ordering is neutral, which created a problem for supporters of sequential designs: they disagreed about the ordering. Thus there was little support for any one sequential design even though a majority of the economists initially supported sequential designs.

Another serious problem of sequential designs is timing. Proponents of sequential designs generally considered selling dozens of licenses per day. Because some of the most valuable licenses were expected to—and did—sell for hundreds of millions of dollars, a sequential design required making billion-dollar decisions in the course of a single day. Although companies can execute a billion-dollar decision in a day, they cannot reasonably incorporate new information in the process because changing a billion-dollar decision usually requires days or even weeks of deliberation at the senior management level. Running sequential auctions in a timely manner—completing hundreds in a month or two—would generally reduce the utility of information gleaned from the auctions themselves, forcing bidders into a prespecified set of strategies. This reduction vitiates the major advantage of ascending auctions: information release.

In contrast to sequential auctions, simultaneous designs were not well understood, and proponents had to solve a variety of problems. The most famous simultaneous design, the "silent auction" used by charities, has physical locations for each of the items for sale. Because bidding closes on all items at the same time, this design requires bidders to have as many bidding agents as the number of items they desire. The alternative, simultaneous multiple-round bidding (SMR), was proposed as a solution to this problem. In SMR all the licenses are available for bidding in each of discrete rounds. The minimum bid on any one license is increased over the previous round by a percentage. Bidders can bid on any or all the licenses in a given round, and the maximum bids from the previous round become the basis for the next round of bidding. This solution created a different problem. A bidder would like to see first what others are willing to pay and then choose the items that represent the best value. That is, every bidder has an optimal strategy of waiting until the others have completed their bidding. Were all the bidders to follow this strategy, of course, there would be no bidding at all. The standard solution in the literature, due to Charles Plott (see, e.g., Plott, Wit, and Yang, 2003), involves a positive probability of ending the auction, which itself creates a probability of inefficiency, regret, and frustration by participants and government alike.

The solution invented by Paul Milgrom and Robert Wilson is the activity rule—each bidder must be active (have the standing high bid or make a new bid) in every round on a specified fraction of the licenses it hopes to win. Thus a bidder that seeks twelve licenses would, under a 50% activity rule, be required to bid on at least six licenses. (After the first auction activity was defined in terms of bidding units to account for differences in license sizes. Each license was assigned bidding units equal to the product of the amount of spectrum in MHz and population in the license area.) This puts pressure on bidders to bid but still allows them the flexibility to substitute to other licenses if the licenses on which they are currently bidding become too expensive.

The magnitude of the activity rule determines the ease of substitution. With a low activity requirement, bidders can readily substitute from one set of licenses to another because they hold few of the licenses they hope to purchase and thus have lots of "purchasing capacity." If bidders are generally bidding only on the licenses required to maintain activity, price increases will stall when the potential demand for licenses at current prices is about one over the amount of the activity rule times the available amount of spectrum. Thus the activity rule needs to be tightened over the course of the auction, or prices will come to a stop even though excess demand remains. The first auctions used a three-phase system: initially a 33% activity requirement, then a 67% requirement, followed by a 100% requirement.[5]

This design, created primarily by academic economists, has become known as the FCC auction. The key advantages of this auction design relative to all others are that it promotes (1) the timely release of information and (2) substitution by buyers. If a price increase on one or more licenses renders that group more expensive, a buyer can switch to another group, usually with no penalty but at worst with a modest penalty. This substitution is facilitated by several complementary features, including the activity rule itself, which directly permits substitution, the gradual tightening of the activity rule,[6] the design of the licenses for sale into "similar-sized" units, and the modest withdrawal penalty that forces bids to be meaningful expressions of willingness to pay while still encouraging the assembly of efficient aggregations.

The success of the FCC auction is perhaps most dramatically illustrated by the second narrowband (paging-frequency) licenses. Here thirty licenses were sold. Six frequency bands were sold in each of five geographic regions. Four of the sets of regional licenses were aggregated into national licenses, and similar licenses sold for similar prices; indeed, the single price anomaly was the consequence of a failed attempt to game the auction, resulting in a withdrawal and a low price for that license. (With the withdrawal penalty, the license sold for a similar price.) Bidders were able to aggregate the licenses they desired, and prices appeared competitive.

Combinatorial Bids

A combinatorial bid involves the ability to bid on a package of licenses as an all-or-nothing bid. Various combinatorial bidding methods were promoted by academic economists. The two main forms initially proposed were (1) to permit bidding on any subset and allow the bidders to revise their bids, using an SMR format, until bidding stopped, or (2) have individual licenses plus a national license.

Combinatorial auctions have the advantage that bidders can express their demands directly—a bidder who wants three licenses can bid on them as a unit. Combinatorial auctions provide a solution to the exposure problem identified earlier. However, combinatorial auctions are more complex because there are many potential combinations. There is also the "threshold" or "free-rider" problem—the potential that bidders on subsets of a larger package will not be able to combine their bids to beat the bid on the larger package even when the sum of the value of the subsets exceeds the value of the package. As with all free-rider problems, there is a risk that the bidders will fail to bid enough. The risk of lower revenue and inefficiency due to the threshold problem, along with the potential complexity of implementing a combinatorial auction, deterred the FCC from selecting it in spite of serious support among academic economists. Nevertheless, combinatorial auctions remain a vibrant area of research and a continuing interest of the FCC. Indeed, since 1996, significant experimental and theoretical research has suggested ways to mitigate the threshold problem (see, e.g., DeMartini et al. 1998; Marx and Matthews 2000; and Ausubel, Cramton, and Milgrom 2006).

Reserve Prices

In the traditional theory of auctions, reserve prices represent a trade-off between revenue and efficiency; efficient reserve prices are the seller's value, usually set to zero as a modeling artifact, while the monopoly reserve price is substantially in excess of the seller's value. Economists divided on the issue of reserve prices along the lines of the importance they gave to efficiency and revenue.

From a static point of view, any positive reserve price conflicts with efficiency when a license is not sold.[7] However, a new, dynamic view of reserve prices emerged from the FCC auctions. A seller who fails to sell has the option of selling in the future; thus the seller's value may not be the seller's use value but instead the value of a buyer not yet present. If the seller expects to sell at a higher price in the future, it may be efficient not to sell today. This may be the case when new technologies are possible, technologies that will be resisted by incumbents because they supplant existing services. The question then is whether private parties or the FCC should keep this "option value." In light of allegations of stockpiling of spectrum by incumbents, reserving spectrum for future technologies could be important. The threat of stockpiling by incumbents provides a rationale for public rather private holding of idle spectrum,[8] but there is by no means a consensus on this point.

Size of Increments

The use of rounds of bidding forces a decision on a bid increment—what is the minimum increase between rounds? If it is too small, the auction will take too many rounds, wasting time and effort. If it is too large, the auction will allocate the licenses inefficiently. The consensus recommendation was created by an insight of Paul Milgrom. Halving the step size or increment approximately doubles the time required to complete the auction. However, inefficiency arises only when the bidder with the second-highest value wins because the high-value bidder is unwilling to pay the second-highest value plus an increment. The loss in value is at most an increment and, moreover, occurs only when the second-highest value is close to the highest value, which has a probability proportional to the size of the increment, so the loss is approximately proportional to the bid increment squared. Consequently, even quite large increments—say, 10%—have an efficiency impact proportional to the square of the increment, or 1%. Milgrom's argument persuaded most economists that substantial increments were not very costly to efficiency and hence represented the best way to speed up auctions. The exception to the consensus was, by and large, from those in favor of continuous-time auctions.

In spite of the consensus among economists, business and the FCC remained leery of large increments. The FCC instead employed an increment accelerator rule, which determined the size of the increment by the amount of competition present in preceding rounds.

Bidder Preferences

An innovative feature of the FCC auction was the use of price preferences or bidder credits, in addition to set-asides, to favor designated entities. A bidder credit is akin to the idea of handicapping in sports. Suppose that a designated entity, because of lack of capital or expertise, has a 10% lower value on average. Then the auction can level the competition by providing a 10% bidder credit—that is, charging the designated bidder only 90% of its bid.

Bidder credits are advantageous over set-asides for at least seven distinct reasons. First, bidder credits rather than set-asides increase competition in an SMR auction. The designated entities become more effective bidders thanks to the handicapping, while the nondesignated entities are some competition for the licenses that would otherwise be set aside. Second, bidding credits set a price or value for promotion of designated entities, thereby permitting resale at the cost of refunding the bidder credit.[9] Third, the inefficiency of promoting the designated entities may be reduced because designated entities win auctions only when they are close to the willingness to pay of the other firms, relative to a set-aside. Fourth, revenues may increase over the levels that would prevail without any bidder credits because for small levels of bidder credit, the increase in competition outweighs the inefficient allocation.[10] Of course, revenue will fall as the bidder credit becomes larger than the disadvantage of the designated group. Fifth, the tendency for set-asides is to create very small licenses, so-called ghetto licenses, perhaps because nondesignated entities lobby hard to prevent the setting aside of valuable licenses that could lead to meaningful competition. Thus a universal modest bidder credit, applicable to all licenses, will prevent the creation of ghetto licenses and permit the designated entities to compete effectively for all licenses. Sixth, price preferences are a versatile instrument, capable of giving distinct levels of preference to different categories of designated entities; for example, the credit may vary with the size of the small business, although the Supreme Court has ruled price preferences like bidder credits for telecommunications auctions illegal.[11] Seventh, price preferences naturally apply to partial ownership by giving partial credit.

The FCC used 25% bidder credits in the first narrowband auction, but none of the licenses were won by designated entities. The credit level was increased to 40% in the second narrowband auction, and all the licenses available for bidder credit were won by designated entities. It is not clear, unfortunately, whether the success in the second auction was due to the increased bidder credit or the increased time to prepare; some of the designated entities seem to be firms that came into existence to take advantage of the bidder credits. Indeed, supporting the "designer-firm" theory, the actual prices paid for the licenses net of the bidder credit were just slightly below the prices paid for licenses not eligible for bidder credits, suggesting that the designated entities were nearly competitive with the nondesignated entities.

Spectrum Caps

Spectrum caps—a limit on the amount of spectrum any one participant may hold in a given geographic area—are a simple means of ensuring adequate competition in the final product market. The existing structure of the wireless market was a duopoly by design. The sale was intended to foster competition, and the spectrum caps were set such that an incumbent could not purchase a 30 MHz license in its existing footprint; this guaranteed at least three new entrants in every market. The FCC aimed to have five competing firms in every geographic market.[12] An important characteristic of spectrum caps is that they are substantially easier to enforce than antitrust laws.

Revealing Bidder Identity

In a standard oral auction it is difficult, although not impossible, to conceal the identities of the bidders. However, in an auction with multiple rounds of bidding done on computers, it becomes possible to conceal the identity of the bidders from other bidders. Concealment can be accomplished by reporting only the price bid on each license and not the identity of the firm that bid, or by giving bidders identification numbers and revealing the bidder number but not the mapping from real bidders to bidder identifications.

The disadvantage of concealing bidder identities is that there is information content not just in what was bid but in who did the bidding. In particular, a bid from a company completing a national license by bidding on a "hole" may be a less significant indicator of value than a bid by a start-up. Perhaps more empirically relevant, there are technological economies of scale, so knowing whether a large Global System for Mobile communications (GSM) technology carrier is bidding may matter substantially to the smaller carriers, who hope to have access to handsets that will become available only if a large player buys spectrum. Thus the identity of other bidders could potentially affect valuation. A second disadvantage, which was entertaining if not economically significant in the first narrowband auction and potentially significant in later auctions, is that bidders spend a lot of time trying to figure out which bidder identification corresponds to which bidder.

There are two main advantages to reporting only prices. First, because concealed identities make defection from a cartel agreement harder to punish, concealing identities should reduce the likelihood of behavior ranging from price-fixing to "tacit understandings." Second, concealed identities make it much harder to "game" the auction. An example of such gaming occurred in the Australian spectrum auctions in which one bidder was attempting to assemble five adjoining licenses and the spoiler continued to bid on the middle license in a strategy that became known as "giving the middle finger." When all that is observable is the price, such a punishment strategy is much less likely to succeed. For a description of the use of such strategies in an FCC auction, see Cramton and Schwartz (2002). In the end, the FCC chose to conceal identities but to reveal bidder identifications in the first auction. Because this auction was run by bidding in a booth like a polling booth, it was relatively easy to deduce which bidder identification went with which company.

How to Design Efficient and High-Revenue Auctions

How well did the economists do in designing the auctions, and what have we learned since? The FCC has run over seventy auctions since 1994. From this wealth of experience we can distill several key lessons and principles. In summary form, these principles are the following:

- Promote information revelation:
  Use ascending auctions.
  Provide bidding tools for analyzing bids.
- Promote substitution:
  Sell licenses simultaneously.
  Make the licenses similarly sized.
  Squash and "round" license sizes for the auction activity-rule
    calculations.
  Progressively tighten activity rules.
- Make the problem to be solved by participants easier:
  Use fixed increments.
  Conceal identities of bidders.
  Allow enough time between rounds for good decisions.
- Design simple, transparent rules.

Conclusion

Academic economists, working with FCC staff and especially FCC economist Evan Kwerel, created an auction form that has been used to sell over

$100 billion dollars of spectrum in dozens of countries. The design reflected trade-offs that were understood only because of the development of auction theory in the 1980s and thus implemented recent innovations in economic analysis. The FCC auction performed well by a variety of measures and seems to have balanced revenue and efficiency.

The FCC auction has rightfully been credited as an important impetus to the adoption of game-theoretic techniques in the business world. The usefulness of economists in the private sector, long a subject of derision, was forcefully demonstrated by the application of sophisticated game theory in this real-world setting.

The role of economics and economists in the FCC auctions was not to prove a theorem that provided an optimal mechanism for some particular setting. Instead, it was to use existing theory to identify the most important factors, design a system that accommodates the needs of market participants, generally in as simple a manner as possible, and identify the features that may be important. Theory, then, is a guide, not a destination.

Notes

John McMillan passed away before this chapter was complete, so it does not reflect his gift for engaging exposition. This chapter does not necessarily represent the views of our employers.

1. *Omnibus Reconciliation Act of 1993*, U.S. Public Law 103-66, 103rd Cong., 1st sess., August 10, 1993.
2. Section 309(j) of the *Communications Act*, 47 U.S.C. § 309(j).
3. A Vickrey (or second-price) auction is a sealed-bid auction in which the high bidder winning but paying the second highest bid. See McAfee and McMillan (1987 p. 710). It is equilibrium behavior only in the relatively specialized private-values environment.
4. MCI, the only major telephone company with no existing spectrum holdings, was a strong proponent of the national license. This was one of the most obvious examples of self-interested lobbying.
5. A literal 100% requirement, when applied to unequally sized licenses, is bad because of integer problems. Integer problems themselves gave bidders headaches in FCC auctions. The Mexican spectrum auctions had the additional problem that Mexico City was a huge portion of the entire country. As a result, the modern design "squashes" or levels the license size, preferably to values that are easy to combine into substitutes. In Mexico the license "sizes," for the purposes of evaluating the activity rule, were set at 1, 2, 3, 4, 6, 12 (Guadalajara), and 24 (Mexico City) to promote substitution. These are quite different from population sizes; the squashing makes it easier to substitute between Mexico City and a group of other licenses.

6. A 100% activity rule makes substitution difficult. Suppose that a bidder seeks six contiguous licenses but does not care where the six are. At 100% a bidder can move without risk of penalty only on the licenses whose prices increased; if prices of three increased, the bidder faces a substantial risk of being left either paying penalties or stuck with the remaining three.

7. Unused spectrum is lost. Use of the spectrum does not inhibit future use of the spectrum. Thus social efficiency calls for full use. This full use is mitigated by an installed base of equipment to use the spectrum, and the sale of spectrum interacts with standards on use.

8. See Cramton, Skzyracz, and Wilson (2007).

9. The amount of the bidder credit should not be confused with the social value of favoring the designated entities or with the size of the disadvantage they face. Generally, optimal bidder credits will be somewhat less than the social value of favoring the entities because the bidder credit must trade off the revenue obtained against the desire to increase participation by the entities. Second, the bidder credit may be larger or smaller than the disadvantage faced by the entities. Revenue maximization requires bidder credits that are positive but smaller than the disadvantage because fully compensating for the disadvantage causes the designated entities to win too often. See McAfee and McMillan (1996, p. 167).

10. Allocative inefficiency has a zero first-order effect, while the change in competition has a first-order effect, when the credit is small.

11. *Adarand v. Pena*, 15 S. Ct. 2097 (1995).

12. The FCC subsequently abolished the ownership cap and drafted industry-specific merger review guidelines that were never released.

References

Ausubel, Larry, Peter Cramton, R. Preston McAfee, and John McMillan. "Synergies in Wireless Telephony." *Journal of Economics and Management Strategy*, 6, no. 3 (Fall 1997), 497–527.

Ausubel, Larry, P. Cramton, and P. Milgrom. "The Clock-Proxy Auction: A Practical Combinatorial Auction Design." Chapter 5 in Peter Cramton, Yoav Shoham, and Richard Steinberg, eds., *Combinatorial Auctions*. Cambridge, Mass.: MIT Press, 2006.

Coase, Ronald H. "The Federal Communications Commission." *Journal of Law & Economics*, 2 (October 1959), 1–40.

Cramton, Peter, and Jess Schwartz. "Collusive Bidding in the FCC Spectrum Auctions." *Contributions to Economic Analysis & Policy*, 1, no. 1 (2002).

Cramton, Peter, Andrzej Skrzypacz, and Robert B. Wilson. Available from www.cramton.umd.edu/papers2005-2009/cramton-skrzypacz-wilson-competition-in-700-mhz-auction.pdf.

DeMartini, Christine, Anthony M. Kwasnica, John O. Ledyard, and David Porter. "A New and Improved Design For Multi-object Iterative Auctions." HSS Working Paper 1054, California Institute of Technology, 1998.

Gandal, Neil. "Sequential Auctions of Interdependent Objects: Israeli Cable Television Licenses." *Journal of Industrial Economics,* 45 (September 1997), 227–244.

Marx, Leslie, and Steve Matthews. "Dynamic Voluntary Contribution to a Public Project." *Review of Economic Studies,* 67 (2000), 327–358.

McAfee, R. Preston, and John McMillan. "Auctions and Bidding." *Journal of Economic Literature,* 25, no. 2 (June 1987), 699–738.

———. "Government Procurement and International Trade." *Journal of International Economics,* 26 (1989), 291–308.

———. "Analyzing the Airwaves Auction." *Journal of Economic Perspectives,* 10 (Winter 1996), 159–175.

McMillan, John. "Selling Spectrum Rights." *Journal of Economic Perspectives,* 8, no. 3 (Summer 1994), 145–162.

Milgrom, Paul. "Auctions and Bidding: A Primer." *Journal of Economic Perspectives,* 3 (Summer 1989), 3–22.

———. *Putting Auction Theory to Work.* Cambridge: Cambridge University Press, 2004.

Milgrom, Paul, and Robert Weber. "A Theory of Auctions and Competitive Bidding." *Econometrica,* 50, no. 5 (September 1982), 1089–1122.

Plott, Charles, J. Wit, and W. C. Yang. "Parimutuel Betting Markets as Information Aggregation Devices: Experimental Results." *Economic Theory,* 22 (2003), 311–351.

Safire, William. "Essay; The Greatest Auction Ever." *New York Times,* Thursday, March 16, 1995, Section A, p. 25.

COMMENT

Jeremy Bulow

Why was the simultaneous multiple-round (SMR) auction design so successful in the 1995 FCC AB auction and in many other settings? Ironically, one reason is that its structure almost guaranteed the sequential closure of markets, with the biggest and most valuable markets closing first. Activity rules made it easier to move from larger licenses to smaller ones in the late bidding rather than the other way around. This probably raised revenue and helped with problems of complementarity.

To see the revenue point, consider Example 1, in which there are two licenses and three bidders with the following valuations.

Example 1

	License A	License B
Bidder 1	10	20
Bidder 2	20	40
Bidder 3	30	60

Say each bidder is allowed to buy only one license. If the licenses are sold sequentially, with the smaller A sold first, prices will be 10 for license A (won by bidder 2) and 20 for license B (won by 3, competing only against 1). If B is sold first, then the prices will be 30 for license B (sold to 3 competing against 2, whose alternative is to win license A at a price of 10), and

10 for A. Auction rules that make it much easier to move from bigger licenses to smaller ones than to go the other way often effectively assure that smaller licenses will not clear before the bigger ones.[1]

Having larger licenses clear first provides a further advantage for aggregation. In packing a car trunk, most people put the big suitcases in first. Similarly, in forming an aggregation, most bidders will focus on the largest, most valuable licenses in a package. A bidder interested in greater New York may regard a partial aggregation that includes the city but not all suburbs as a success and one that contains all the suburbs but not the city as a disastrous failure.[2]

A second reason to like the SMR is that it has some significant advantages over a pure Vickrey auction, in which each bidder writes down its value for all license combinations and a computer calculates the value-maximizing allocation, each bidder receiving a surplus equal to its marginal contribution to total value. The authors discuss how multiple-round bidding allows bidders to learn information through the auction, allowing them to bid more efficiently than in a one-shot auction. But there is a second disadvantage to a Vickrey approach.[3]

Assume that bidders have the valuations listed in Example 2.

Example 2

Bidder	Value of A only	Value of B only	Value of AB
1	o	o	10
2	9	o	9
3	o	9	9

The Vickrey auction will award the licenses to bidders 2 and 3 at prices of 1 each. (Since the total value in the auction is 18, and it would be only 10 without either 2 or 3 they each receive a surplus of 8). This means that if these bidders each have actual values of 6 instead of 9 for their licenses, they can gain by colluding by raising their bids to 9 each (lowering their prices from 4 to 1), and if they have values of 2 each, they can still profit by bidding 9 on the licenses. The Vickrey auction is thus deeply susceptible to collusion, because jointly raised bids can allow the colluders to acquire more licenses at lower prices. Furthermore, the "collusion" can take the form of one entity submitting bids as two—if bidders 2 and 3 were treated as one bidder, they would have to pay 10 to buy the licenses.

Of course all mechanisms will fail if bidders can collude. The difference is that in most economic models, for collusion to be successful it must be "collusion in the large." The competitive model works well because in most settings collusion requires the participation of almost all bidders. With Vickrey-Clark-Groves mechanisms one may only require "collusion in the small"; given the top bid for a package, two players bidding on individual licenses may be able to profitably collude on their own. (In fact, the bids in Example 2 constitute a Nash Equilibrium even with low bidder values, although collusion would be required under some refinements.)[4]

Finally, even when the SMR is theoretically optimal, as in European 3G spectrum auctions, where each bidder was limited to one license, successes (the United Kingdom) and failures (Switzerland, Italy) depended on whether the number of licenses and other ancillary rules encouraged entry and deterred collusion. The ultimate goal of any auction design, which the SMR often but not always achieves, must be to facilitate vigorous and relatively efficient bidder competition. The SMR's designers performed a valuable service for consumers and taxpayers around the world, but as with any prescription, it must be used with care.

Notes

1. Of course, the key is that the gaps in value are larger for the big licenses, not the absolute values, but this should usually be true.
2. Some of the largest aggregation problems are solved by the initial specification of licenses: if all agree that New York City should be sold to one bidder then the auction will likely bundle the boroughs into one license.
3. There are other disadvantages to the Vickrey auction, for example when bidders have common values or budget constraints or are risk averse.
4. I originally raised these points about the Vickrey auction in a presentation at the FCC Combinatorial Bidding Conference in Wye River, MD, May 5, 2000. The presentation was based on discussions with Paul Klemperer.

CHAPTER EIGHT

Air-Transportation Deregulation

Elizabeth E. Bailey

Air-passenger deregulation was driven in no small measure by purveyors of ideas. Academics identified the regulation of the airline industry as a candidate for reform. They were able to show that air-passenger fares were lower by half in states with little regulation. An academic political entrepreneur was influential in designing hearings in 1975 that made the regulation issue visible and opened a policy window for reform. A mediagenic scholar who was both intellectually powerful and charismatic led administrative reform at the Civil Aeronautics Board (CAB) in 1977 and 1978 and provided confidence in airline deregulation, which was signed into law on October 28, 1978 (Public Law 95-504). The reform issue was framed as both providing the consumer of air travel with lower fares and freeing business from the "dead hand of regulation." The poster child of the success of air-passenger deregulation has been Southwest Airlines. Southwest, a low-cost carrier, has provided the impetus for lower consumer prices while serving as a model of business success. Its market value grew to $10.52 billion in 2007, compared with $5.99 billion for American Airlines and $5.81 billion for United Airlines.

Air-cargo deregulation was signed into law on November 9, 1977 (Public Law 95-163), a year before passage of air-passenger deregulation. A comprehensive passenger and cargo reform bill had stalled because of interest-group concerns on the air-passenger side. Passenger carriers, which provided air-cargo service in the belly of their planes, were focused on influencing the pace and direction of air-passenger reform and were silent on air-cargo reform. In contrast, air-cargo deregulation was supported by the four publicly traded air-cargo airlines: Federal Express, Airlift, Seaboard, and Tiger. Moreover, the air-cargo bill proposed to make this one of the few industries from which all economic controls would be removed. Therefore, it was instructive for the larger air-passenger reform that followed the next year. Federal Express, whose operations had been limited to small aircraft, has innovated with its overnight express service to become a shipping giant, handling more than 6 million packages a day across the world, and with a market value of $25.9 billion in 2007. The express segment has filled a need for transporting high-priority items for all economic sectors: commercial, government, and consumer.

It is hard to overemphasize how important deregulation has been. Congress moved methodically to reform regulation across many infrastructure industries, such as trucking, railroads, telecommunications, cable television, gas pipelines, stock brokerage, banking, natural gas, and utilities. Just as the regulatory movement of the 1930s reflected the view that market failure was pervasive, so the deregulation movement of the late 1970s and early 1980s reflected the view that economic regulation of prices and entry was a government failure, generating misallocations and inefficiencies. In markets where universal service had been achieved, markets, not regulators, would be better allocators of society's resources. Deregulation enabled the birth of new industries, such as overnight shipping, and increased the flexibility of existing industries to remake themselves.

Air-Passenger Regulation as a Candidate for Reform

The Herbert Hoover administration bid out a system of routes for private airmail carriage in the late 1920s. Route authority was awarded along linear systems that followed major railroad tracks, with United Airlines being granted the east-west route through Chicago, Trans World Airlines the east-west route through St. Louis, and so forth. The Civil Aeronautics Board (CAB) was established in 1938, and its entry policies reflected this pattern of division of the market into systems. Major dense markets were reserved for trunk carriers. The CAB selected among these carriers for new nonstop service or for first competitive service. Over the years the CAB rejected scores of applications to start new airlines to serve these routes. Local-service airlines provided subsidized service to smaller communities. They were restricted to nonoverlapping regions of the country and were a reliable source of feeder traffic for the trunks. The key assumption underlying this pattern of route authority was that airlines were like railroads, where competition requires duplication of facilities. This assumption was misplaced. The "sunk costs" for air travel are airports and airspace systems controlled by government, not airways. By the 1970s, eleven trunk carriers were still in operation, along with ten local-service carriers.

Economic studies developed a critique of regulation. They provided policy makers with evidence that reform would be beneficial for consumers. Richard Caves (1962) could find no evidence of economies of scale at a system level in the airline industry and thus no evidence of any need for federal control over entry. Michael Levine (1965) and William Jordan (1970) chronicled the successful performance of the largely unregulated intrastate airline markets in California. These carriers charged fares that were about half as high as those offered by CAB-certificated airlines, and they offered high-load-factor (percentage of seats filled), frequent service. In markets such as Los Angeles–San Francisco that had been considered fully developed, traffic grew when the intrastate carriers entered. This growth was at a much higher rate than in other similar markets that the regulated carriers served. Moreover, the low-price intrastate carriers in California were generally profitable, as was, beginning in the early 1970s, Southwest Airlines, operating within Texas. Thus the experience of the intrastate carriers supported the view that regulation was preventing low-fare options for consumers.

Other persuasive evidence came from a study by George Douglas and James Miller (1974). They, among others, began to build more sophisticated models of airline competition. These models showed that the existing regulatory regime, in which regulators set prices by a formula based on distance, but carriers were free to determine frequency of flights, was resulting in too many flights and load factors that were too low. Customers might prefer lower-quality service (more crowded planes) with lower prices to higher-quality service with higher prices, but the regulatory regime was not willing to provide the low-price/low-quality combination. Moreover, the introduction of jet airliners, including wide-bodied jets, lowered costs of longer-haul service relative to shorter-haul service, while the regulatory price formula lagged. Hence prices tended to be set more above costs the longer the length of the haul. Instead of added profits from these longer-haul flights, load factors on them just became lower. In contrast, a model of an efficient airline system would have load factors that both would be higher than those under regulation and would increase with length of haul. The reasoning on higher load factors overall was that when price and service could both vary, price discounts would be offered to fill planes better. The reasoning on higher load factors for longer hauls was that passengers were not as time sensitive on longer-haul flights. For example, if an individual wants to go from Los Angeles to San Francisco in the morning, it matters a lot whether the plane leaves at 7:30 A.M. or at 10:00 A.M. However, this difference matters a lot less if the individual is flying from Los Angeles or San Francisco to New York. During the decade or more before regulatory reform, load factors for all certificated carriers had hovered in the range of 50% to 55%.

Air-Passenger Regulatory Reform Hearings in 1975

The decade before 1975 was characterized by double-digit inflation and high unemployment, so-called stagflation. Wage and price controls had been tried and had failed. The stage was set for economic regulatory reform (see Greenspan 2007). The political trigger for reform in the airline industry occurred in 1975 when Stephen Breyer (then on leave from Harvard Law School, now a Supreme Court justice) marshaled evidence in a series of highly visible hearings held by Senator Edward Kennedy. These hearings focused on three questions: Were CAB fares too high? Had the CAB blocked entry? Would reform hurt small communities? Each of these questions involved a detailed empirical investigation whose purpose was to create a widespread conviction that reform was desirable. A political coalition needed to be formed around the issue, and to achieve this coalition, the issue had to be made visible.

The question "Are CAB fares too high?" provides a concrete example of how the hearings worked. The intrastate experience in California was portrayed using 1974 fares. The academic studies of the 1960s were thus updated. A passenger flying 338 miles between San Francisco and Los Angeles on Pacific Southwest Airlines (PSA) paid $18.75; a traveler (such as Senator Kennedy) flying the 399 miles between Boston and Washington on CAB-regulated carriers paid $41.67 (see Breyer 1982, Chapters 11 and 16), more than twice as much. An analysis was done in great detail to identify what the fare difference reflected. The same plane, a Boeing 727-200, was on average 55% full when it was flown with 121 seats by American Airlines, but was 60% full when it was flown with 158 seats by PSA. Thus the price difference reflected fuller planes and more dense seating. The two routes were shown to have similar density (roughly 915,000 passengers on the West Coast route and 981,000 passengers on the East Coast route), so the price differences did not reflect different traffic densities. The Federal Aviation Administration presented data showing no additional costs due to weather. The Air Transport Association was asked to provide an independent study of the causes of the fare differences and could account for only roughly $6 of the $20 to $30 difference on most routes. At the end of the investigation, the point "Yes, CAB fares are too high" was validated by the public policy debate.

Each of the major objections to reform was dealt with in a similar manner. "Has the CAB blocked entry?" was addressed in two ways. The CAB was shown to have had a route moratorium in the early 1970s in which it refused as a matter of policy to entertain any applications for new route authority. From 1938 to 1976 the CAB was found not to have certified a single new trunk carrier. The question "Will reform hurt small communities?" generated a similar amount of study. Residual concern about this issue meant that small-community air service would continue to receive subsidies as part of the reform package.

The road to reform did not end with the Kennedy hearings. The hearings raised the bar by having reform reach major-issue status. President Gerald Ford and President Jimmy Carter, as well as Senators Kennedy and Howard Cannon, continued to work the reform issue. There were still powerful groups who had vested interests against reform, mainly the major certificated air carriers and their unionized employees. Smaller communities receiving subsidized air service were concerned about service. Airport operators wanted to protect their ability to raise capital on the security of long-term leases with certificated carriers.

Prevailing scholarship indicated that political forces with stability (such as incumbent firms and labor unions) would gain over time ever more influence over the agencies that regulated them. George Stigler (1971) and Sam Peltzman (1989) predicted capture of regulatory agencies by such constituencies. Indeed, the blocking of new entry into the industry by the CAB can be interpreted as capture of the agency by the incumbent carriers. Yet the regulatory reform movement itself would seem to adhere more to the entrepreneurial political competition model of James Wilson (1980), in which a political entrepreneur would advocate for consumers and influence the policy debate even when the costs of reform were likely to be narrowly concentrated on the industry and its unionized employees (but see also Levine 2007).

Air-Cargo Regulation as a Candidate for Reform

On the air-cargo side, the CAB permitted cargo to be carried in the belly of any type of aircraft over any route for which an airline had passenger authority. The combination aircraft was scheduled during the day to suit passenger needs rather than during the night, which would better suit cargo demands. In addition, there were four publicly traded all-cargo carriers. Three of these were certificated all-cargo carriers. They tended to have both domestic and international authority. The fourth was an unregulated commuter (air taxi) aircraft operator, Federal Express. Federal Express could use only very small aircraft (7,500 pounds of payload capacity or less), such as Falcon jets. By comparison, a Boeing 727 (small combination aircraft) could carry a payload of 40,000 pounds.

Between 1956 and 1977 no new all-cargo airlines were certificated. Essentially the all-cargo carriers were confined to the routes they had received when they had first been certificated in the late 1940s and early 1950s to prevent them from competing with passenger carriers. A new applicant was required to bear the burden of proof that its service would meet the test of "public convenience and necessity." This meant that incumbent carriers could block competitive entry on their routes. The CAB rejected petitions, such as those of Flying Tiger and others, that requested route extensions. The CAB also rejected petitions, such as that in 1975 from Federal Express, to operate five larger-capacity aircraft, so Federal Express had to fly many small planes wingtip to wingtip in its denser markets. Rate regulation was onerous and slow. CAB-regulated prices were set by rate averaging based solely on shipment size and distance, not on timely delivery. The CAB also set rates of air cargo carried in the belly of passenger aircraft to divert traffic from all-cargo to combination aircraft. The Domestic Air Freight Rate Investigation, begun in 1970 by the CAB, was still open in 1977. Further, the Interstate Commerce Commission (ICC) prohibited airlines from transporting air cargo by truck except within twenty-five miles of an airport. This distortion meant that there was a need to contract with regular motor carriers for pickup and delivery. Yet the ICC, like the CAB, did not allow higher prices for faster service. Moreover, coordination between truck and air schedules introduced inefficiencies. Just as passengers prefer single-carrier service, so too such service is an element of efficient delivery in freight distribution and logistics.

In June 1976 the CAB, under Chairman John Robson, proposed to Congress that cargo be treated independently of passenger operations and be subject to full economic regulatory reform. Such complete reform went beyond measures then offered by Senator Kennedy and by the Ford administration. Entry would immediately be fully free for the certificated all-cargo carriers and existing commuter all-cargo carriers. New carriers would enter one year later. Rates were to be considered legal unless they were found to be unjustly discriminatory or predatory. Hearings were held in 1977 on a comprehensive (air-passenger and air-cargo) reform bill. Air-passenger regulatory reform was still controversial because of the interest groups that feared that they would be harmed by reform. However, the certificated all-cargo and commuter all-cargo carriers had joined together in a call for regulatory reform. The combination carriers (trunks and local service) did not weigh in on the cargo reform issue. Thus the stage was set for successful client politics, in Wilson's terminology. All-cargo carriers who stood to gain voiced strong support for air-cargo reform, while opposition was diffused. Lawyers for Flying Tiger and Federal Express worked actively with congressional committees, and when it appeared that the comprehensive bill would not go through unless reform of air-passenger service was removed from it, an amendment was introduced by Senator Howard Cannon that would deregulate only the all-cargo air-transportation mode. This amendment was approved on October 20, 1977. The amended bill was signed into law by President Carter on November 9, 1977 (Public Law 95-163). The bill allowed the all-cargo carriers to use larger aircraft, schedule them without geographic restrictions, and set prices according to market forces.

As described by Andrew Carron (1981), air-cargo deregulation was an immediate success for the all-cargo carriers. Federal Express saw its share price rise from $9.16 in October 1977 to $34.75 by December 1977. Flying Tiger rose from $11.13 to $16.38 in the same two months. Meanwhile, the Dow Jones transportation index (which had lost 2.2% the year before cargo deregulation) increased some 5.5% during those same months. Federal Express immediately began acquiring jet freighters, each seven times the size of its largest aircraft under regulation. In the first year after air-cargo deregulation, freight service expanded sharply, with cities that had lost freighter service gaining the most when deregulation opened those markets. Federal Express, for example, expanded total shipments by 38% in 1978, compared with 15% in 1977. Predictions of transitional chaos were not fulfilled. Thus air-cargo deregulation joined the experiments in deregulation of air-passenger service in California and Texas as a success. The experiment made passage of a more comprehensive air-passenger deregulation bill the following year a lot easier.

Air-Passenger Deregulation in 1978

Alfred Kahn arrived as chairman of the CAB in the summer of 1977. Kahn had academic credentials as the author of the preeminent academic treatise on the economics of regulation (Kahn 1971), but he was also effective in testifying before Congress and having access to the White House. He has been dubbed "the Father of Deregulation." Kahn brought together a team that included myself (as a commissioner), former academics Michael Levine and Darius Gaskins (as senior staff members), Philip Bakes (a congressional staff member who became CAB general counsel), and later Mary Schuman (now Mary Boies) of the White House domestic policy staff. The CAB members of the team adopted "sunshine" rules for its weekly meetings and proactively brought forth policies that would accomplish deregulation administratively. On the pricing side, the CAB provided immediate opportunities for discount fare flexibility by asking carriers to "show cause" why up to 35% of all fares should not be sold at a rate that would permit carriers to fill empty seats during off-peak periods. Permitting downward pricing flexibility before upward pricing flexibility would generate gains for consumers and, in the short run at least, gains for the carriers as well. The thinking was that such win-win strategies would provide evidence of success from deregulation and make Congress more comfortable with passage of an airline deregulation bill. On the entry side, there was a need to open the system to new entry in a manner that was consistent with administrative procedure. An idea that was adopted involved underserved airports. If an airport such as Newark, Baltimore, Midway, or San Jose was underserved in its metropolitan area, carriers should "show cause" why the CAB should not permit any carrier to enter any route to and from that airport. Again, the idea was to come up with a win-win strategy for both industry and communities that would make Congress more comfortable with the deregulatory agenda (see Bailey, Graham, and Kaplan 1985).

The commitment and dynamism of the CAB team were helpful in turning the tide toward passage of the deregulation bill in 1978. The success of air-cargo deregulation also helped. Air-passenger deregulation was signed on October 28, 1978 (Public Law 95-504). The law proposed a gradual reduction in CAB regulation, with entry deregulation to be completed by December 31, 1981, and price regulation to cease two years later. The CAB would "sunset" its operations entirely by January 1985. The remaining CAB responsibilities for international negotiations and small-community air service would shift to the Department of Transportation. Antitrust authority would be shifted to the Department of Justice. Safety regulation remained at the Federal Aviation Administration.

Welfare Effects Following Air-Passenger Deregulation

Deregulation removed regulatory price controls. The result was lower average prices. The popular press (*Economist*, June 16, 2007; *USA Today*, July 24, 2007) reports that the average fare paid in cents per mile has been cut in half since 1977 in inflation-adjusted terms. Prices passengers paid to fly one mile went from 10.08 cents in 1970 down to 4.20 cents by the end of 2006 (in 1978 cents per passenger mile). Price deregulation has preserved and deepened the downward trend of airfares even as prices for other big-ticket items (like college tuition) have risen. Overall, the depth of the price decline is perceived to be of the same magnitude as the one that took place within unregulated states (California and Texas) in the 1960s and early 1970s. Economists, however, have conducted more sophisticated studies that result in significant but somewhat lower welfare benefits from fare reductions. Morrison and Winston (1995) devised a carefully constructed counterfactual model using the regulatory standard industry fare level (SIFL). The idea is that the correct comparison is between the average prices that would have been set by the regulatory agency if it had continued and the prices in the deregulated marketplace. The counterfactual model has been updated to 2005 by Borenstein and Rose (2008), who show that actual fares were only about 30% lower than SIFL-formula fares in 2005. This lower reduction still suggests a consumer welfare increase of about $28 billion in that year. In addition, load factors also improved much as had been predicted, from 60% in the mid-1980s to well into the 70% range by the 1990s.

There has been enormous price dispersion from deregulation both within and across routes. Across routes, fares have fallen more on long routes than on short routes, as was anticipated by Douglas and Miller. The dispersion within routes was unanticipated and was mostly due to creation of sophisticated yield-management systems by airlines to differentiate business from leisure travelers using devices such as the Saturday-night-stay restriction. Frequent-flyer programs, in contrast, favor business travelers and seek to build brand loyalty through upgrades and free tickets. Other business innovations in the early years after deregulation included creation of computer reservation systems and, more recently, ticketing through the Internet.

Another unanticipated aspect of airline deregulation was the almost immediate transformation of airline networks from linear point-to-point systems created by the CAB into hub-and-spoke networks. These networks enabled improved scheduling of flights so consumers could conduct business by leaving early in the morning and returning home in the evening. Morrison and Winston (1986) found that many of the gains of deregulation for business travelers were due to improved frequency of scheduling. But the creation of hub-and-spoke delivery systems also meant that a single carrier could create a degree of monopoly power at a hub airport.

Contestability theory, as put forth most fully by William Baumol, John Panzer, and Robert Willig (1982), argues that market segments that appear to have elements of natural monopoly can be unbundled from direct regulation because entry (threat or actual) will discipline pricing of an incumbent monopolist. A majority of airline routes are served by one airline. Moreover, it was thought that airplanes were "marginal costs with wings" that could readily be moved from market to market. Instead, entry did not serve to mitigate monopoly pricing during the 1980s and 1990s, particularly at hub airports where one carrier had 50% or more of the scheduled passenger traffic. A price premium of roughly 20% was typical (see Borenstein and Rose 2008 for a history of scholarship on this point). An interesting exception to this finding is presented in a study by Goolsbee and Syverson (2006). They find that potential entry by Southwest Airlines into point-to-point routes where Southwest is present at both airports serves to lower prices about 60% of what actual entry would provide. So Southwest Airlines has provided a degree of contestability in the deregulated marketplace. Indeed, the fare disparities at hub airports have narrowed in recent years because of the growth in market share of the low-cost new-entrant carriers. Low-cost carriers grew in market share from less than 5% in 1980 to about 10% in 1995 and nearly 30% in 2007.

Welfare gains have also been achieved through new nonstop service to some 26% of cities. This change corresponds to the widespread introduction of regional jets, which grew from almost none in 1997 to nearly one-third of all domestic commercial flights in 2005. The rapid introduction of this new technology demonstrates the flexibility of the deregulated industry in remaking itself (see Borenstein and Rose forthcoming).

Industry structure was dramatically altered between 1978 and 2007. Many of the former trunk carriers bought the local-service carriers concentrated in their hub cities (e.g., Northwest bought Republic, Continental bought Frontier, and Trans World bought Ozark). These purchases may have been motivated in part by the stable and positive (rather than cyclical) earnings of the local-service carriers (see Bailey and Williams 1988). Because passengers strongly prefer single-carrier service for their travel, the strategy of serving the full domestic marketplace was also a factor in merger activity (e.g., Delta bought Western, and US Airways bought PSA and Piedmont). Consolidations have also included many takeovers of former low-cost new entrants. Today, of seven remaining major carriers (market share of 5% or more), two are managed by the new low-cost entrants, Southwest Airlines and US Airways (acquired by America West).

There has been financial distress and exit, not just new entry and consolidation, in air-passenger service. A number of airlines have been liquidated (e.g., Braniff, Eastern, and Pan American). Others (e.g. Continental, Northwest, United, US Airways, and Delta) have used the bankruptcy code, not to exit the industry, but instead to break labor contracts and/or remove legacy pension costs from carriers' books to the government. Airport and air traffic control systems (both under government ownership) have lagged behind the industry growth that has taken place following deregulation. Moreover, carriers at hub airports may optimize their networks with some expected delays built in (see Mayer and Sinai 2003). Not surprisingly, when delays have become unreasonable, Congress has considered a degree of reregulation, at least to the extent of declaring truth in airline scheduling in the late 1980s or considering a passenger bill of rights today. Levine (2007) offers an interesting perspective on the difficulties of reregulation in the air-passenger case where the independent regulatory agency has been disbanded and the industry no longer speaks with one voice (legacy versus new-entrant carriers). Another complaint has been the inconvenience caused by added security since September 11, 2001. There was a financial bailout of the industry at that time, and subsequently the federal government has taken over the security function at airports.

Finally, welfare benefits associated with air-passenger deregulation include the spillover effect that lower U.S. fares and greater airline efficiency has had on the international scene. Many foreign airlines had been government owned. The privatization movement (e.g., British Airways in 1983) has been driven in part by the need of foreign airlines to compete better with the deregulated U.S. airlines. The emergence of low-fare carriers has also been a factor internationally (e.g., Laker, Ryanair, and Virgin), as it has been domestically. Within the European Union, freedom of entry was finally established in 1997. There remains a goodly amount of regulation on the international scene, however, with restrictions on foreign ownership and restrictions of access to international airports by carriers wishing to offer new service. In the face of these restrictions, many airlines have formed alliances that enable sharing of frequent-flyer benefits and more efficient scheduling.

Welfare Effects Following Air-Cargo Deregulation

When the U.S. Congress deregulated air-cargo transport in 1977 and interstate trucking in 1980, it created opportunities for certificated air-cargo carriers and express air-cargo carriers. Merger activity was an important structural adjustment following air-passenger deregulation. It was also important on the air-cargo side. Flying Tiger merged with Seaboard and in

1981 sought to take over Airlift's international routes. In 1989 Federal Express bought Flying Tiger in order to secure landing rights at major international airports so that it could operate a seamless domestic and international system. The other major private U.S. cargo carrier is United Parcel Service, which had its initial public offering in 1999 and a market capitalization of $71 billion in 2007.

The focus on building hub-and-spoke systems was an important feature following air-passenger deregulation. So, too, hub-and-spoke systems were important in air express service. Federal Express established Memphis as its nighttime hub. In terms of logistics change, it put all package-related information in a central computerized system in 1979, installed digitally assisted dispatch systems in its trucks in 1980, and established delivery guarantees at 10:30 A.M. in 1982. It offered online tracking in 1994 and formed a public-private alliance with the U.S. Postal Service (see Birla 2005). It also received an exception to the private express statutes that enabled the delivery by private carriage of urgent communications as long as the price charged was at least $3.00 or twice as much as the first-class rate (see Crew 1996). There is strong demand for priority shipping services that save time even if a premium must be paid. Yet, as we have seen, time was not a consideration at the CAB or the ICC in setting rates, so the huge success of express services would not have been possible absent air-cargo deregulation.

When the air-cargo industry was deregulated, the CAB suspended many data-reporting requirements. Therefore, it has not proved possible to set up a counterfactual study on pricing, as has been done on the passenger side using the SIFL. However, Hummels (2007) has attempted to construct a data set that displays air-cargo rates over time. He shows that air-cargo rates rose through the 1970s until 1980 (due to oil price increases), and thereafter prices declined 2.52% per year from 1980 to 1993. Another index shows inbound air freight falling 2.5% per year from 1990 to 2001 and thereafter rising because of greater security costs after September 11, 2001. Air shipping, according to his data, grew between 1955 and 2004 from an insignificant share of trade to a third of U.S. imports by value. These trends are due in part to technological change in aircraft (the shift to wide-bodied planes) and in ocean shipping (containerization). They are also due to shifts in consumer tastes, so that more expensive items have become a higher portion of trade. Hummels (2007) considers the example of importing a bottle of wine from France. Air shipping costs of $8 are assumed to be twice ocean shipping costs of $4. If the bottle of wine costs $16, this added cost represents a 25% increase, but if the bottle of wine costs $160, the added transport cost of air shipment goes down to 2.5%.

A consumer is more willing to use the more expensive mode of transportation if the percentage effect on delivered price is smaller.

Evans and Harrigan (2005) study a case where the demand for timeliness comes from producers rather than from consumers. When restocking is frequent, lean retailing requires bar codes to keep track of daily sales of each item, electronic data interchange between retailers and suppliers, and modern distribution centers. The essence of lean retailing is rapid response to demand fluctuations in lieu of holding large inventories. Just-in-time and air express are in the forefront of this new era. Consistent and predictable overnight cargo delivery on a national—and, later, international—scale was a major breakthrough for both retailers and producers. Implementation was a major challenge in transport logistics. Custodial treatment of packages, absolutely accurate records, and instantaneous tracking were new business capabilities. Air express service had been suppressed under regulation because of the restrictions on plane size. It has flourished under deregulation and has been part of a new, high-value-added, technology-intensive service. Evans and Harrigan do not study the deregulation issue but instead focus on the increased importance of timeliness in helping explain the effect of distance on trade patterns. Products where timeliness matters grew much faster from nearby countries than they did from Asia, at least for U.S. apparel imports.

Conclusion

Air-transportation regulation appeared to favor incumbent carriers. It suppressed new entrants, whether low-cost air-passenger carriers, like Southwest Airlines, or carriers concerned with timely delivery, like Federal Express. Deregulation has permitted such carriers to flourish and has led to greatly lowered prices for air-passenger travel and to more timely delivery modes for air cargo.

With respect to the anticipated and less anticipated aspects of reform, economists were pretty accurate on the welfare gains from lower prices. Senator Kennedy based his reform agenda on this outcome, and he was not disappointed. Economists were less successful at forecasting business issues like marketing (building brand loyalty), operations (optimal flow of traffic through networks), and innovations in logistics (just-in-time inventory systems).

Air carriers are no longer in the same straitjacket that they were in during the days of economic regulation. But deregulation has not moved the air-transportation industry quickly into a new equilibrium configuration.

Instead, deregulation has enabled a plethora of creative innovations. New industries and firms have been born and reconfigured. Operations have been redesigned. Consumers have gained enormously from lower fares. Deregulation has enabled a dynamic, not a static, marketplace.

References

Bailey, Elizabeth E., David R. Graham, and Daniel R. Kaplan. *Deregulating the Airlines.* Cambridge, Mass.: MIT Press, 1985.

Bailey, Elizabeth E., and Jeffrey R. Williams. "Sources of Economic Rent in the Deregulated Airline Industry." *Journal of Law and Economics* 31 (1988): 173–202.

Baumol, William J., John C. Panzer, and Robert Willig. *Contestable Markets and the Theory of Industry Structure.* New York: Harcourt Bruce Jovanovich, 1982.

Birla, Madan. *FedEx Delivers.* Hoboken, N.J: John Wiley & Sons, 2005.

Borenstein, Severin, and Nancy L. Rose. "How Airline Markets Work . . . or Do They? Regulatory Reform in the Airline Industry." In Nancy L. Rose, ed., *Economic Regulation and Its Reform: What Have We Learned.* Boston: National Bureau of Economic Research, (forthcoming).

Breyer, Stephen. *Regulation and Its Reform.* Cambridge, Mass.: Harvard University Press, 1982.

Carron, Andrew S. *Transition to a Free Market: Deregulation of the Air Cargo Industry.* Washington, D.C.: Brookings Institution, 1981.

Caves, Richard. *Air Transport and Its Regulators: An Industry Study.* Cambridge, Mass.: Harvard University Press, 1962.

Crew, Michael A. "Competition in Postal Service: International Perspectives." In Edward L. Hughes, ed., *The Last Monopoly: Privatizing the Postal Service for the Information Age.* Washington, D.C.: Cato Institute, 1996, 91–102.

Douglas, George W., and James C. Miller III. *Economic Regulation of Domestic Air Transport: Theory and Policy.* Washington, D.C.: Brookings Institution, 1974.

Evans, Carolyn L., and James Harrigan. "Distance, Time and Specialization: Lean Retailing in General Equilibrium." *American Economic Review,* 95(1) (March 2005): 292–313.

Goolsbee, Austan, and Chad Syverson. "How Do Incumbents Respond to the Threat of Entry? Evidence from Major Airlines." National Bureau of Economics Working Paper 11072, revised, 2006.

Greenspan, Alan. *The Age of Turbulence.* New York: Penquin Press, 2007.

Hummels, David. "Transportation Costs and International Trade in the Second Era of Globalization." *Journal of Economic Perspectives* 21(3) (Summer 2007): 131–154.

Jordan, William A. *Airline Regulation in America: Effects and Imperfections.* Baltimore: John Hopkins Press, 1970.

Kahn, Alfred E. *The Economics of Regulation: Principles and Institutions.* New York: John Wiley & Sons, 1971.

Levine, Michael E. "Is Regulation Necessary? California Air Transportation and National Regulatory Policy." *Yale Law Journal* 74 (July 1965): 1416–1447.

———. "Regulation, the Market, and Interest Group Cohesion: Why Airlines Were Not Reregulated." In Mark K. Landy, Martin A. Levin, and Martin Shapiro, eds., *Creating Competitive Markets: The Politics of Regulatory Reform.* Washington, D.C.: Brookings Institution, 2007, 215–246.

Mayer, Christopher, and Todd Sinai. "Network Effects, Congestion Externalities and Air Traffic Delays; or, Why Not All Delays Are Evil." *American Economic Review* 93(4) (2003): 1194–1215.

Morrison, Steven, and Clifford Winston. *The Economic Effects of Airline Deregulation.* Washington, D.C.: Brookings Institution, 1986.

———. *The Evolution of the Airline Industry.* Washington, D.C.: Brookings Institution, 1995.

Peltzman, Sam. "The Economic Theory of Regulation after a Decade of Deregulation." *Brookings Papers on Economic Activity: Microeconomics,* 1989, 1–41.

Stigler, George. "The Theory of Economic Regulation." *Bell Journal of Economics and Managerial Science* 3 (1971), 3–21.

Wilson, James Q., ed. *The Politics of Regulation.* New York: Basic Books, 1980.

COMMENT

Nancy L. Rose

As Elizabeth Bailey's chapter aptly describes, it would be difficult to over-state the significance of U.S. air-transportation deregulation in the late 1970s. Air-transportation deregulation was in the vanguard of a revolution that spread deregulation, restructuring, and the adoption of market-based regulatory reforms across broad sectors of the global economy. It was a victory for public policy, yielding substantial direct and indirect benefits that not only transformed U.S. air-passenger and cargo markets but also served as a model for reforms in airline markets around the world and facilitated logistics and other innovations that transformed the way business is organized. And it was a triumph for economics, which provided both the critical analysis that pushed air deregulation onto the policy agenda and many of the key policy makers who helped drive reform to a successful conclusion. One might, with little hyperbole, count this as one of the finest hours of empirical microeconomics.

How did economics contribute to overturning decades of regulatory policy and entrenched opposition to reform? Three factors merit particular emphasis. The first was the existence of a rich body of research that married microtheoretic models with rigorous institution-based empirical analysis. This chapter highlights some of the best-known work: Caves's 1962 thorough case study *Air Transport and Its Regulators*, Levine's (1965) and Jordan's (1970) compelling comparisons of the enormous fare differentials between unregulated intrastate and Civil Aeronautics Board–regulated interstate routes, and Douglas and Miller's (1974) structural analysis that demonstrated the inherent futility of CAB efforts to increase air-carrier profits through higher fares, given the prevalence of nonprice frequency competition. These studies, however, were just the tip of a substantial iceberg of economic research on regulation broadly and airline regulation in particular (see, for example, Kahn's 1971 two-volume treatise *The Economics of Regulation*).

I believe that the second factor was the dominance of "one-handed" economists among those studying economic regulation. The conclusions of economics regulatory research were generally clear and consistent, with no "other hand" to distract from, detract from, or confuse the message. As Roger Noll testified, "The nice thing about being a student of industrial organization and regulation is that you . . . never have to run the risk of being dead wrong saying regulation has been foolish in a particular sector. I know of no major industrial scholarly work by an economist . . . in the past 10 years that reaches the conclusion that a particular industry would operate less efficiently and less equitably [without] than with regulation" (Derthick and Quirk 1985, 54).

James Q. Wilson (1980) highlights the role of "policy entrepreneurs" in producing reforms such as this. Senator Edward Kennedy's decision to push airline deregulation onto the political agenda, influenced by the substantial and consistent economics literature demonstrating that CAB regulation led to higher prices, was crucial(Breyer 1982). Elected officials were not, however, the only entrepreneurs to contribute to airline deregulation. The third important factor was the presence of economists well versed in industrial organization and regulatory economics in key policy positions, and their determination to use their roles, in concert with political reformers, to effect change. The Gerald Ford administration appointed economists such as George Eads, Paul MacAvoy, James Miller, and John Snow to a variety of posts from which they pursued the administration's procompetition agenda and supported policy makers like CAB chair John Robson, who experimented with relaxing regulatory restrictions from within the agency. The starring role in airline deregulation was undoubtedly played by Jimmy Carter appointee Fred Kahn and his colleagues at the CAB, including cocommissioner (and author of this chapter) Elizabeth Bailey and bureau chiefs Darius Gaskins and Michael Levine. Kahn's decision to implement competitive reform from within the CAB was critical to the ultimate success of the Airline Deregulation Act of 1978. The CAB's administrative "deregulation" of prices and expansion of entry opportunities demonstrated the efficacy of greater competition in airline markets while fundamentally altering the constellation of political interests in the battle over deregulation legislation (see Thomas McCraw's chapter on Kahn in *Prophets of Regulation*, 1984).

A voluminous economics literature assesses the impact of airline deregulation in the thirty years that have followed the Airline Deregulation Act of 1978. The bulk of this research finds substantial benefits. Despite these results, periodic calls for reregulation continue. The industry does face numerous challenges: pricing complexity alienates many passengers, airport congestion and travel delays impose substantial monetary and convenience costs, financial volatility leads to swings in profitability and financial distress, and persistent regulation of most international aviation markets continues to limit global competition. Some of these challenges stem from the "messiness" of competition, although it is important to recognize that its benefits far surpass "tidier" regulated outcomes. This is a lesson well worth repeating. Others, such as congestion costs from distortions in airport pricing and inadequate investment in aviation infrastructure, owe more to the persistent vestiges of 1970s-style regulation of airports and air traffic infrastructure. This suggests an opportunity for economists to make continued contributions.

References

Breyer, Stephen. 1982. *Regulation and Its Reform*. Cambridge, Mass.: Harvard University Press.

Caves, Richard E. 1962. *Air Transport and Its Regulators*. Cambridge, Mass.: Harvard University Press.

Derthick, Martha, and Paul J. Quirk. 1985. *The Politics of Deregulation*. Washington, D.C.: Brookings Institution.

Douglas, George, and James C. Miller III. 1974. *Economic Regulation of Domestic Air Transport*. Washington, D.C.: Brookings Institution.

Jordan, William A. 1970. *Airline Regulation in America: Effects and Imperfections*. Baltimore: Johns Hopkins Press.

Kahn, Alfred E. 1971. *The Economics of Regulation*. 2 vols. New York: John Wiley & Sons.

Levine, Michael. 1965. "Is Regulation Necessary? California Air Transportation and National Regulatory Policy." *Yale Law Journal* 74 (July 1965): 1416–1447.

McCraw, Thomas K. 1984. *Prophets of Regulation*. Cambridge, Mass.: Harvard University Press.

Wilson, James Q., ed. 1980. *The Politics of Regulation*. New York: Basic Books.

CHAPTER NINE

Deferred-Acceptance Algorithms: History, Theory, Practice

Alvin E. Roth

Both a theoretical and an applied literature grew from the article "College Admissions and the Stability of Marriage" (Gale and Shapley 1962; henceforth GS). Gale and Shapley proposed a simple model of two-sided matching in which men and women (or students and colleges) each had preferences over individuals in the other set to whom they might be matched. They also proposed an algorithm for finding a "stable" matching, in which no man or woman is matched to an unacceptable mate, and no man and woman who are not matched to each other would both prefer to be. GS used this algorithm to prove not only that the set of stable outcomes is nonempty for all preferences of the kind they considered, but that when preferences are strict, there always exists, for each side of the market, a stable matching that is optimal for agents on that side of the market in the surprisingly strong sense that every agent likes the optimal stable matching for his or her side of the market as well as any stable matching. After appropriate caveats about the abstraction of their model from actual college admissions, they stated in closing that "it is our opinion, however, that some of the ideas introduced here might usefully be applied to certain phases of the admissions problem" (14).

This opinion has turned out to be justified. In the past several years admissions to high schools in New York City and to all public schools in Boston have been reorganized through clearinghouses that use deferred-acceptance algorithms adapted to local needs, which solve serious problems encountered by the previously used systems (Abdulkadiroglu, Pathak, and Roth 2005; Abdulkadiroglu et al. 2005). It turns out that well before GS similar ideas had been incorporated in the early 1950s into the successful clearinghouse through which most American doctors still obtain their first jobs (Roth 1984). These ideas turned out to be generalizable to the design of the clearinghouse that organizes the contemporary medical marketplace (Roth and Peranson 1999).

We now know that deferred-acceptance algorithms have been independently discovered a number of times, in part because they capture a folk idea of how markets operate. A deferred-acceptance algorithm works by having agents on one side of the market make proposals (offers or applications) to agents on the other, proposing first to their first choice. Those who receive more proposals than they can accept reject their least preferred but do not immediately accept those they do not reject; they instead hold them without commitment, and acceptances are deferred until the end of the algorithm. In the meantime agents who have been rejected make new proposals, which lead to new rejections (including rejections of proposals that were held at an earlier period but are less preferred than a new proposal), until there are no rejected agents who wish to make further proposals. At this point all proposals that are being held are finally accepted to produce a matching.

Although deferred-acceptance algorithms have some similarity to market behavior, seeing how clearinghouses that use them operate differently from the less centralized marketplaces they replace has yielded new insights into the tasks that markets have to perform to work well, whether they are centralized or decentralized.

The Marriage and College-Admissions Models

GS presented two closely related models of two-sided matching, differing only in whether the agents on each side each wish to be matched with one other agent of the opposite sort (the "marriage model"), or the matching is many-to-one (the "college-admissions" model). In the marriage model there are two disjoint sets of agents, "men" and "women," each of whom has preferences over the individuals on the other side (and the possibility of being unmatched). If agent k (on either side of the market) prefers to remain single rather than be matched to agent j, then j is said to be *unacceptable* to k. If an agent is not indifferent between any two acceptable mates or between being matched to an acceptable mate and being unmatched, his or her preferences will be called *strict*. Strict preferences can be represented as rank-order lists of acceptable mates.

An outcome matches agents on one side to agents on the other side, or to themselves, and if w is matched to m, then m is matched to w. Agents' preferences over outcomes are determined by their preferences for their own mates at those outcomes.

A matching μ is *blocked by an individual k* if *k* prefers being single to being matched with his or her mate at μ, μ(*k*). A matching m is *blocked by a pair of agents* (*m, w*) if they each prefer each other to the partner they receive at μ, that is, if *m* prefers *w* to μ(*m*) and *w* prefers *m* to *μ(w)*.

A matching μ is *stable* if it is not blocked by any individual or pair of agents. Gale and Shapley proved that a stable matching exists for every marriage market by presenting and analyzing the following algorithm.

GS Deferred-Acceptance Algorithm, with men proposing

o. If some preferences are not strict, arbitrarily break ties (e.g., if some *m* is indifferent between w_i and w_j, order them consecutively in alphabetic order). Different agents may break ties differently; for example, tie break-ing can be random or can be decentralized by having each agent fill out a strict preference list.

1a. Each man *m* proposes to his first choice (if he has any acceptable choices). b. Each woman rejects any unacceptable proposals and, if more than one acceptable proposal is received, holds the most preferred and re-jects all others.

*k*a. Any man rejected at step *k* − 1 makes a new proposal to his most preferred acceptable mate who has not yet rejected him. (If no acceptable choices remain, he makes no proposal.)

b. Each woman holds her most preferred acceptable offer to date and rejects the rest.

STOP: when no further proposals are made, and match each woman to the man (if any) whose proposal she is holding.

The matching produced in this way is stable because no man ever pro-poses to an unacceptable woman, and no woman ever holds the offer of an unacceptable man; if some man would prefer to be matched to a woman other than his assigned mate, he must, according to the algorithm, have al-ready proposed to her, and she must have rejected him, which implies that she has a man she strictly prefers; hence they cannot form a blocking pair.

GS observed that which side of the market proposes in a deferred-acceptance algorithm has consequences. In particular,

when all men and women have strict preferences, there always exist an M-optimal stable matching (one that every man likes at least as well as any other stable matching) and a W-optimal stable matching. Furthermore, the matching $μ_M$ *produced by the deferred-acceptance algorithm with men pro-*

posing is the M-optimal stable matching. The W-optimal stable matching is the matching μ_W produced by the algorithm when the women propose.

GS proved this by showing that in the course of the deferred-acceptance algorithm, no man is ever rejected by a woman who could be matched to him in a stable matching.

GS also formulated a many-to-one college-admissions model populated by a set of colleges and a set of students that was identical to the marriage model except that each college C_i wished to be matched to some number $q_i \geq 1$ students, while each student was interested in being matched to only one college. That is, each student had a preference over colleges, each college had a preference over individual students, and a matching was a function that assigned each student to no more than one college and each college C_i to no more than q_i students. They observed that essentially the same deferred-acceptance algorithm (with college C_i proposing at each point to its q_i most preferred students who had not yet rejected it in the college-proposing version or rejecting all but the q_i most preferred applications it had received at any point of the student-proposing version) would produce a stable matching defined as before. That is, the outcome produced by the algorithm would not admit any student-college blocking pairs defined precisely as in the marriage model.[1]

Strategic Behavior

Strategic Properties of the Marriage Model

A different kind of question about stable matching, which has proved to be of critical importance in market design, concerns the strategic properties of a market organized via a clearinghouse. If a clearinghouse is organized along the lines of the deferred-acceptance algorithm, we can ask whether participants will find it in their interest to provide the private information about their preferences on which the algorithm depends. To put the question another way, is it possible to design a clearinghouse in which a stable matching is produced from participants' stated rank-order lists in such a way that it will not sometimes be in someone's interest to submit a rank-order list different from her or his true preferences? It turns out that there are limits on what any mechanism that produces stable matchings can accomplish in this regard, but there is a sense in which the deferred-acceptance algorithm performs up to those limits.

In particular, call a rule for making a matching a *stable matching mechanism* if, for any stated preferences, it produces a matching that is stable with respect to those preferences. In Roth (1982a) I showed an "impossibility" result:

> *There does not exist any stable matching mechanism that makes stating the true preferences always best for each agent, no matter what preferences are stated by others.*

However, I also showed in that article (as did Dubins and Freedman 1981) that it is possible to design the mechanism so that one side of the market can never do any better than to state their true preferences:

> *When a matching will be determined by the man-proposing deferred-acceptance algorithm, no man can ever do better than to state his true preferences, regardless of what preferences others (men or women) may state.*

Models of Many-to-One Matching

The college-admissions model and its descendants with and without explicit price formation remain very useful for focusing on the matching aspects of markets.[2] The question that arose as economists began to think about using these models to study actual markets was how and to what extent the college-admissions model outlined in GS could be extended to a well-defined game involving many-to-one matching. A model of such a game would, of course, require that the preferences of all the participants be specified over possible outcomes, so colleges would need to have preferences defined not just over individual students but over sets of students with whom they might be matched. Colleges would also have strategies available that would not be available in one-to-one matching.

Roth (1985) examined a "minimal" extension of the GS college-admissions model that would preserve the main properties of the marriage model to the extent possible and allow strategic issues to be explored. Consider a model consisting of colleges (which seek to match with multiple students) and students (who seek to match with a single college). In addition to the definitions given in GS, let a college C_i with quota q_i have preferences over sets of students with the property that when comparing two possible sets of students S and S' that differ only by one individual student, the college prefers the set that has the more preferred individual. That is, the college's preferences over groups of students are *responsive* to its preferences over individual students. (Preferences defined in this way are a special case of preferences in which students are substitutes rather than complements in colleges' preferences; i.e., there is no student who is desirable only if some other student is also in the entering class).[3]

In this model of many-to-one matching, the colleges and students are not symmetric, and we have the following possibility and impossibility results (from Roth 1985):

> No stable matching mechanism exists that makes it always best for each college to state its true preferences. But when a matching is determined by the student-proposing deferred-acceptance algorithm, no student can ever do better than to state his or her true preferences, regardless of what preferences others (students or colleges) may state.

Colleges with multiple seats to fill have more strategic options than just how they rank individual students; they also need to reveal how many students they wish to admit. Sönmez (1997) considered the strategic decisions faced by colleges that were constrained by some maximum capacity (and that in fact preferred to fill that capacity if they could get the students they preferred) but were free to admit fewer students, and proved the following impossibility result:[4]

> No stable matching mechanism makes it always best for a college to reveal its full capacity.

Deferred-Acceptance Algorithms in Practice

Labor Markets for Doctors

The first position taken by American doctors after graduation from medical school is now called a residency, and these positions are the backbone of hospitals' labor force and a critical part of physicians' education and career. From 1900 to 1945 one way that hospitals competed for new residents was to try to hire residents earlier than other hospitals. This moved dates of appointment earlier and earlier, until by 1945 it was customary for residents to be hired almost two years before they would graduate and begin work. When I described this in Roth (1984), I was not yet familiar with other markets that had seen this kind of "unraveling" of appointment dates, but today we know that unraveling is a common and costly form of market failure. (Unraveling, in which offers become not only increasingly early but also dispersed in time and of increasingly short duration, has occurred in other medical labor markets in the United States, Canada, and the United Kingdom and in numerous other kinds of markets; see Roth and Xing 1994 for an account of many unraveled markets).[5]

In 1945 medical schools agreed not to release information about students before a specified date. This helped control the date of the market, but a new problem emerged: hospitals found that if some of the first offers they made were rejected, the candidates to whom they wished to make their next offers had often already accepted other positions. This led to exploding offers to which candidates had to reply immediately, before they could learn what other offers might be available, and to a chaotic market that shortened in duration from year to year and resulted not only in missed agreements but also in broken ones. This kind of congestion also has since been seen in other markets, and in the extreme form it took in the American medical market by the late 1940s, it also constituted a form of market failure (see Roth and Xing 1997 and Avery et al. 2007 for detailed accounts of congestion in labor markets in psychology and law).

Faced with a failing market, the various American medical associations (of hospitals, students, and schools) agreed to employ a centralized clearinghouse to coordinate the market. After students had applied to residency programs and been interviewed, instead of having hospitals make individual offers to which students had to respond immediately, students and residency programs would instead be invited to submit rank-order lists to indicate their preferences. That is, hospitals (residency programs) would rank the students they had interviewed, students would rank the hospitals (residency programs) they had interviewed, and a centralized clearinghouse—a matching mechanism—would produce a matching from the preference lists. Today this centralized clearinghouse is called the National Resident Matching Program (NRMP).

The original algorithm proposed for the medical clearinghouse (Mullen and Stalnaker 1952) was an unstable mechanism that also made it obviously risky for students to list their true preferences. It was replaced with another algorithm, adapted from a prior regional clearinghouse called the Boston Pool Plan (see Roth 2003), and this was the algorithm employed in 1952, the first year that matches were decided through the clearinghouse. Roth (1984) showed that the algorithm adopted in 1952 is equivalent to the hospital-proposing deferred-acceptance algorithm as a matching mechanism in the sense that it produces the hospital-optimal stable matching when applied to a simple college-admissions market (see Roth 1984, 2008a).

Over the years changes in the medical marketplace made a simple deferred-acceptance algorithm less able to accommodate the requirements of the market. One such change involved the growing number of married couples graduating from American medical schools and wishing to be matched to jobs in the same vicinity. This had not been a problem when the match was created in the 1950s, when virtually all medical students were men. In an early attempt to accommodate couples, both members of the couple were asked to submit rank-order lists as individuals and to declare one of their members the "leading member," with the preference list of the other member then being edited to facilitate matching to the same community. Although this mechanism often matched the members of the couple to positions in the same city, couples often declined to take these positions and instead managed to arrange positions they preferred. In Roth (1984) I observed that if couples were modeled as having preferences over pairs of positions, this could be understood as responding in a natural way to the instability of the resulting matching.[6] I further observed that when couples had preferences over pairs of positions, the set of stable matchings could be empty.

In 1995 I was invited to direct the redesign of the medical match.[7] As a designer, I would no longer have the luxury of simply observing that some problems are hard: for example, more than 1,000 people go through the match each year as members of couples. And the empirical evidence was clear that stability was important to the success of matches. Roth (1990, 1991) had studied the clearinghouses that had been tried in the various regions of the British National Health Service (NHS) after those markets unraveled in the 1960s. A royal commission had recommended that clearinghouses be established on the American model, but because the American medical literature did not describe in detail how the clearinghouse worked, each region of the NHS had adopted a different algorithm for turning rank-order lists into matches, and the unstable mechanisms had largely failed and been abandoned, while the stable mechanisms had succeeded and survived.[8]

Roth and Peranson (1999) report on the new clearinghouse algorithm we designed, a generalized applicant-proposing deferred-acceptance algorithm that allows couples to state preferences over pairs of positions and also deals with some other complications in the market. Unlike the deferred-acceptance algorithm for simpler matching markets, this does not produce a stable matching on the first pass through agents' preferences. Instead, a list of potential blocking pairs is accumulated (e.g., every time one member of a couple is displaced from a position and causes the other member of the couple to be withdrawn from a position), and the algorithm attempts to satisfy these pairs one at a time, using a class of algorithms explored in Roth and Vande Vate (1990). This is a generalization of the deferred-acceptance algorithm in the sense that if all hospitals and applicants submitted simple preferences (without couples or other special features of the medical match), the algorithm would produce the applicant-optimal stable matching. The new algorithm has been used by the NRMP

Table 9.1   Labor markets that adopted the Roth-Peranson clearinghouse design after 1998 (and date of first use of a centralized clearinghouse of some sort)

Postdoctoral dental residencies in the United States:
  Oral and maxillofacial surgery (1985)
  General practice residency (1986)
  Advanced education in general dentistry (1986)
  Pediatric dentistry (1989)
  Orthodontics (1996)

Psychology internships in the United States and Canada (1999)

Neuropsychology residencies in the United States and Canada (2001)

Osteopathic internships in the United States (before 1995)

Pharmacy practice residencies in the United States (before 1994)

Articling positions with law firms in Alberta, Canada (1993)

Medical residencies in the United States (NRMP) (1952)

Medical residencies in Canada (CaRMS) (before 1970)

Specialty Matching Services (SMS/NRMP):
  Abdominal transplant surgery (2005)
  Child and adolescent psychiatry (1995)
  Colon and rectal surgery (1984)
  Combined Musculoskeletal Matching Program (CMMP)
    Hand surgery (1990)
  Medical Specialties Matching Program (MSMP)
    Cardiovascular disease (1986)
    Gastroenterology (1986–1999; rejoined in 2006)
    Hematology (2006)
    Hematology/oncology (2006)
    Infectious disease (1986–1990; rejoined in 1994)
    Oncology (2006)
    Pulmonary and critical medicine (1986)
    Rheumatology (2005)
  Minimally invasive and gastrointestinal surgery (2003)
  Obstetrics/gynecology
    Reproductive endocrinology (1991)
    Gynecologic oncology (1993)
    Maternal-fetal medicine (1994)
    Female pelvic medicine and reconstructive surgery (2001)
  Ophthalmic plastic and reconstructive surgery (1991)
  Pediatric cardiology (1999)
  Pediatric critical-care medicine (2000)
  Pediatric emergency medicine (1994)
  Pediatric hematology/oncology (2001)
  Pediatric rheumatology (2004)
  Pediatric surgery (1992)
  Primary-care sports medicine (1994)

Table 9.1 *(continued)*

Radiology
    Interventional radiology (2002)
    Neuroradiology (2001)
    Pediatric radiology (2003)
Surgical critical care (2004)
Thoracic surgery (1988)
Vascular surgery (1988)

---

since 1998 and has subsequently been adopted by over three dozen labor-market clearinghouses (see Table 9.1).

American law now recognizes the use of deferred-acceptance algorithms as part of a procompetitive market mechanism. In 2002 over a dozen law firms representing three former medical residents brought an antitrust suit challenging the use of matching for medical residents. The theory of the suit was that matching was a conspiracy to hold down wages for residents and fellows, in violation of the Sherman Antitrust Act. (Niederle and Roth 2003a observed that empirically the wages of medical specialties with and without centralized matching in fact do not differ.) An interesting game-theoretic aspect of the suit itself was that it was a double class-action suit that sought not only to represent the class of all former medical residents but to sue a class of defendants that included all hospitals that employ residents, including several dozen named defendants. This had the effect of making the legal defense costs very high because lawyers for the many defendants had to coordinate with one another in each of many preliminary motions and hearings expected to stretch over years. Thus the strategy of the plaintiffs seemed aimed at forcing a financial settlement before the otherwise lengthy process reached trial. However, the same strategy that made legal defense costly made it possible for the defendants to seek legislative relief from the suit because virtually every senator and congressman has a hospital in his or her district. The struggle thus shifted to Washington, and Public Law 108-218 (2004) notes that the medical match is a procompetitive market mechanism, not a conspiracy in restraint of trade.

School Choice in New York City and Boston

A different area of application involves clearinghouses that use deferred-acceptance algorithms to assign children to schools. The clearinghouses designed for New York City high schools and for Boston public schools at all levels are described in Abdulkadiroglu, Pathak, and Roth (2005,

2009) and Abdulkadiroglu et al. (2005, 2006). The New York City clearinghouse has been in operation since 2003 (for students entering high school in September 2004), and the Boston clearinghouse went into operation in 2005–2006 for students entering school in September 2006. The problems that these designs were intended to solve were quite different.

In New York the school-choice system is a two-sided market in which the schools are active players. The prior system for assigning students to schools was a partially decentralized system in which students applied to schools by rank-ordering them on preference lists and schools made offers of admission to students through the mail. This system was too congested to serve adequately the almost 100,000 students per year who enter ninth grade in New York City, and about 30,000 had to be assigned administratively, without regard to their preferences. The old system also made it risky for students to list their true preferences. The resulting matching was unstable, and schools withheld capacity from the system in order to be able to admit students at the last minute. These problems have largely vanished since the adoption of a centralized clearinghouse that uses a student-proposing deferred-acceptance algorithm, modified to reflect particular features of school matching (see Abdulkadiroglu, Pathak, and Roth 2009).

In Boston the schools are passive, and so school choice in Boston is a one-sided market of the type studied by Abdulkadiroglu and Sönmez (2002), who observed that deferred-acceptance algorithms might often be sensible even when stability was not required to stop blocking pairs from forming.[9] In Boston, in particular, where the new clearinghouse uses a straightforward student-proposing deferred-acceptance algorithm, the central issue in its adoption was that it would give students and their families a dominant strategy to state their true preferences. School choice in Boston had previously been organized through a centralized clearinghouse that was not at all strategy proof,[10] and one of the reasons for adoption of the new system was that it was intended to eliminate the need for students and families to "game the system" and avoid the harm done to those who did not.[11]

Thomas Payzant, then superintendent of schools, wrote, in a 2005 memo to the school committee, "The most compelling argument for moving to a new algorithm is to enable families to list their true choices of schools without jeopardizing their chances of being assigned to any school by doing so." Payzant further wrote, "A strategy-proof algorithm levels the playing field by diminishing the harm done to parents who do not strategize or do not strategize well."

Matching and Market Design

Although I have focused in this chapter on the application of the deferred-acceptance algorithm to the design of clearinghouses for labor markets and school choice, I will end by briefly indicating some of the larger questions in economics that are illuminated by studying the kinds of markets in which deferred-acceptance clearinghouses are used. Why have clearinghouses that use the deferred-acceptance algorithm (as well as other kinds of clearinghouses) been helpful in markets? What are the kinds of market failure for which such a clearinghouse is a solution? To put it another way, what do we learn about markets and about clearinghouses organized around deferred-acceptance algorithms from the markets that have employed such clearinghouses?[12]

In Niederle and Roth (forthcoming) and Roth (2008b) evidence was marshaled from a variety of market failures suggesting that to work well, marketplaces need to do the following:

1. Provide thickness—that is, they need to attract a sufficient proportion of potential market participants to come together ready to transact with one another.
2. Overcome the congestion that thickness can bring by providing enough time, or by making transactions fast enough, so that market participants can consider enough alternative possible transactions to arrive at satisfactory ones.
3. Make it safe to participate in the market as simply as possible
   a. as opposed to transacting outside the marketplace or
   b. as opposed to engaging in strategic behavior that reduces overall welfare.

These problems, together or separately, are often the reasons that markets adopt a clearinghouse. When offers are made through an algorithm, congestion problems can be solved because algorithms operate very fast. Furthermore, using a deferred-acceptance algorithm makes it safe for those on the proposing side of the market to reveal their true preferences, and if the market is large, this is true for both sides of the market.[13] Therefore, if there is sufficient participation in the centralized clearinghouse, the market is thick, uncongested, and safe even for strategically unsophisticated participants.

Although much of market design has so far concentrated on market failures that can be fixed with centralized clearinghouses of one sort or another (see, e.g., Roth 2002 and Milgrom 2004), there is often a decentralized market or potential market in the background that must also be understood. One promising area of research will be to understand better how the problems of providing thickness, dealing with congestion, and making markets safe are dealt with in decentralized markets.[14]

Notes

A more detailed version of this chapter can be found in Roth (2008a).

1. Ostrovsky (2008) looks at a model of "supply chains" of agents that are stable if there are no "blocking chains" and manages to produce many of the classical results of two-sided matching models (cf. Roth and Sotomayor 1990) without the two-sided structure of these models.

2. In the college-admissions model, prices are implicitly modeled as part of each college's description and reflected in the preferences, but very similar results obtain when price adjustment is modeled explicitly, as in the models of Shapley and Shubik (1972) and Becker (1981) and in a variety of generalizations that unify the two classes of models, for which see, e.g., Kelso and Crawford (1982), Roth and Sotomayor (1990), Hatfield and Milgrom (2005), and Hatfield and Kojima (2008).

3. Note that there may be many different preferences over groups of students that are responsive to the same preferences over individuals; for example, a college with responsive preferences over pairs of students could prefer to receive choices 1 and 4 rather than choices 2 and 3, or vice versa.

4. See Sönmez (1999) for some related results.

5. On the costs of such unraveling in some markets for which unusually good data have been available, see Niederle and Roth (2003b, forthcoming) on the market for gastroenterology fellows, and Fréchette, Roth, and Ünver (2007) on the market for postseason college football bowls. For some recent unraveled markets, see Avery, Fairbanks, and Zeckhauser (2003) on college admissions, and Avery et al. (2001) on appellate court clerks.

6. Happy couples are of course subject to the iron law of marriage that one cannot be happier than one's spouse (at least not in equilibrium).

7. I had at this point studied medical matches and related clearinghouses for a number of years and had become known to some of the medical match officials when I communicated with some of them. In this respect, my 1990 article in *Science* proved more accessible to many medical policy makers than did my various articles in economics journals.

8. Of course, there are other differences between regions of the British health service than how they organized their medical clearinghouses, so there was also room for controlled experiments in the laboratory on the effects of stable and unstable clearinghouses; see Kagel and Roth (2000).

9. In school choice an important fact is that many students have the same priority at a given school, and ties must be broken. How this is done raises some

new theoretical questions; see, e.g., Abdulkadiroglu, Pathak, and Roth (2009), Erdil and Ergin (2006, 2007), and Kesten (2004, 2006).

10. The old Boston system had the effect of heavily penalizing families that failed to be matched to their first choice, and so it put a premium on selecting a "first choice" that was attainable. In general, a great deal can be learned by studying flawed existing allocation systems. See also, e.g., Balinski and Sonmez (1999), Ergin and Sönmez (2006), and Pathak and Sönmez (2007).

11. Although the Boston public schools adopted a deferred-acceptance algorithm, the one-sided nature of choice in Boston gave them other attractive, strategy-proof options. In particular, we also proposed (Abdulkadiroglu et al. 2005) an algorithm based on the top-trading-cycles algorithm discussed by Shapley and Scarf (1974), which was shown to be strategy-proof in Roth (1982b), and which was generalized and studied from multiple perspectives in Abdulkadiroglu and Sönmez (1998, 1999, 2002) and Sönmez and Ünver (2005).

12. Muriel Niederle and I have gotten a privileged view of this by studying the market for gastroenterology fellows and helping gastroenterologists reorganize it. The market for gastroenterology fellows was organized through a centralized fellowship match from 1986 to the mid-1990s. The arrangement fell apart (see McKinney, Niederle, and Roth 2005 for an investigation of the causes of this collapse), and for the next decade the market operated in a decentralized way. It reestablished a match in 2006 (see Niederle, Proctor, and Roth 2006, and Niederle and Roth forthcoming).

13. On large markets, see Roth and Peranson (1999), Immorlica and Mahdian (2005), and Kojima and Pathak (forthcoming).

14. Regarding congestion in decentralized markets, the Ad Hoc Committee on the Job Market of the American Economic Association (AEA) is charged with suggesting changes in the job market for new Ph.D. economists (the committee members are John Cawley, Phil Levine, Muriel Niederle, John Siegfried, and myself). In 2005 the committee instituted a "scramble" webpage on which, late in the market, applicants and departments still on the market could announce themselves. This was intended to help make the latter part of the market thick. In 2006 the AEA instituted a system by which applicants could send, through the AEA, up to two signals of interest to departments they wished to interview. This is intended to avoid coordination failures resulting from congestion in that market, in which departments receive many more applications than they can conduct interviews.

References

Abdulkadiroglu, Atila, Parag A. Pathak, and Alvin E. Roth (2005). "The New York City High School Match." *American Economic Review, Papers and Proceedings*, 95, 2, May, 364–367.

——— (2009). "Strategy-Proofness versus Efficiency in Matching with Indifferences: Redesigning the NYC High School Match." *American Economic Review*, 99, 5, December.

Abdulkadiroglu, Atila, Parag A. Pathak, Alvin E. Roth, and Tayfun Sönmez (2005). "The Boston Public School Match." *American Economic Review,* Papers and Proceedings, 95, 2, May, 368–371.

——— (2006). "Changing the Boston School Choice Mechanism." Working paper, January.

Abdulkadiroglu, Atila, and Tayfun Sönmez (1998). "Random Serial Dictatorship and the Core from Random Endowments in House Allocation Problems." *Econometrica* 66, May, 689–701.

——— (1999). "House Allocation with Existing Tenants." *Journal of Economic Theory,* 88, 233–260.

——— (2002). "School Choice: A Mechanism Design Approach." *American Economic Review,* 93, 729–747.

Avery, Christopher, Andrew Fairbanks, and Richard Zeckhauser (2003). *The Early Admissions Game: Joining the Elite.* Cambridge, Mass.: Harvard University press.

Avery, Christopher, Christine Jolls, Richard A. Posner, and Alvin E. Roth (2001). "The Market for Federal Judicial Law Clerks." *University of Chicago Law Review,* 68, 3, Summer, 793–902.

——— (2007). "The New Market for Federal Judicial Law Clerks." *University of Chicago Law Review,* 74, Spring, 447–486.

Becker, Gary S. (1981). *A Treatise on the Family.* Cambridge, Mass.: Harvard University Press.

Dubins, L. E., and D. A. Freedman (1981). "Machiavelli and the Gale-Shapley Algorithm." *American Mathematical Monthly,* 88, 485–494.

Erdil, Aytek, and Haluk Ergin (2006). "Two-Sided Matching with Indifferences." Working paper.

——— (2008). "What's the Matter with Tie-Breaking? Improving Efficiency in School Choice." *American Economic Review,* 98, 3, June, 669–689.

Ergin, Haluk, and Tayfun Sönmez (2006). "Games of School Choice under the Boston Mechanism." *Journal of Public Economics,* 90, 215–237.

Fréchette, Guillaume, Alvin E. Roth, and M. Utku Ünver (2007). "Unraveling Yields Inefficient Matchings: Evidence from Post-Season College Football Bowls." *Rand Journal of Economics,* 38, 4, Winter, 967–982.

Gale, David, and Lloyd Shapley (1962). "College Admissions and the Stability of Marriage." *American Mathematical Monthly,* 69, 9–15.

Hatfield, John William, and Fuhito Kojima (2008). "Matching with Contracts: Comment," *American Economic Review* 98, 1189–1194.

Hatfield, John William, and Paul Milgrom (2005). "Matching with Contracts." *American Economic Review,* 95, 4, September, 913–935.

Immorlica, Nicole, and Mohammad Mahdian (2005). "Marriage, Honesty, and Stability." SODA 2005, 53–62.

Kagel, John H., and A. E. Roth (2000). "The Dynamics of Reorganization in Matching Markets: A Laboratory Experiment Motivated by a Natural Experiment." *Quarterly Journal of Economics,* February, 201–235.

Kelso, Alexander S., Jr., and Vincent P. Crawford (1982). "Job Matching, Coalition Formation, and Gross Substitutes." *Econometrica,* 50, 1483–1504.

Kesten, Onur (2004). "Student Placement to Public Schools in US: Two New Solutions." Working paper, Carnegie Mellon University.

———— (2006). "On Two Competing Mechanisms for Priority Based Allocation Problems." *Journal of Economic Theory*, 127, 155–171.

Kojima, Fuhito (2007). "Matching and Price Competition: Comment." *American Economic Review*, 97, 3, June, 1027–1031.

Kojima, Fuhito, and Parag Pathak (forthcoming). "Incentives and Stability in Large Two-sided Matching Markets." Working paper.

McKinney, C. Nicholas, Muriel Niederle, and Alvin E. Roth (2005). "The Collapse of a Medical Labor Clearinghouse (and Why Such Failures Are Rare)." *American Economic Review*, 95, 3, June, 878–889.

Milgrom, Paul (2004). *Putting Auction Theory to Work*. Cambridge: Cambridge University Press.

Mullin, F. J., and John M. Stalnaker (1952). "The Matching Plan for Internship Placement: A Report of the First Year's Experience." *Journal of Medical Education*, 27, 193–200.

Niederle, Muriel, Deborah D. Proctor, and Alvin E. Roth (2006). "What Will Be Needed for the New GI Fellowship Match to Succeed?" *Gastroenterology*, 130, January, 218–224.

Niederle, Muriel, and Alvin E. Roth (2003a). "Relationship between Wages and Presence of a Match in Medical Fellowships." *JAMA: Journal of the American Medical Association*, 290, 9, September 3, 1153–1154.

———— (2003b). "Unraveling Reduces Mobility in a Labor Market: Gastroenterology with and without a Centralized Match." *Journal of Political Economy*, 111, 6, December, 1342–1352.

———— (2005). "The Gastroenterology Fellowship Market: Should There be a Match?" *American Economic Review, Papers and Proceedings*, 95, 2, May, 372–375.

———— (forthcoming). "The Effects of a Central Clearinghouse on Job placement, Wages, and Hiring Practices: Gastroenterology Fellows as a Case Study." NBER volume.

Ostrovsky, Michael (2008). "Stability in Supply Chain Networks." *American Economic Review*, 98, 3, June, 897–923.

Pathak, Parag, and Tayfun Sönmez (2007). "Leveling the Playing Field: Sincere and Strategic Players in the Boston Mechanism." Working paper.

Public Law 108–218, *Pension Funding Equity Act of 2004*, sec. 207. www.frweb gate.access.gpo.gov/cgi-bin/getdoc.cgi?dbname=108_cong_public_laws& docid=f:publ218.108.pdf.

Roth, A. E. (1982a). "The Economics of Matching: Stability and Incentives." *Mathematics of Operations Research*, 7, 617–628.

———— (1982b). "Incentive Compatibility in a Market with Indivisible Goods." *Economics Letters*, 9, 127–132.

———— (1984). "The Evolution of the Labor Market for Medical Interns and Residents: A Case Study in Game Theory." *Journal of Political Economy*, 92, 991–1016.

———— (1985). "The College Admissions Problem Is Not Equivalent to the Marriage Problem." *Journal of Economic Theory*, 36, 277–288.

——— (1990). "New Physicians: A Natural Experiment in Market Organization." *Science*, 250, 1524–1528.

——— (1991). "A Natural Experiment in the Organization of Entry Level Labor Markets: Regional Markets for New Physicians and Surgeons in the U.K." *American Economic Review*, 81, June, 415–440.

——— (2002). "The Economist as Engineer: Game Theory, Experimental Economics and Computation as Tools of Design Economics." Fisher Schultz Lecture. *Econometrica*, 70, 4, July, 1341–1378.

——— (2003). "The Origins, History, and Design of the Resident Match." *JAMA: Journal of the American Medical Association*, 289, 7, February 19, 909–912.

——— (2008a). "Deferred Acceptance Algorithms: History, Theory, Practice, and Open Questions." *International Journal of Game Theory*, Special Issue in Honor of David Gale, March, 537–569.

——— (2008b). "What Have We Learned from Market Design?" Hahn Lecture. *Economic Journal*, March, 285–310.

Roth, A. E., and E. Peranson (1999). "The Redesign of the Matching Market for American Physicians: Some Engineering Aspects of Economic Design." *American Economic Review*, 89, 4, September, 748–780.

Roth, A. E., and M. Sotomayor (1990). *Two-Sided Matching: A Study in Game-Theoretic Modeling and Analysis*. Econometric Society Monograph Series. Cambridge: Cambridge University Press.

Roth, A. E., and J. H. Vande Vate (1990). "Random Paths to Stability in Two-Sided Matching." *Econometrica*, 58, 1475–1480.

Roth, A. E., and X. Xing (1994). "Jumping the Gun: Imperfections and Institutions Related to the Timing of Market Transactions." *American Economic Review*, 84, September, 992–1044.

——— (1997). "Turnaround Time and Bottlenecks in Market Clearing: Decentralized Matching in the Market for Clinical Psychologists." *Journal of Political Economy*, 105, April, 284–329.

Shapley, Lloyd S., and Herbert Scarf (1974). "On Cores and Indivisibility." *Journal of Mathematical Economics*, 1, 23–28.

Shapley, Lloyd S., and Martin Shubik (1972). "The Assignment Game I: The Core." *International Journal of Game Theory*, 1, 111–130.

Sönmez, Tayfun (1997). "Manipulation via Capacities in Two-Sided Matching Markets." *Journal of Economic Theory*, 77, 1, November, 197–204.

——— (1999). "Can Pre-arranged Matches Be Avoided in Two-Sided Matching Markets?" *Journal of Economic Theory*, 86, 148–156.

Sönmez, Tayfun, and M. Utku Ünver (2005). "House Allocation with Existing Tenants: An Equivalence." *Games and Economic Behavior*, 52, July, 153–185.

COMMENT

Peter Cramton

Economists are increasingly being asked to design markets. Alvin Roth provides a beautiful summary of this activity in matching markets. Here I extend the discussion to auction markets and emphasize connections between auctions and matching.

Auctions determine who gets the goods and at what prices. The assignment of goods is simply a match. The key difference is that prices—formed from the bids—mediate the match. Auctions are matching with prices.

Interestingly, the major matching results have close analogs in auctions. In matching, stability is important. We do not want people to object to the match. Fortunately, stability is easily achieved with the deferred-acceptance algorithm. Incentives are important. We do not want people to game. Although there is no strategy-proof stable mechanism, if markets are thick enough, then the deferred-acceptance algorithm performs extremely well and provides optimal incentives. In auctions, stability is still important. We do not want an outcome where a group of bidders could offer the seller a better deal. Incentives are still important. Again, there is no strategy-proof mechanism that always satisfies the stability property. However, if markets are thick enough, a variant of the deferred-acceptance algorithm will minimize gaming opportunities and achieve highly efficient outcomes.

Auction applications are rapidly expanding. Communication and computational advances have certainly played an important role, but the development of simple and powerful auction methods has been important too. Market designers now have a much richer set of tools to address more complex problems.

One example is a package auction (or combinatorial auction) in which bidders can bid on packages of items. In a package auction bidders can express preferences for complementary items without running the risk that they will win just some of what they need. This is important, for example, in spectrum auctions in which different technologies require that the spectrum be organized in different ways. In the past, the regulator has been forced to decide how the spectrum is organized with a specific band plan—effectively deciding how much spectrum is available for each technology. A package auction enables the regulator to conduct a technology-neutral auction, which lets the bidders determine the band plan through their competitive bids. A good example is the United Kingdom's 2.6 GHz auction in 2009: the quantity of paired versus unpaired spectrum is determined in the auction, not by the regulator.

One of the challenges of package auctions is finding an effective way for bidders to convey preferences. There are simply too many packages to ask for preferences for all possible packages. A common approach is to begin with a clock auction. The auctioneer names a price for each product, and bidders respond with their most preferred packages. The price is then raised on all products with excess demand, and the bidding continues. This price-discovery process focuses the bidders' attention on packages that are most relevant. Once this price discovery is over, the bidders are in a much better position to submit any additional bids, as well as improve the bids already submitted. An optimization is then done to determine the value-maximizing assignment, as well as competitive prices that satisfy the stability constraints. Typically, there are many such prices, so a further optimization is done to find the prices that provide the best incentives for truthful bidding.

Package auctions are also proposed for auctioning takeoff and landing rights at congested airports, such as the three New York City airports. The goal of the auction is to make the best use of scarce runway capacity. Left to their own devices, airlines will overschedule flights during peak hours, creating congestion and costly delay. The package auction enables each airline to bid for its preferred package of slots. The resulting competitive prices motivate airlines to substitute away from expensive slots, either by shifting flights to less expensive times or by using larger aircraft to carry the same number of passengers with less runway use.

Another example of market design is electricity markets. Modern electricity markets are organized as a number of auction markets. The markets, taken together, are designed to provide reliable electricity at the least cost to consumers. Spot markets determine how much each supplier is generating on a minute-by-minute basis; forward energy markets enable customers and suppliers to lock in medium-term prices for electricity; and long-run investment markets coordinate new entry to cover any expansion in electricity demand. These auction markets must be carefully designed to work together to achieve the goal of least costly, reliable supply. Design failures can be quite costly, as the California electricity crisis of 2000–2001 demonstrated. When the stakes are high, an important step in market design is building prototypes and then testing those prototypes in the experimental lab or in the field before full-scale implementation.

One exciting aspect of market design is working on the forefront of theory and bringing that theory to practice. In both auctions and matching, solving real problems has proved to be an excellent way to develop new theory. The applications benefit from the improved markets, and the theory is enriched in the process.

CHAPTER TEN

Economics, Economists, and Antitrust: A Tale of Growing Influence

Lawrence J. White

> Over the years, our courts have increasingly turned to economic principles to guide their interpretation of the antitrust laws ... Relying on economic analysis is now routine for U.S. courts in the antitrust arena—a salutary development helping our courts make sound decisions ... Another area where economics has a profound impact is within the Antitrust Division.
>
> —THOMAS O. BARNETT (2007)

Antitrust policy in the United States is an amalgam. The body of legislated law starts with the Sherman Act of 1890, the Clayton Act of 1914, and the Federal Trade Commission Act of 1914. Because the language in these statutes is extraordinarily broad and terse, court decisions during more than a century have interpreted and given specific meaning to the broad language of the statutes. Decisions by the federal enforcement agencies—the Antitrust Division of the U.S. Department of Justice (DOJ) and the Federal Trade Commission (FTC)—on whether to pursue cases or to decline their prosecution provide another facet to antitrust policy.

Finally, economics and economists play an important role (Kovacic 1992; FTC 2003; Barnett 2007). In their modern interpretation the antitrust laws are intended to encourage competition, thwart cartels and price-fixing, and discourage the unwarranted creation and exercise of market (or monopoly) power.[1] Competition and monopoly have been bedrock concepts in the liturgy of microeconomics for over a century. The influence of economics on antitrust policy would seem to be a natural phenomenon.

However, the influence of economics on antitrust policy is a relatively recent development; it was not considered to be "natural" as recently as three or four decades ago. As of the early 1960s the two enforcement agencies employed few well-trained economists, and the appearance of an economist as an expert in support or testifying on behalf of the plaintiffs or defendants in antitrust litigation was rare. Today, by contrast, both agencies have sizable staffs of well-trained economists, and most antitrust cases of any kind have economists involved on one or both sides.

A Brief Overview of U.S. Antitrust Policy

There are three major thrusts to modern antitrust enforcement in the United States.[2] The first consists of efforts to prevent "collusion": explicit price-fixing, bid rigging, or cartel formation.[3] These efforts mostly consist of lawsuits brought by the DOJ and by private parties under Section 1 of the Sherman Act, which forbids "every contract, combination in the form of trust or otherwise, or conspiracy, in restraint of trade or commerce among the several States or with foreign nations." Violations of the Sherman Act are felonies, and the DOJ often seeks prison terms against individuals and sizable fines against companies. Private parties that claim to have been harmed directly by price-fixers can also bring suits (regardless of whether there have been any suits by the DOJ or the FTC), and any proven damages are automatically trebled.

Second are efforts to prevent mergers where their effect would be to cause a significant lessening of competition. These are primarily suits brought by the DOJ or the FTC under Section 7 of the Clayton Act, which forbids mergers "where in any line of commerce in any section of the country, the effect of such acquisition may be substantially to lessen competition, or to tend to create a monopoly." The goal of such a suit is simply to gain an injunction to stop the merger from proceeding.[4]

Third are efforts to restrain the unilateral exercise of market power. These are suits brought by the DOJ, the FTC, or private parties. Section 2 of the Sherman Act forbids acts that "monopolize, or attempt to monopolize . . . any part of the trade or commerce among the several States, or with foreign nations." Felony convictions are again possible, although the DOJ more often brings civil suits seeking injunctions. Again, private treble-damages lawsuits can be brought.

In addition, under Section 5 of the Federal Trade Commission Act, the FTC has the ability to prevent "unfair methods of competition in or affecting commerce, and unfair or deceptive acts or practices in or affecting commerce." Finally, the DOJ, the FTC, and private parties can bring suits aimed at tying, bundling, exclusive dealing, and similar vertical restraints under Section 3 of the Clayton Act.

In addition to prosecuting antitrust law violations, the DOJ and the FTC pursue procompetitive policies in three other ways. First, they frequently file amicus curiae (friend-of-the-court) briefs in privately filed antitrust cases that have reached appellate levels, especially cases that have reached the Supreme Court. Because the number of private cases filed annually is approximately ten times the number brought by the two enforcement agencies, and private cases can yield binding legal precedents, these amicus briefs give the agencies the opportunity to lobby the courts in favor of pro-competitive decisions.

Second, the DOJ and the FTC engage in "competition advocacy": the advocacy of procompetitive policies for other federal agencies in regulatory proceedings and for the fifty states in their regulatory actions.

Third, as other countries (especially in the wake of the transition of the countries of Eastern Europe to market-oriented economies) have become interested in developing antitrust policies of their own, the two U.S. enforcement agencies have provided international advice and technical assistance.

Economics and Economists' Involvement in Antitrust: A Brief History

The influence of economics on antitrust policy has occurred along three paths: (1) advances in microeconomics thinking—theoretical developments and empirical testing—that undergird antitrust; (2) economists' direct involvement in antitrust litigation and policy development at the enforcement agencies and in the service of private parties involved in antitrust cases; and (3) economists' writings about specific antitrust cases, including those in which they provided litigation support.

The Development of Economics Thinking

It would be difficult to identify a body of economics thought before the 1930s that could called "industrial organization" (IO).[5] By the end of the 1930s, however, the field was coalescing.[6] This was due partly to the influence of Edward Mason at Harvard University (Mason 1939, 1957) and his colleagues and doctoral students[7] and partly to the industrial data collection and analyses that emerged from the Temporary National Economic Committee (TNEC).[8]

The field continued to develop over the next few decades. By the 1950s the structure-conduct-performance (S-C-P) model—with the central role of seller concentration as a determinant of industry conduct and performance—was the mainstay of IO thinking. In addition, formal thinking about oligopoly (Chamberlin 1929; 1956, chap. 3; Fellner 1949; Stigler 1964), aided by insights from game theory (Shubik 1959; Schelling 1960) and especially the "prisoner's dilemma,"[9] helped support the central role of concentration.

The role of entry in the model gained prominence in the 1950s (Bain 1956). Empirical testing of the relationship between industry profit rates as a dependent variable and structural characteristics of the various industries as the independent variables, using the *Censuses of Manufactures* as the central data source, provided empirical support for the S-C-P model (Bain 1951), as did a large number of industry study monographs (Grether 1970). At the end of the 1950s Bain's (1959) IO text laid out the S-C-P paradigm in systematic form, while Kaysen and Turner's (1959) treatise on antitrust policy provided an extensive application of the paradigm to antitrust.[10] This latter book's strong structuralist deconcentration remedies for oligopolistic industries rested heavily on Bain's (1956) finding that, although economies of scale were a significant barrier to entry in many industries, they did not appear to extend to the sizes of the largest firms in these industries, with the implication that antitrust-forced divestitures would involve little sacrifice in productive efficiencies.

A second strand of IO analysis was also developing in the 1950s under the intellectual leadership of Aaron Director at the University of Chicago (Peltzman 2005). This strand was more skeptical of the S-C-P paradigm, more sympathetic to vertical restraints, and generally more supportive of market outcomes.

Government antitrust victories and the judicial opinions that supported those victories in Sherman Section 1 and Section 2 cases in the 1940s and 1950s involving the aluminum, cigarette, movie, and shoe-machinery industries reflected these developments of the S-C-P paradigm. Only in the movie industry, however, were there major divestitures as remedies, but these involved vertical separations, not the horizontal divestitures envisioned by Kaysen and Turner.[11]

Further, after being largely dormant because of unduly restrictive wording in its original legislative language, Section 7 of the Clayton Act was revived by the Celler-Kefauver Amendment in 1950.[12] A remarkable two-decade series of government challenges to mergers—mostly victorious—followed, based largely on S-C-P grounds (although some elements of populist fears of bigness were also present). *Brown Shoe Co. v. United States* (1962) was the emblematic case of this series, in which the DOJ succeeded in challenging a merger between two shoe manufacturers/retailers in a relatively unconcentrated industry.

The 1960s and early 1970s saw further elaborations of the S-C-P paradigm and more extensive testing of the profitability-concentration relationship, including entry conditions (Mann 1966; Comanor and Wilson 1967; Collins and Preston 1968),[13] advertising (Comanor and Wilson 1974), foreign trade (Esposito and Esposito 1971), the structural conditions on the buyers' side of the market (Lustgarten 1975), risk (Bothwell and Keeler 1976), and the presence of a critical concentration ratio (White 1976).[14] But a "Chicago school" counterrevolution was brewing as well (Demsetz 1974), which argued that high concentration might be causing high profit rates because of economies of scale (contrary to the earlier claims by Bain). The famous face-off of S-C-P advocates versus the Chicago school in the early 1970s led to a widely read and cited conference volume (Goldschmid, Mann, and Weston 1974).

A further blow to the profit-concentration empirical support for the S-C-P model came in the early 1980s from attacks (Benston 1982; Fisher and McGowan 1983; Fisher 1987) on the use and reliability of the accounting data that measured the profit rates used in the studies and on whether relative profit rates were even the appropriate indicators of market power. Profit-based tests of the S-C-P paradigm slackened and were replaced by price-based studies drawn from individual industries (Weiss 1989; Audretsch and Siegfried 1992), which showed a similar positive relationship between prices and concentration. In addition, empirical studies of auctions indicated that the number of bidders at auctions (which, in procurement auctions, would be an approximate equivalent to the number of sellers in a market) had the same type of effect on prices.

In the area of vertical relationships, too, there was a clash between the Harvard and Chicago traditions. The former was suspicious of—and tended to hostility toward—vertical mergers (e.g., between suppliers and customers) and vertical restraints (e.g., tying, bundling, exclusive dealing, territorial sales restraints, and resale price maintenance). The Chicago school was more sympathetic.

Finally, a number of IO-oriented professional economics journals came into existence, which provided specialized vehicles for dissemination of research in IO:[15] *Journal of Industrial Economics* (1952), *Antitrust Bulletin* (1955), *Journal of Law & Economics* (1958), *Rand Journal of Economics* (1970), *Review of Industrial Organization* (1977), *International Journal of Industrial Organization* (1984), *Journal of Regulatory Economics* (1984), and *Journal of Economics and Management Strategy* (1992). Also, a first-ever *Handbook of Antitrust Economics* (Buccirossi 2007) is another milestone in the maturation of economics thought as applied to antitrust.

The Role of Economists at Enforcement Agencies and in Antitrust Litigation

Economists' direct involvement in antitrust extends back at least to the beginning of the twentieth century,[16] although their role before the 1970s was often limited to simple litigation support—in a sense, as "hewers of wood and haulers of water"—rather than as participants in the development of case theories and the formulation of policy. The U.S. Bureau of Corporations, which had been established in 1903 within the Department of Commerce and Labor and which had economists on its staff, provided valuable research support for some of the early successful antitrust prosecutions undertaken by the DOJ, including *United States v. Standard Oil* (1911) and *United States v. American Tobacco* (1911) (Scherer 1990).

An early testimony, possibly the first, by an economist in an antitrust case was in *United States v. U.S. Steel* (1920). The Supreme Court's decision (against the DOJ) disparagingly cited the testimony of "an author and teacher of economics whose philosophical deductions had, perhaps, fortification from experience as Deputy Commissioner of Corporations and as an employee in the Bureau of Corporations." When the FTC was created in 1914, its Economic Department (which eventually became the Bureau of Economics) inherited the Bureau of Corporations' research and investigative role, as well as absorbing the specific office accommodations and personnel of its predecessor agency (Scherer 1990).

At the DOJ the responsibility for antitrust enforcement was placed in a separate Antitrust Division in 1933.[17] Within three years the division hired its first economists. Until the early 1970s, however, the economics group within the division was used primarily for data gathering and statistical support in litigation. Posner's (1971, 532) study of the division offered the following description: "The Division's economists today are handmaidens to the lawyers, and rather neglected ones at that." Another study of the division in the early 1970s (Green 1972, 128) characterized economists there as "second-class citizens. They have little or no say in the type of cases brought, the legal theories used, or the relief sought. In general, they neither conduct long-range studies nor work closely with the policy-planning staff. Mostly they aid attorneys in the preparation of statistical data for trial, and they occasionally testify. They are technicians—'statisticians,' as nearly all of the lawyers call them—and act like it." A later study (Weaver 1977) mentioned economists only in passing—again an indication of their subsidiary role.

In the mid-1960s the assistant attorney general for antitrust, Donald Turner (who had a doctorate in economics from Harvard, as well as a law degree), established the position of Special Economic Assistant to the Assistant Attorney General, and a series of young IO economists served one-year terms in the position (Williamson 2003). But until the early 1970s little was done to strengthen the quality and position of the staff economists at the division.

At the FTC the tradition that had started at the Bureau of Corporations served economics and economists somewhat better. The Bureau of Economics (BE) was able to attract trained leaders with doctorates, and during the 1960s the size and budget of the BE expanded considerably. Nevertheless, at the end of the 1960s outside reviews of the FTC (ABA 1969; Green 1972) commented unfavorably on the low quality of the BE's personnel and on the BE's lack of influence on policy and decision making within the agency.[18]

The 1970s brought a general strengthening of the position of economists at the two enforcement agencies and in litigation support. At the FTC a reorganization and reform of the agency strengthened the position and status of the BE. Commentaries at the beginning of the 1980s (Katzmann 1980; Clarkson and Muris 1981) noted the strengthened position of the BE. At the DOJ in 1973 that year's Special Economic Assistant persuaded the division to strengthen the Economics Section and transform it into the Economic Policy Office, with authority to expand its personnel and recruit doctoral-level economists to staff positions.

More generally, involvement of economists in antitrust cases increased in the 1970s. The DOJ's major suits against IBM (initiated in 1969) and AT&T (initiated in 1974) eventually involved large numbers of economists on both sides, and this widespread exposure of economists to antitrust may well have been influential in encouraging participation in other cases.

The involvement of economists in antitrust policy, as well as litigation support, took a sharp turn upward in the early 1980s with the arrival at the Antitrust Division and the FTC of leaders who were sympathetic to the role and message of microeconomics in the development of antitrust policy and in litigation.[19] For the first time there were FTC commissioners who were economists, including the chairman during the first few years of the Ronald Reagan administration. The FTC continued to have an economist as at least one of its five commissioners during 1981–1985 and 1991–1995. At the division an indication of the rising importance of economists in the mid-1980s was the elevation of the position of director of the Economic Policy Office to a deputy assistant attorney general.

As of the first decade of the twenty-first century, economists are playing prominent roles at both agencies (FTC 2003; Barnett 2007; Carlton and

Heyer 2007; Salinger, Ippolito, and Schrag 2007). At the DOJ there are approximately sixty doctoral-level economists, headed by a deputy assistant attorney general who is usually a leading academic IO economist and who typically serves for about two years in the position. Similarly, at the FTC the BE is staffed by approximately seventy doctoral-level economists (although they spend about a quarter of their time on consumer protection issues), and the bureau's director is usually a leading academic economist who spends about two years in the position.

Economists' Writings about Specific Antitrust Cases

The tradition of economists' writing specifically about major antitrust cases extends at least as far back as a 1949 symposium in the *American Economic Review* (Adelman 1949; Nicholls 1949); Nicols 1949). Most of the antitrust discussions before the 1970s were by economists who had simply become interested in the details and implications of a particular antitrust case.

A notable exception was Carl Kaysen, who in 1950 as a doctoral student of Edward Mason at Harvard provided a unique form of antitrust litigation support: he was appointed as a law clerk by Charles Wyzanski, a federal district court judge, to provide economic counseling to the judge in the DOJ's monopolization trial of the United Shoe Machinery Company. Kaysen served for two years and wrote a lengthy report for Judge Wyzanski, which subsequently became Kaysen's doctoral dissertation and a monograph (Kaysen 1956).

By the 1970s economists were actively participating in antitrust cases more frequently and then writing about those cases. The IBM and AT&T cases provided fertile opportunities for such writings, but other suits and investigations also proved sufficiently interesting to yield publications.[20] Since the 1970s economists' participation in antitrust litigation has become substantially more frequent (Kovacic 1992; Barnett 2007), and articles reflecting that participation also continue to appear (Kwoka and White 2009 and earlier editions).

Special Achievements

Economists' achievements in bringing changes in antitrust enforcement and policy are especially noteworthy in three areas: merger analysis, vertical relationships and restraints, and predatory pricing.[21]

Merger Analysis

Almost all modern antitrust merger analysis takes as its starting point the DOJ-FTC *Horizontal Merger Guidelines*.[22] The guidelines, first published in 1982 and subsequently revised in 1987, 1992, and 1997,[23] establish two approaches under which a merger might be deemed to have anticompetitive consequences: "coordinated effects" and "unilateral effects."

1. Coordinated effects are a direct application of the S-C-P model, with the special emphases provided by Stigler (1964). The primary concern is that oligopolistic sellers will, after a merger, be able implicitly to coordinate their behavior so as to achieve significantly higher prices (or to effect other changes in conduct variables) and higher profits.

Seller concentration, as measured by the Herfindahl-Hirschman Index (HHI),[24] occupies the center stage (as it does in the S-C-P model) for at least two reasons: first, seller concentration is the most readily measured structural attribute; second, the immediate effect of any horizontal merger is to increase seller concentration. The guidelines also bring into the analysis the other important components of the S-C-P model: conditions of entry; the buyer side of the market; the nature and complexity of the product; the transparency of price and other market information; and the antitrust history of the sellers in the market.

A particular problem with implementing merger enforcement before 1982 was defining the relevant product and geographic markets. The S-C-P model assumes that an appropriate market has been specified, so that the *market shares* of the leading firms provide a meaningful indication of the likelihood that the firms will collectively exercise market power. But the S-C-P model itself provides no guidance for delineating appropriate markets.

The guidelines address this problem as follows: a relevant market is a product or group of products that are sold by a group of sellers who, if they acted in concert (i.e., as a "hypothetical monopolist"), could achieve a "small but significant and nontransitory increase in price" (SSNIP); that SSNIP is designated as 5% for one year. This is equivalent to defining a relevant market as one in which market power can be exercised (or one in which market power can be enhanced). The smallest group of sellers that satisfies the SSNIP test is usually designated as the relevant market. These principles apply to the determination of product markets and geographic markets. The determining factor in the analysis is whether sufficient numbers of buyers would switch to other sellers (of other goods or located in other areas) to thwart the price increase.

The logic of this approach follows from the goal of preventing mergers that create or enhance market power. The SSNIP test identifies the smallest group of sellers who could exercise such power. With one exception the market-definition paradigm focuses on sellers (because it is sellers who exercise market power). That exception arises when a group of sellers may be able to practice price discrimination and raise prices significantly for an identifiable group of buyers (defined by a geographic area or by a business function). In this case that group of buyers may also be considered a relevant market. This market-definition paradigm has proved enduring.

2. Unilateral effects. The 1992 revision to the *Horizontal Merger Guidelines* added "unilateral effects" as an area of concern: a significant post-merger price increase that could occur solely because of the actions of the merged entity. This unilateral price increase could occur if the two merging firms produced products that were moderately close substitutes for each other (but not perfect substitutes), and a significant number of the customers of each firm had as their runner-up choice the products of the merger partner. If the products of all other firms were distant-enough third choices for these customers, the merged entity would likely find a general price increase worthwhile, and it could do even better if it could identify and target these "trapped" customers and thereby practice selective price discrimination against them.[25]

The anticompetitive effects of this type of merger do not arise because of cooperation or collusion among the firms that compete with the merged entity. Instead, the competitive harm occurs because the merged firm is better able to internalize the benefits of a price increase. For this analysis the issues of market definition and market shares are largely irrelevant; what matters is the extent to which customers have the two merging firms as their first and second choices (and the extent to which other firms are distant third choices).

Vertical Relationships and Restraints

The Harvard IO tradition was hostile toward vertical relationships and vertical restraints. Kaysen and Turner (1959), for example, had a generally negative view of vertical mergers and of vertical restraints such as tying, bundling, exclusive dealing, requirements contracts, full-line forcing,[26] territorial restraints, and resale price maintenance (RPM).[27]

The Chicago tradition, however, under the intellectual guidance of Aaron Director, began offering a different view of vertical restraints. Bowman (1957) and Burstein (1960a) argued that tying was often a vehicle for monitoring buyers' use of the tied product and thus served as an alternative mechanism for effecting price discrimination (of which the welfare effects are generally ambiguous); Burstein (1960b) argued the same for full-line forcing.[28] Telser (1960) argued that RPM could be a means by which a manufacturer (or other "upstream" entity) could overcome the potential free-riding problems that accompany the provision of product information to customers and thereby induce more point-of-sale service from retailers.[29] The free-riding argument for RPM has been extended to the provision of other retailer services (Marvel and McCafferty 1984; Mathewson and Winter 1984; Marvel 1985). Free-riding problems have also been offered as a justification for territorial restraints (White 1981) and for exclusive dealing (Marvel 1982). Furthermore, there was a widespread Chicago attack on the idea that vertical integration could generally have serious anticompetitive consequences.

Before the mid-1970s the Supreme Court's antitrust legal decisions on vertical restrictions and vertical mergers were consistent with the harsh Harvard view. Early on, the Court condemned RPM as a per se violation of Section 1 of the Sherman Act in *Dr. Miles Medical Co. v. John D. Park & Sons Co.* (1911) and reaffirmed that position through the 1980s.[30]

Tying came under attack in *Motion Picture Patents v. Universal Film Manufacturing* (1917), with reaffirmations in the following decades. In 1949 the Court condemned tying as a per se illegal offense in *Northern Pacific Railway v. United States* (1949) and declared that "tying agreements serve hardly any purpose beyond the suppression of competition" in *Standard Oil Co. of California v. United States* (1949).

Similarly, the Court attacked requirements contracts in *Standard Oil Co.* (1949) and in *Richfield Oil v. United States* (1952). Earlier the Court had attacked exclusive dealing in *Standard Fashion v. Magrane-Houston* (1922) and repeated that attack in *Standard Oil* (1949). Later, in *United States v. Arnold Schwinn* (1967), the Court condemned territorial restraints as a per se violation of the Sherman Act. The Court condemned vertical mergers in *United States v. du Pont* (1957), *Brown Shoe* (1962), and *Ford Motor v. United States* (1972).

The tide turned after the mid-1970s, with Chicago arguments largely carrying the day.[31] Two 1977 decisions highlighted the change. In *Continental T.V. v. GTE Sylvania* (1977) the Court declared that territorial restraints should be examined under a rule of reason rather than being automatically condemned as per se illegal under the rule of *Schwinn* just ten years earlier. In *U.S. Steel v. Fortner Enterprises* (1977) the Court found (reinforcing *United States v. Jerrold Electronics* [1961]) that the absence of market power in the tying market meant that a tying arrangement was acceptable (despite the per se rule of *Northern Pacific*, which remained in place).

The 1980s saw further progress. Although the Supreme Court continued its per se condemnation of RPM in *Monsanto v. Spray-Rite* (1984) and in *Business Electronics v. Sharp Electronics* (1988), it raised the standard of proof that plaintiffs needed to prevail. In *Jefferson Parish Hospital District No. 2 v. Edwin G. Hyde* (1984) the Court again found that the absence of market power meant that a tying arrangement was acceptable; and a minority opinion signed by four members of the Court argued that the per se rule for tying should be superseded by a rule-of-reason approach.

In the 1990s the Court took a step back on tying in *Eastman Kodak v. Image Technical Services* (1992), in which the Court (on a motion for summary judgment) found that Kodak must stand trial on a tying claim. However, later in the decade, in *State Oil v. Khan* (1997) the Court declared that maximum RPM should be judged under the rule of reason (and not condemned as a per se violation).

The first decade of the twenty-first century has been auspicious for a more enlightened approach to vertical restraints. In *Illinois Tool Works v. Independent Ink* (2006) the Court decided that the presence of a patent on the tying product does not automatically mean that the seller has market power. In *Leegin Creative Leather Products v. PSKS* (2007) the Court decided that minimum RPM—the "plain vanilla" version of RPM that had been condemned as per se illegal in *Dr. Miles*—should also be judged under a rule of reason.

In sum, antitrust law with respect to vertical restraints has made great progress since the 1970s, building on advances in economics thinking. With luck, in the not-too-distant future the Supreme Court will see the wisdom of formally reversing *Northern Pacific* and judging tying cases under the rule of reason as well.

Predatory Pricing

Before the 1970s the "treatment of predatory pricing in the cases and the literature . . . commonly suffered from two interrelated defects: failure to delineate clearly and correctly what practices should constitute the offense, and exaggerated fears that large firms will be inclined to engage in it" (Areeda and Turner 1975, 697–698). Similar defects could be ascribed to allegations of price discrimination (where predation claims were often also lurking), as exemplified by FTC enforcement actions and Supreme Court decisions (e.g., *Utah Pie v. Continental Baking* [1967]). Common to enforcement actions and judicial decisions were findings of "pricing below cost" as incriminating behavior, where "below cost" was either vaguely defined or defined as below average costs (which usually also meant using some arbitrary method of distributing joint costs across multiple products, such as using the relative sales revenues of the products as the relative weights).

Academic work to clarify predatory issues and to cast doubt on the empirical frequency of predation began at Chicago (under Aaron Director's influence) in the late 1950s (McGee 1958; Telser 1966; Peltzman 2005). The paradigm of envisioning predation as an "investment" (an initial sacrifice) and then a subsequent recoupment period (higher prices permitting a profits return on the initial investment) became clear.

Building on this base, Areeda and Turner (1975) offered a powerful critique and a proposal that pricing at or above marginal cost (with average variable cost serving as a proxy for the usually unmeasurable marginal cost) should generally be considered a "safe harbor" for firms in alleged predatory situations.[32] This subsequently became known as the "Areeda-Turner rule." Subsequent Supreme Court decisions—*Matsushita v. Zenith* (1986); *Brooke Group v. Brown & Williamson* (1993); and *Weyerhaeuser v. Ross-Simmons* (2007)—were clearly influenced by the investment-plus-recoupment paradigm and by the price-above-marginal-cost test.

At about the same time that economists in antitrust were clarifying notions of predation, economists in regulatory areas (Baumol 1968; Baumol and Walton 1973) were writing about similar pricing issues in those areas and were nudging regulatory criteria and decisions—for example, in telecommunications and transportation—away from the use of fully distributed cost and toward the use of incremental costs.

Conclusion

The influence of economics on antitrust legal decisions and policy over the past two to three decades has been substantial. This influence has occurred through developments in economics thinking, the elevation of economists' status and positions at the DOJ and the FTC, and the wider participation of economists in antitrust litigation generally. Reasonable economists can differ about the wisdom of some of these developments and about the particular stringency of enforcement (or lack thereof) over the past few decades, but few can argue against the proposition that economists' influence has increased.[33]

Nirvana has not yet arrived, however. In at least four areas creative economics thinking could encourage better antitrust decisions and policy. First is the ongoing dilemma of how to take into account the efficiencies that may accompany a proposed merger. The trade-offs of the potential welfare losses from heightened market power against the potential improved efficiencies have been apparent at least since Williamson (1968). But improved efficiencies are easy to promise and may be difficult to deliver;

and "unscrambling the eggs" of a merger a few years after it has been approved and the efficiencies have failed to appear may be difficult or impossible (in addition to the difficulties of measuring whether efficiencies have indeed appeared).

Second, unilateral predatory behavior needs a more nuanced approach. Current antitrust decisions portray predation as a narrow strategy of an initial investment in below-marginal-cost pricing that will be recouped in higher prices and profits after the target firm departs from the market. Lost in this narrow approach are the larger issues of whether achieving a reputation for below-cost pricing might deter future entry or deter fringe firms that might otherwise be inclined to be mavericks. Achieving this reputation could make the action worthwhile, even if the narrow costs and benefits would not appear to be profitable (Brodley, Bolton, and Riordon 2000). Further, applying even this narrow cost-benefit paradigm to nonprice behavior has proved difficult. And the issue of bundled discounts, as portrayed in *LePage's v. 3M* (2003), has roiled antitrust thinking.

Clear economics thinking can surely help. For example, the concept of "no economic sense"—that a price or nonprice action should be condemned if it makes no economic sense for the firm undertaking it unless the target firm disappears from the market or will otherwise be disciplined (Ordover and Willig 1981; Werden 2006)—is one direction that is worth pursuing (although it does not encompass the strategic reputation issues raised earlier). There may well be other directions that good economics thinking can uncover.

Third, the issue of market definition in monopolization cases under Section 2 of the Sherman Act remains in an unsatisfactory state. The *Horizontal Merger Guidelines* market-definition paradigm generally does not work for monopolization cases because that paradigm is forward looking, whereas most monopolization cases hinge on the issue of whether the defendant already has market power. Perhaps creative thinking can yield a breakthrough in this area, as it did for mergers.[34]

Fourth, economists need to lead the effort to make a retrospective assessment of the efficacy of antitrust enforcement, especially merger enforcement. Are the DOJ and the FTC drawing the right "lines" in their decisions whether to challenge or approve mergers?

The answer to this question cannot be learned from examining the number of merger challenges per year or the characteristics of the mergers that are challenged or are successfully challenged (because one can never know the counterfactual—that is, what would have otherwise occurred in the absence of a challenge—with respect to those latter mergers). But postmerger pricing studies of those mergers that are allowed to proceed—especially those mergers that are close calls (as indicated by whether the agencies made a second request for additional information from the merger proponents)—should yield useful information. If these studies indicate that postmerger prices have not increased (ceteris paribus), merger policy has been too strict; if the studies instead indicate that postmerger prices have increased significantly, merger policy has been too lenient.

In sum, antitrust economics still has important tasks before it. I hope that supply will respond to this demand.

Notes

The author was the chief economist in the Antitrust Division of the U.S. Department of Justice, 1982–1983. An earlier version of this chapter was presented at the American Economic Association (AEA) session "Better Living through Economics (V)," New Orleans, January 5, 2008. Readers can find more complete references, legal citations, and details in White (2008a). Thanks are due to Kenneth Elzinga, the discussant at that session, and to William Baumol, William Comanor, Frank Fisher, George Hay, Roger Noll, Sam Peltzman, F. M. Scherer, Geoffrey Shepherd, John Siegfried, Martin Spechler, and Oliver Williamson for helpful comments on an earlier draft.

1. Historically, a populist strain, with its fears of bigness and its goal of keeping economic institutions small and locally oriented, was also present. That strain has disappeared from current enforcement and interpretation.

2. Arguably, there is a fourth thrust as well: restrictions on price discrimination under the Robinson-Patman Act, which was a 1936 strengthening of Section 2 of the Clayton Act. However, the DOJ has not brought a Robinson-Patman lawsuit since the early 1960s, and the FTC's suits have declined almost (but not quite) to zero; private plaintiffs rarely win the few cases that they bring.

3. Although most antitrust enforcement efforts are phrased in terms of preventing anticompetitive acts by sellers, antitrust enforcement applies (in principle) equally to anticompetitive acts by buyers (and thus to the exercise of monopsony power as well as monopoly power).

4. Such suits may be settled by agreements by the merging parties to divest sufficient assets to maintain a sufficiently competitive environment.

5. I have been unable to determine when the phrase "industrial organization" was first used to describe the specific field of microeconomics that has now come to be associated with that phrase or when the phrase came into common use for describing the field. A 1937 journal article title comes close: "The Organization of Industry and the Theory of Prices" (Burns 1937). Marshall (1920) has five chapters (bk. 4, chaps. 8–12) that have the words "industrial organization" in their titles, but these chapters focus on issues of the firm (such as economies and diseconomies of scale) rather than on issues of industry and Markets. Schumpeter (1954, 948–950), in discussing the "contributions of the

applied fields" to the development of economics thought "from 1870 to 1914 (and later)," briefly discusses the category of "railroads, public utilities, 'trusts,' and cartels," but all of his discussion is focused on railroad and public utility economics. See more generally the discussion in de Jong and Shepherd (2007).

6. The American Economic Association reprinted fifteen articles on IO-oriented topics that had been published between 1934 and 1940 in *Readings in the Social Control of Industry* (1942). None of the articles had "industrial organization" in its title, although the Burns (1937) article was among them; but the preface to the volume (Homan 1942, v–vi) mentioned that the selection of the articles followed "the principle of confining attention to the more general problems of public policy toward industrial organization and control." See also Peltzman (2007).

7. See Shepherd (2007); and see de Jong and Shepherd (2007) more generally for brief biographies of some of the leading figures in IO during the 1930s and after.

8. The TNEC was created by an act of Congress in June 1938 and ended in April 1941. In its three years of existence it generated thirty-seven volumes of testimony, two volumes of recommendations, and forty-three monographs. Its data-collection efforts provided the precedent for the *Census of Manufactures*, which first published data for 1947.

9. The "prisoner's dilemma" is a game situation that illustrates that individual choices, though apparently optimal when selected in isolation, can yield joint outcomes that make the multiple players worse off than if they had made different choices originally. The name comes from the "story" that usually accompanies the game: The dilemma of two prisoners, each interrogated separately, who each have the incentive to confess; but when both confess, they are both worse off than if they had both remained silent. See, for example, Schelling (1960, p. 214).

10. By the late 1950s and early 1960s the S-C-P paradigm was also being applied to regulated industries; see, e.g., Meyer et al. (1959) and Caves (1962).

11. Also, in *United States v. du Pont* (1957) the Supreme Court ruled that du Pont had to divest its 23% stock ownership in General Motors, but again, this was a vertical separation.

12. This amendment to the Clayton Act took its name from the two lawmakers who were its chief proponents: Representative Emanuel Celler (Dem., NY) and Senator C. Estes Kefauver (Dem., TN).

13. Later surveys of entry can be found in Siegfried and Evans (1994) and Geroski (1995).

14. See Weiss (1971, 1974), Bresnahan (1989), Schmalensee (1989), and Caves (2007) for summaries.

15. The first year of publication is in parentheses.

16. As Letwin (1965, 71–77) and Scherer (1970, 424) have noted, economists in the 1880s were generally unconcerned about the rise of the "trusts" and thus were not advocates of passage of the Sherman Act.

17. The DOJ acquired antitrust enforcement authority under the Sherman Act in 1890. Until 1903 enforcement was carried out directly within the Office of the Attorney General, and from 1903 to 1933 it was carried out within the Office of the Assistant to the Attorney General.

18. Mueller (2004) offers a different view.

19. Also in the late 1970s and the 1980s the number of economics consulting firms that had extensive antitrust litigation support practices increased substantially. Often these firms were led and staffed by alumni from the economics staffs of the two enforcement agencies.

20. White (2008a) provides an array of examples.

21. In addition to the major achievements mentioned in the text, honorable mention for antitrust economists might include (1) being early advocates of sensible economic deregulation of securities and banking markets, transportation markets, telecommunications markets, and energy markets; (2) being major advocates for larger fines and the continuation of treble damages in private antitrust suits as instruments for deterrence; and (3) being major advocates of the repeal of the Robinson-Patman Act.

22. Accessed at www.usdoj.gov/atr/public/guidelines/hmg.htm.

23. An earlier set of DOJ guidelines was published in 1968 but proved unsatisfactory and was largely scrapped when the 1982 guidelines were adopted.

24. The HHI was used as the measure of seller concentration in the guidelines, rather than the four-firm concentration ratio (which was far more commonly used before 1982), partly because it is a more complete measure of the shares of all firms in the market and partly because Stigler (1964) showed that it could serve as an indicator of the ease with which sellers who were trying to coordinate their pricing could distinguish between random market-share fluctuations and market-share changes that could occur as a consequence of a surreptitious price cut.

25. Unilateral effects could also occur if a dominant firm merged with one of its rivals, even in a homogeneous goods industry (Stigler 1965). The guideposts on postmerger concentration (and merger-induced change in concentration) would probably be sufficient to catch such mergers, but to be on the safe side, the guidelines also indicate that any merger involving a firm that has a market share of 35% or higher will receive special scrutiny.

26. Full-line forcing is a business practice whereby a supplier (e.g., producer) insists that, in order for a dealer to sell any of the products in the supplier's range of products, the dealer must carry and sell the full line.

27. At least part of the reason for many economists' harsh view of RPM was the experience of the 1930s, when small retailers (and especially pharmacists) lobbied for protection against "unfair" competition from large chain stores. One legislative reaction, noted earlier, was the Robinson-Patman Act of 1936, which strengthened the Clayton Act's Section 2 prohibitions on price discrimination (because, the small retailers alleged, chain stores were extracting discounts from manufacturers that were unavailable to smaller retailers). Another response, the Miller-Tydings Act of 1937, authorized the states to legalize RPM (which also went by the name "fair trade") so that the small retailers could

persuade manufacturers to impose RPM and thus force the chain stores to sell at the same prices as the smaller retailers.

28. It was also argued that tying and similar vertical restraints could be a way of making sure that the product functioned properly and thus of preserving the goodwill of the manufacturer and of dealing with potential free-riding problems.

29. See also Bowman (1955). Telser acknowledged that RPM could be a cover for a retailers' or manufacturers' cartel. What was important, however, was his demonstration that a manufacturer unilaterally might find RPM to be in its interest.

30. However, in *United States v. Colgate* (1919) the Court decided that it was legal for a manufacturer to decide what the retail price of an item should be and then unilaterally decline to deal with any retailer that failed to adhere to that price. The tension between *Dr. Miles Medical* and *Colgate* remained a problem until the *Leegin* decision in 2007, which I describe later.

31. There were exceptions to the pre-1970s pattern described earlier. For example, in *Tampa Electric v. Nashville Coal* (1961) the Court declined to condemn a requirements contract and declared that exclusive dealing should be judged by a rule of reason. That same year, in *United States v. Jerrold Electronics* (1961), the Court affirmed a lower-court opinion that allowed tying for a start-up situation. But these and a few other cases were exceptions.

32. As I noted earlier, Turner had a Ph.D. in economics, as well as a law degree, and thus he can legitimately be included in this list of economists' accomplishments.

33. Why the legal profession—at the enforcement agencies, in private practice, and in the judiciary—was willing to accept the expanded influence of economics and economists on its legal terrain is an interesting question. A few potential (and potentially complementary) explanations are offered in White (2008a).

34. Elaboration on this problem and some suggestions are offered in White (2008b).

References

Adelman, Morris A. "The A & P Case." *American Economic Review*, 39 (May 1949), 280–283.

American Bar Association (ABA). "Report of the ABA Commission to Study the Federal Trade Commission." September 15, 1968. Reprinted in *Journal of Reprints for Antitrust Law and Economics*, 1 (Winter 1969), 885–1009.

American Economic Association. *Readings in the Social Control of Industry*. Philadelphia: Blakiston, 1942.

Areeda, Philip, and Donald F. Turner. "Predatory Pricing and Related Practices under Section 2 of the Sherman Act." *Harvard Law Review*, 88 (February 1975), 697–733.

Audretsch, David B., and John J. Siegfried, eds. *Empirical Studies in Industrial Organization: Essays in Honor of Leonard W. Weiss*. Dordrecht: Kluwer Academic Publishers, 1992.

Bain, Joe S. "Relation of Profit Rate to Industry Concentration: American Manufacturing, 1936–1940." *Quarterly Journal of Economics,* 65 (May 1951), 293–324.

———. *Barriers to New Competition.* Cambridge, Mass.: Harvard University Press, 1956.

———. *Industrial Organization.* New York: John Wiley & Sons, 1959.

Barnett, Thomas O. "Competition Law and Policy Modernization: Lessons from the U.S. Common-Law Experience." Presentation to the Lisbon Conference on Competition Law and Economics, Lisbon, Portugal, November 16, 2007. www.usdoj.gov/atr/public/speeches/227755.htm.

Baumol, William J. "Reasonable Rules for Rate Regulation: Plausible Policies for an Imperfect World." In Almarin Phillips and Oliver E. Williamson, eds., *Prices: Issues in Theory, Practice, and Public Policy.* Philadelphia: University of Pennsylvania Press, 1968, 101–123.

Baumol, William J., and Alfred G. Walton. "Full Costing, Competition and Regulatory Practice." *Yale Law Journal,* 82 (March 1973), 639–655.

Benston, George J. "Accounting Numbers and Economic Values." *Antitrust Bulletin,* 27 (Spring 1982), 161–215.

Bothwell, James L., and Theodore E. Keeler. "Profits, Market Structure, and Portfolio Risk." In Robert T. Masson and P. David Qualls, eds., *Essays in Industrial Organization in Honor of Joe S. Bain.* Cambridge, Mass.: Ballinger, 1976, 71–88.

Bowman, Ward S., Jr. "The Prerequisites and Effects of Resale Price Maintenance." *University of Chicago Law Review,* 22 (Summer 1955), 825–873.

———. "Tying Arrangements and the Leverage Problem." *Yale Law Journal,* 67 (November 1957), 19–36.

Bresnahan, Timothy F. "Empirical Studies of Industries with Market Power." In Richard Schmalensee and Robert Willig, eds., *Handbook of Industrial Organization,* vol. 2. Amsterdam: North-Holland, 1989, 1011–1057.

Brodley, Joseph F., Patrick Bolton, and Michael H. Riordon. "Predatory Pricing: Strategic Theory and Legal Policy." *Georgetown Law Journal,* 88 (August 2000), 2239–2330.

Buccirossi, Paolo, ed. *Handbook of Antitrust Economics.* Cambridge, Mass.: MIT Press, 2007.

Burns, Arthur R. "The Organization of Industry and the Theory of Prices." *Journal of Political Economy,* 45 (October 1937), 662–680.

Burstein, Meyer L. "The Economics of Tie-in Sales." *Review of Economics and Statistics,* 42 (February 1960a), 68–73.

———. "A Theory of Full-Line Forcing." *Northwestern University Law Review,* 55 (March–April 1960b), 62–95.

Carlton, Dennis W., and Ken Heyer. "The Year in Review: Economics at the Antitrust Division, 2006–2007." *Review of Industrial Organization,* 31 (September 2007), 121–137.

Caves, Richard E. *Air Transport and Its Regulators.* Cambridge, Mass.: Harvard University Press, 1962.

———. "In Praise of the Old I.O." *International Journal of Industrial Organization,* 25 (February 2007), 1–12.

Chamberlin, Edward H. "Duopoly: Value Where Sellers Are Few." *Quarterly Journal of Economics*, 44 (November 1929), 63–100.

———. *The Theory of Monopolistic Competition*. 7th ed. Cambridge, Mass: Harvard University Press, 1956.

Clarkson, Kenneth W., and Timothy J. Muris. "Commission Performance, Incentives, and Behavior." In Kenneth W. Clarkson and Timothy J. Muris, eds., *The Federal Trade Commission since 1970*. Cambridge: Cambridge University Press, 1981, 280–306.

Collins, Norman R., and Lee E. Preston. *Concentration and Price-Cost Margins in Manufacturing*. Berkeley: University of California Press, 1968.

Comanor, William S., and Thomas A. Wilson. "Advertising, Market Structure, and Performance." *Review of Economics and Statistics*, 49 (November 1967), 423–440.

———. *Advertising and Market Power*. Cambridge, Mass.: Harvard University Press, 1974.

De Jong, Henry W., and William G. Shepherd, eds. *Pioneers of Industrial Organization: How The Economics of Competition and Monopoly Took Shape*. Cheltenham: Edward Elgar, 2007.

Demsetz, Harold. "Two Systems of Belief about Monopoly." In Harvey J. Goldschmid, H. Michael Mann, and J. Fred Weston, eds., *Industrial Concentration: The New Learning*. Boston: Little, Brown, 1974, 164–184.

Esposito, Louis, and Frances F. Esposito. "Foreign Competition and Domestic Industry Profitability." *Review of Economics and Statistics*, 53 (November 1971), 343–353.

Evans, David S., ed. *Breaking up Bell: Essays on Industrial Organization and Regulation*. New York: North-Holland, 1983.

Federal Trade Commission. "FTC History: Bureau of Economics Contributions to Law Enforcement, Research, and Economic Knowledge and Policy." Roundtable with former directors of the Bureau of Economics, Federal Trade Commission, September 4, 2003. www.ftc.gov/be/workshops/directorsconference/docs/directorstableGOOD.pdf.

Fellner, William J. *Competition among the Few*. New York: Knopf, 1949.

Fisher, Franklin M. "On the Mis-use of the Profits-Sales Ratio to Infer Monopoly Power." *Rand Journal of Economics*, 18 (Autumn 1987), 384–396.

Fisher, Franklin M., and John J. McGowan. "On the Misuse of Accounting Rates of Return to Infer Monopoly Profits." *American Economic Review*, 73 (March 1983), 82–97.

Geroski, Paul A. "What Do We Know about Entry?" *International Journal of Industrial Organization*, 13 (December 1995), 421–440.

Goldschmid, Harvey J., H. Michael Mann, and J. Fred Weston, eds. *Industrial Concentration: The New Learning*. Boston: Little, Brown, 1974.

Green, Mark J. *The Closed Enterprise System*. New York: Grossman, 1972.

Grether, Ewald T. "Industrial Organization: Past History and Future Problems." *American Economic Review*, 60 (May 1970), 83–89.

Homan, Paul T. Preface to American Economic Association, *Readings in the Social Control of Industry*. Philadelphia: Blakiston, 1942, v–vi.

Katzmann, Robert A. *Regulatory Bureaucracy: The Federal Trade Commission and Antitrust Policy.* Cambridge, Mass.: MIT Press, 1980.

Kaysen, Carl. *United States v. United Shoe Machinery Corporation: An Economic Analysis of an Anti-trust Case.* Cambridge, Mass.: Harvard University Press, 1956.

Kaysen, Carl, and Donald F. Turner. *Antitrust Policy: An Economic and Legal Analysis.* Cambridge, Mass.: Harvard University Press, 1959.

Kovacic, William E. "The Influence of Economics on Antitrust." *Economic Inquiry,* 30 (April 1992), 294–306.

Kwoka, John E., Jr., and Lawrence J. White, eds. *The Antitrust Revolution.* 5th ed. New York: Oxford University Press, 2009.

Letwin, William. *Law and Economic Policy in America.* New York: Random House, 1965.

Lustgarten, Steven H. "The Impact of Buyer Concentration on Manufacturing Industries." *Review of Economics and Statistics* 57 (May 1975), 125–132.

Mann, H. Michael. "Seller Concentration, Barriers to Entry, and Rates of Return in Thirty Industries, 1950–1960." *Review of Economics and Statistics,* 48 (August 1966), 296–307.

Marshall, Alfred. *Principles of Economics.* 8th ed. London: Macmillan, 1920.

Marvel, Howard P. "Exclusive Dealing." *Journal of Law & Economics,* 25 (April 1982), 1–25.

———. "How Fair Is Fair Trade?" *Contemporary Policy Issues,* 3 (Spring 1985), 23–36.

Marvel, Howard P., and Stephen McCafferty. "Resale Price Maintenance and Quality Certification." *Rand Journal of Economics,* 15 (Autumn 1984), 346–359.

Mason, Edward S. "Price and Production Policies of Large-Scale Enterprise." *American Economic Review,* 29 (March 1939, supplement), 61–74.

———. *Economic Concentration and the Monopoly Problem.* Cambridge, Mass.: Harvard University Press, 1959.

Mathewson, G. Frank, and Ralph A. Winter. "An Economic Theory of Vertical Restraints." *Rand Journal of Economics,* 15 (Spring 1984), 27–38.

McGee, John S. "Predatory Price Cutting: The Standard Oil (N.J.) Case." *Journal of Law & Economics,* 1 (October 1958), 137–169.

Meyer, John R., Merton J. Peck, John Stenason, and Charles Zwick. *Competition and the Transportation Industries of the United States.* Cambridge, Mass.: Harvard University Press, 1959.

Mueller, Willard F. "The Revival of Economics at the FTC in the 1960s." *Review of Industrial Organization,* 25 (August 2004), 91–105.

Nicholls, William H. "The Tobacco Case of 1946." *American Economic Review,* 39 (May 1949), 284–296.

Nicols, Alfred. "The Cement Case." *American Economic Review,* 39 (May 1949), 297–310.

Ordover, Janusz A., and Robert D. Willig. "An Economic Definition of Predation: Pricing and Product Innovation." *Yale Law Journal,* 91 (November 1981), 8–53.

Peltzman, Sam. "Aaron Director's Influence on Antitrust Policy." *Journal of Law & Economics*, 48 (October 2005), 313–330.

———. "George Joseph Stigler." In Henry W. de Jong and William G. Shepherd, eds., *Pioneers of Industrial Organization: How the Economics of Competition and Monopoly Took Shape*. Cheltenham: Edward Elgar, 2007, 239–244.

Posner, Richard A. "A Program for the Antitrust Division." *University of Chicago Law Review*, 38 (Spring 1971), 500–536.

Salinger, Michael A., Pauline M. Ippolito, and Joel L. Schrag. "Economics at the FTC: Pharmaceutical Patent Dispute Settlements and Behavioral Economics." *Review of Industrial Organization*, 31 (September 2007), 85–105.

Schelling, Thomas C. *The Strategy of Conflict*. Cambridge, Mass.: Harvard University Press, 1960.

Scherer, F. M. *Industrial Market Structure and Economic Performance*. Chicgo: Rand McNally, 1970.

Scherer, F. M. "Sunlight and Sunset at the Federal Trade Commission." *Administrative Law Review*, 42 (Fall 1990), 461–487.

Schmalensee, Richard. "Inter-industry Studies of Structure and Performance." In Richard Schmalensee and Robert Willig, eds., *Handbook of Industrial Organization*, vol. 2. Amsterdam: North-Holland, 1989, 951–1009.

Schumpeter, Joseph S. *History of Economic Analysis*. New York: Oxford University Press, 1954.

Shepherd, William G. "Edward S. Mason." In Henry W. de Jong and William G. Shepherd, eds., *Pioneers of Industrial Organization: How the Economics of Competition and Monopoly Took Shape*. Cheltenham: Edward Elgar, 2007, 209–210.

Shubik, Martin. *Strategy and Market Structure*. New York: Wiley, 1959.

Siegfried, John J., and Laurie Beth Evans. "Empirical Studies of Entry and Exit: A Survey of the Evidence." *Review of Industrial Organization*, 9 (April 1994), 121–155.

Stigler, George J. "A Theory of Oligopoly." *Journal of Political Economy*, 72 (February 1964), 55–69.

———. "The Dominant Firm and the Inverted Price Umbrella." *Journal of Law & Economics*, 8 (October 1965), 167–172.

Telser, Lester G. "Why Should Manufacturers Want Fair Trade?" *Journal of Law & Economics*, 3 (October 1960), 86–105.

———. "Cutthroat Competition and the Long Purse." *Journal of Law & Economics*, 9 (October 1966), 259–277.

Weaver, Suzanne. *Decision to Prosecute: Organization and Public Policy in the Antitrust Division*. Cambridge, Mass.: MIT Press, 1977.

Weiss, Leonard W. "Quantitative Studies of Industrial Organization." In Michael D. Intriligator, ed., *Frontiers of Quantitative Economics*. Amsterdam: North-Holland, 1971, 362–403.

———. "The Concentration-Profits Relationship and Antitrust." In Harvey J. Goldschmid, H. Michael Mann, and J. Fred Weston, eds., *Industrial Concentration: The New Learning*. Boston: Little, Brown, 1974, 184–233.

———, ed., *Concentration and Price*. Cambridge, Mass.: MIT Press, 1989.

Werden, Gregory J. "Identifying Exclusionary Conduct under Section 2: The 'No Economic Sense Test.' " *Antitrust Law Journal,* 73, no. 2 (2006), 413–434.

White, Lawrence J. "Searching for the Critical Concentration Ratio: An Application of the 'Switching of Regimes' Technique." In Stephen M. Goldfeld and Richard E. Quandt, eds., *Studies in Nonlinear Estimation.* Cambridge, Mass.: Ballinger, 1976, 61–76.

———. "Vertical Restraints in Antitrust Law: A Coherent Model." *Antitrust Bulletin,* 26 (Summer 1981), 327–345.

———. "The Growing Influence of Economics and Economists on Antitrust: An Extended Discussion." Working Paper EC-08-03, Stern School of Business, New York University, January 2008a. w4.stern.nyu.edu/emplibrary/economics%20&%20antitrust.pdf.

———. "Market Power and Market Definition in Monopolization Cases: A Paradigm is Missing." In Wayne D. Collins, ed., *Issues in Competition Law and Policy,* Vol. II. Chicago: American Bar Association, 2008b, 913–924.

Williamson, Oliver E. "Economies as an Antitrust Defense: The Welfare Tradeoffs." *American Economic Review,* 58 (March 1968), 18–36.

———. "Economics and Antitrust Enforcement: Transition Years." *Antitrust,* 17 (Spring 2003), 61–65.

COMMENT

Kenneth G. Elzinga

Professor White is one of the few antitrust economists who could write this chapter. He is the optimal age and he has the optimal experience.

If White were younger, he probably would not care about how antitrust economics got where it is today. Most young economists cannot distinguish Alfred Marshall from Thomas Malthus. But White's chapter offers a rich minihistory of antitrust and economists. He is old enough to care about these things.

If White had remained only in the academy and had not served at the Antitrust Division in a policy role, he might not fully realize how advanced economics has become inside the enforcement agencies. He might think that all the interesting work comes from the academy. And had White spent most of his time in government, he might not fully appreciate the role of what Keynes called "academic scribblers" in transforming antitrust.

On the whole, White's chapter is on target in selecting the three major contributions of antitrust: improvements in merger enforcement; a different understanding of vertical relationships between manufacturers and their downstream distributors; and a new way of assessing predatory pricing.

So what is there to criticize in a chapter whose author is optimally positioned and has drawn the right conclusions? Only a few items.

First, I think that economists who have toiled in the antitrust vineyard deserve more credit for the deregulation of surface transportation industries (rail and truck), the airline industry, and the market for financial services (notably banking and securities brokerage). There were lawyers and economists outside the antitrust community who contributed to deregulation, but several economists used the lens of antitrust to focus on the problems of regulation. It is the propensity of antitrust economics to peer into every nook and cranny of regulation and ask, "Could markets work better here?" that represents their contribution. It may well be that the accomplishment of antitrust economics in deregulation trumps what economics has brought to merger enforcement and vertical relationships.

Second, I think that economists deserve more credit than White gives for changing the penalty structure in antitrust. Fines, the economist's preferred means of deterrence, now are high enough for antitrust violations to get a chief financial officer's attention. Economics contributed to this.

Third, although White mentions the diminishing role of the Robinson-Patman Act, and although attorneys like H. Thomas Austern and F. M. Rowe deserve much of the credit for showing the flaws in the act, economists contributed to the process. One thinks particularly of M. A. Adelman here, but there were also others who explained that price discrimination generally is a manifestation of competition, not an obstacle to it.

Professor White's thesis is that antitrust economics and the work of economists have had a major effect on antitrust enforcement. One is left to wonder: how did all this happen? That is, why did the legal profession, which once had a lock on how antitrust is done, let the door open far enough so that when it comes to antitrust enforcement economists now often occupy front and center stage?

Anyone who knows anything about legal markets knows that the legal profession does not have a propensity or a reputation for ceding ground to outside sources of competition. Lawyers are quick to hop on anyone who appears to be "practicing law without a license," that is, offering competition for their legal services.

My question, how did this happen? is not idle curiosity. Anyone who looks at the world through the Tullock-Krueger lens of rent seeking must wonder: how could it be that some antitrust economists now make more money than many antitrust lawyers? Not only that, antitrust economists have more fun than many antitrust lawyers (for example, economists do not have to travel from city to city taking fact depositions). In addition, antitrust economists get to develop theories about how antitrust should be implemented; and antitrust economists, more than lawyers, get to pick the cases they work on and the issues they address.

The answer that would be congenial to antitrust economists is that the scholarship of antitrust economists has been so profound and so compelling that the agencies and the courts simply could not ignore the contributions of antitrust economists. This fits the old adage "ideas have consequences."

I think that there is some truth to this. But "ideas have consequences" is not an economic theory of how the world is shaped. No public choice economist would be satisfied with this explanation.

Let me offer two other hypotheses, more congenial to economic logic, why lawyers have ceded so much ground to economists in the field of antitrust (but not, so far as I can tell, in other areas of law where the imperialistic bent of economics has not been successful and lawyers continue to have a lock on how the job gets done).

First, not all heads of the Antitrust Division have been traditional antitrust lawyers. Several key players have been law professors. For them, the coin of the realm is different than taking a position with an established law firm after heading an agency. For professors, the coin of the realm involves idea generation and the building of an academic reputation.

So individuals like Donald Turner, Thomas Kauper, and William Baxter (I would put Donald Baker in this group as well, for his time at Cornell Law School) did not plan to enter the world of private practice when their time at the agencies came to an end. They planned to return to the academy, where their tenure in government would be judged by a different metric than the tenure of those who become partners in established law firms.

At the FTC, I would put Robert Pitofsky, James C. Miller, and William Kovacic in this same camp. They are scholars; they want their time in public service to be judged favorably by academic constituencies.

If my first hypothesis is correct, then antitrust economists should applaud those occasions when professors become heads of the agencies. White is spot-on for mentioning how Donald Turner, when he came to the Antitrust Division from Harvard Law School, brought with him into the front office a young economist, William Comanor, to advise him. From this taproot came a string of IO economists who served in this advisory capacity. George Hay, serving under Thomas Kauper, another professor who became assistant attorney general, genuinely transformed the role of economics in the Antitrust Division. Professor White's minihistory of the role of economists would have been very different if Turner and Kauper and Baxter had not been where they were and when.

Second, there is an economic complementarity between economists and lawyers, and antitrust lawyers have been willing to cede a place at the table because, if I can stretch the metaphor, the table has become much larger and more attractively burnished with economists in the room. White mentioned how every major antitrust case now has economists engaged. This has meant a lot to economists. It may mean even more, in the aggregate, to the antitrust bar.

For every pair of opposing economists who write expert reports on class certification, and for every pair who write reports on liability, and for every pair who write reports on damages, there are several lawyers gainfully employed deposing those economists, and lawyers must be involved in shepherding all these reports. And now the antitrust bar has *Daubert* challenges to further increase the demand for their services.

Professor White writes that in the early days economists were the "hewers of wood and haulers of water" for lawyers. In a remarkable revised sequence, lawyers have become the "hewers of wood and haulers of water" for economists. But the hewing and the hauling are well paid. As my former colleague James Buchanan once wrote about his professional life, "It's better than plowing."

Professor White's contribution to this volume is a commendable survey of the literature of antitrust, it is engagingly written, and it should be read by every junior economist who teaches IO or is employed by the FTC or the Antitrust Division or at a litigation consulting firm. I predict that this chapter will be read and cited often. But it will not come without professional peril for the author: meritorious as the chapter is, it also will annoy many antitrust economists who will believe that their particular work deserved more attention in White's chronicle.

CHAPTER ELEVEN

Economics and the All-Volunteer Military Force

Beth J. Asch, James C. Miller III, John T. Warner

An important case in the past half century where the "economic way of thinking" contributed to a major government policy change in the United States was the decision to terminate conscription as the means of staffing the bulk of the U.S. armed forces. After an acrimonious public debate that lasted five years, conscription was ended in 1973. Economists played an important role in the draft debates and in the decision to terminate it. Since then they have been important in the management of the all-volunteer force (AVF). Although their recommendations have not always been heeded, economists and the economic way of thinking they have advanced have helped shape effective military personnel.

The Role of Economics in Ending the Draft

From World War II until July 1973 the draft was a given for male youth in America. Economists said surprisingly little about the draft before the mid-1960s, but that changed with the escalation of the Vietnam War in 1966 and the public debate about it that ensued. Over the next five years economists produced a substantial volume of research on the draft and the feasibility of an AVF. Perhaps the major contributor to this effort was Walter Oi. As an economist working in the Department of Defense (DOD) in 1964, he authored an internal report that pointed to the feasibility of a volunteer force. Although this report was not made public, in subsequent publications Oi refined and expanded his original work (Oi 1967a, 1967b). Other works by economists included those of Stuart H. Altman and Alan E. Fechter (1967), W. Lee Hansen and Burton A. Weisbrod (1967), Anthony C. Fisher (1969), and Altman and Robert J. Barro (1971). In 1968 a group of University of Virginia graduate students wrote a remarkable collection of essays advocating a volunteer army (Miller 1968). This collection included essays by economists David Johnson, Matt Lindsay, Jim Miller, Mark Pauly, Robert Tollison, and Tom Willett, as well as political scientist Joe Scolnick.[1]

As well as contributing formal analyses, economists were participating in the political arena. One of these was Martin Anderson, then a faculty member at Columbia University and now at the Hoover Institution. Anderson broached the possibility of ending conscription to Richard Nixon during his presidential campaign.[2] Impressed by his arguments, Nixon advocated the end of conscription in a speech delivered on October 17, 1968. Some observers believe that this speech was the margin of difference in the 1968 presidential election. Once elected, President Nixon established the President's Commission on an All-Volunteer Armed Force (known as the Gates Commission after its chairman, Thomas Gates) to study the economic feasibility of an AVF. Milton Friedman, already known for his strong views on the draft (Friedman 1962, 1967), became one of the most influential members of the commission. Other prominent members included W. Allen Wallis, president of the University of Rochester, and future Federal Reserve chairman Alan Greenspan. The commission assembled an impressive research staff. William Meckling, dean of Rochester's School of Business, served as its executive director. Research directors included David Kassing, Walter Oi, and Harry Gilman; staff members included Robert Barro and John White, who later became deputy secretary of defense.

In November 1970 the Gates Commission unanimously recommended abolition of the draft and implementation of a volunteer force. At the time of the report, the Gates Commission's members and the economists working on the issue were in the minority; with few exceptions, members of Congress and persons in influential positions within the DOD—military and civilian—remained skeptical of the viability of a volunteer force.

Reasons for a Volunteer Force

Economists writing during the late 1960s used five arguments to conclude that a volunteer force would be more efficient than a draft force. The first was that the opportunity costs of the personnel constituting a volunteer force would always be less than or equal to the opportunity costs of the personnel serving in a mixed force of equal size. Opportunity costs of military personnel consist of their alternative wages plus their net nonpecuniary preferences for civilian life. Volunteers enter military service when the military wage exceeds their opportunity costs, but that is not true for conscripts. Indeed, individuals are conscripts precisely because the military wage does not meet their opportunity costs. There are several special cases in which the opportunity costs of a conscripted force equal the opportunity costs of a volunteer force,[3] but in a draft based on random selection from the pool of youth who meet military entrance standards, the opportunity costs of a conscripted force clearly exceed the opportunity costs of a volunteer force, at least when military service is not universal.

The second source of relative efficiency of a volunteer system derives from the fact that when conscription is imposed, individuals expend resources to evade conscription, and the state must expend resources to prevent evasion (Warner and Negrusa 2005). These costs are avoided in a purely volunteer system.

A third efficiency flows from the lower opportunity costs for volunteers in the aggregate: a volunteer force has higher retention, lower turnover, and consequently less annual demand for new personnel. To lower the burden of conscription, draftees have typically been required to serve for short periods (2 years during Vietnam). Volunteers serve longer terms (now about 4.5 years, on average) and reenlist at much higher rates. Longer initial tours increase the proportion of deployable, trained personnel in the force. The Gates Commission estimated that just reducing personnel in training would permit a 6% reduction in force size without a loss of readiness and would reduce per capita training costs. Moreover, experience growth in the volunteer force brought about by higher retention would further increase the differences in force effectiveness because, other things being equal, more experienced personnel are more productive. Force size differences are further accentuated by the increased complexity of military equipment.

Fourth, efficiency gains from a volunteer force arise from better incentives for personnel and for force managers. Because pay is low in a draft system, performance incentives must necessarily be negative: threats of court-martial, imprisonment, and bad-conduct discharge, all of which penalize personnel after they depart service. Volunteer systems, with positive performance incentives, are likely to produce better results.

Finally, the apparent cheapness of conscripts encourages substitution of conscripts for equipment, resulting in a socially inefficient mix of the two.

Once military equipment is in place, it tends to be used in fixed proportions to personnel. But the rise in the cost of junior enlisted personnel that accompanied the end of conscription has, over time, encouraged the development and adoption of equipment that requires fewer operators and is easier to operate and repair.

Although economists tend to focus on efficiency issues, the question of who should bear the burden of national defense occupied center stage in the U.S. debate about conscription during the 1960s. Advocates of conscription and advocates of a volunteer force had very different concepts of equity in the provision of a military force. In Europe the longtime view was that all citizens had a moral obligation to defend the state and that such obligations outweighed individual freedoms and rights within the state. Balancing the broad concepts of individual freedom and obligation to the state involves ethical judgments beyond the scope of economics. But economics does offer insights about the consequences of conscription and volunteerism for the distribution of income and for who pays for national defense.

Conscription promotes a less equal distribution of income and tends to place the burden of paying for national defense on lower-income groups. Benjamin Franklin recognized this point two centuries ago: "But if, as I suppose is often the case, the sailor who is pressed and obliged to serve for the defence of this trade at the rate of 25s. a month, could have £3.15s, in the merchant service, you take from him 50s. a month; if you have 100,000 in your service, you rob that honest part of society and their poor families of £250,000 per month, or three million per year."[4] Implicit in Franklin's statement is the regressive nature of the conscription tax. This tax is particularly regressive when conscription selects for service the same individuals who would have served in the volunteer system and thereby reduces the extent of direct (and probably progressive) taxation of the general populace.

The move in recent drafts to limit exemptions and deferments and to conscript by lottery derives from the regressivity of the draft tax. A lottery is not a panacea, however. Families with daughters, families without children, and recipients of capital income can avoid the conscription tax but not a general income tax. And although a lottery draft is more equitable ex ante than other forms of conscription, random assignation of a tax burden is not fair either, ex post. The ex post inequity obviously increases as the number to be drafted falls in relation to the number available for conscription. Advocates of conscription have proposed solving this inequity by requiring youth to participate in national service. Economists have unreservedly criticized such schemes.[5] Elimination of the conscription tax has forced more explicit consideration of the cost of military manpower in defense decision making and arguably in public decision making about military action.

Finally, Franklin's observation about the equity effects of the draft raises questions of public choice and the decisions of nations to use their forces. The Gates Commission devoted attention to the question whether a volunteer force would encourage military adventurism abroad (*Report of the President's Commission* 1970, chap. 12). The Gates Commission said no; analyses by Wagner (1972) and Tollison (1972) supported this conclusion. Wagner modeled the decisions of democracies to engage in military action and predicted that democracies with conscription are more likely to initiate military action because of a lower tax price for the median voter under conscription. Furthermore, his analysis indicated that they are more likely to continue military action when they experience adversity on the battlefield. Tollison (1972) reasoned that with the cost of conscription being borne much more by a small minority of voters, those in the majority are more likely to vote in favor of military action because they realize the benefits but bear less of the cost.

Reasons to Draft

For reasons given earlier, the social cost of an AVF tends to be lower than the social cost of conscription. Recent analysis has shown, however, that the analytical case for a volunteer force is not airtight. Work by Lee and McKenzie (1992), Ross (1994), Warner and Asch (1996), and Warner and Negrusa (2005) shows that a volunteer force does not always have lower social cost. When the military force size expands, the military wage bill increases, and the government must increase taxes today (or in the future if it borrows today) to pay the larger bill. But private-sector distortions or deadweight tax losses caused by federal taxation amount to around thirty to forty cents per dollar of federal revenue (Browning 1987). Deadweight losses rise at a faster rate under a volunteer force than under conscription because of faster payroll cost growth as force size increases (because pay must be increased under an AVF but not under a draft).[6] When the force size becomes large enough, it is possible for the excess deadweight tax loss of the AVF to swamp the other savings from it.[7]

At the time of the draft debate, officials inside the DOD and members of Congress expressed skepticism of the volunteer concept. One concern was force quality, which critics thought would decline under an AVF. Some thought that the volunteer force would attract lower-ability individuals than the military would be able to obtain through compulsion. Critics also worried that force quality would decline because of a lack of political support for an AVF. When confronted with competing demands for federal dollars, politicians would permit military pay to decline over time, forcing the armed services to reduce force size or lower entry standards. A third concern was that the higher personnel budget in the volunteer regime would crowd out military research and development and military hardware.

The threat of being drafted kept the nation's reserve forces well manned during the draft era because many youth subject to the draft joined the reserves. The risk of conscription also induced college students to join officer-training programs while in college. Critics worried that elimination of conscription would lead to deterioration of reserve forces and the officer corps.

Still another concern was the social representation of a volunteer force. Fear was expressed that minorities would become overrepresented in the volunteer force, and the armed forces would become less representative of society at large. Because minorities tend to score lower on the Armed Forces Qualification Test (AFQT), they would be concentrated in the warfighting skills such as infantry and would be more exposed to death or injury in wartime.

Finally, some observers supported conscription on public choice grounds, claiming (for example) that the United States would not have undertaken military action in Vietnam if a random draft had been in effect. The notion was that under a random draft with no deferments (or with the extreme of universal service), the perceived cost of military action, to both voters and politicians, would be higher with a draft than with an AVF because everyone's offspring would be at risk, not just the progeny of volunteers. Whether such intergenerational effects would outweigh the opposing effects analyzed by Wagner and Tollison is an open question.

The Final Decision to Terminate Conscription

The Gates Commission submitted its report to President Nixon on February 21, 1970. It recommended not only an increase in pay and an improvement in living conditions for military personnel but also a standby draft. This was important because the major vehicle for reform proved to be the need to extend the draft, which was set to expire on July 1, 1971.

Not all of Nixon's advisors were as sanguine about the feasibility of an AVF as the commission (Rostker 2006, 87–96). Secretary of Defense Melvin

Laird expressed misgivings about the will of Congress to come up with the necessary funds. General Lewis Hershey, the former Selective Service chief, who had been relieved of his position and reassigned as an advisor to the president on military manpower issues, used his influence to oppose any reduction in reliance on conscription. Members of Congress opposed the AVF for a variety of reasons. John J. Ford, staff director of the House Armed Services Committee at the time, said that "a substantial percentage of the members of Congress at that time were veterans of military service . . . They had lived with the Selective Service law in effect virtually all their adult life. They had a sense of the *moral rightness,* if you will, of service to your country, or at least being liable for such service. This feeling of moral rightness is probably also what informed proposals for universal military service that were advanced all through the time of the Selective Service System and continue to be offered in every Congress up to the present time" (Ford 2003; emphasis in original).

On April 23, 1970, President Nixon requested that Congress move toward an AVF while extending the draft. He rejected the timetable for ending the draft recommended by the Gates Commission but supported the goal. The House Armed Services Committee held hearings on the request and heard testimony from many individuals. According to Ford (2003), it was Walter Oi's testimony that finally swayed the committee: "Dr. Oi could not sell his one-year extension. But his candor, knowledge, and willingness to challenge DOD data undoubtedly helped the Committee members feel more comfortable with an all-volunteer approach" (5). The committee took recorded votes on various options. A motion to approve a bill embodying the Gates Commission's recommendation was defeated 28–7. A motion to extend the draft for four years was defeated 29–4. A motion for a one-year extension was defeated 30–9. The final vote on a two-year extension passed 32–4. Legislation to create an AVF, augmented by a standby draft, was signed on September 28, 1971.

Managing the Volunteer Force

The transition to the AVF was not easy. It was plagued by hostility within the army, the service most affected by the switch, and by the legacy of compensation and personnel systems that were geared toward managing a high-turnover force with little differentiation by skill. The era of the AVF can be divided into three distinct periods: (1) the early years, 1973–1980; (2) the Ronald Reagan years, 1981–1989; and (3) the years after the Cold War (1990 to the present).[8] Each period has had unique challenges.

During these periods economics has had a significant influence in shaping the policies that addressed the problems encountered and in how the transitions were managed.

The Early Years, 1973–1980

After estimating the pay raise required to implement an AVF, Oi (1967b) estimated that the AVF would lead to a 30% annual reduction in enlisted-force turnover. Oi's estimate implied an AVF turnover rate of 15%. As enlistment lengths and retention rates both increased in the early period, early AVF turnover fell from about 21% to 16%.[9] The quick improvement in retention and initial recruiting success led to much early euphoria about the AVF, but it was short lived. After the initial retention surge as volunteers replaced conscripts, retention began to decline in the late 1970s. The decline was most pronounced in the navy, where shortages of experienced personnel appeared in the navy's seagoing ratings. Subsequent research (Warner and Goldberg 1984) indicated that the retention decline was a result of a significant drop in relative military compensation due to a federal employee pay freeze that was imposed under the Jimmy Carter administration in an attempt to reduce a growing federal deficit.

Analysis by Gates Commission economists had indicated that the supply of new recruits and reenlistees was elastic: about 1.25 for enlistees (a 10% increase in military pay would result in a 12.5% increase in enlistments). The elasticity of first-term reenlistment was estimated to be even higher, around 2.0 to 3.0. Given these estimates, it is not surprising that the late 1970s were a bad time for the AVF. The experience of the late 1970s was a wake-up call for Congress and the DOD to be more vigilant about monitoring trends in the economy for signs of impending force-management difficulty.

The Reagan Years, 1981–1989

Predictably, the experience of the late 1970s provoked pronouncements of failure from AVF critics. The debate was resolved for the time being by Ronald Reagan's election as president in November 1980. Reagan was a strong proponent of the AVF and had pledged during the campaign to resolve the AVF's problems if he were elected. During the campaign Congress acted on the problems by decoupling the 1981 military and federal civilian pay raises, granting military personnel a 14% basic pay increase. The new administration backed another pay increase, and in January 1982 military basic pay was increased another 11%. Assisted by the recession of

1981–1982, recruiting and retention improved significantly because of these pay raises.

The Reagan years were characterized by a large standing military force whose purpose was to repel the Soviet threat to Western Europe. In meeting the overall quantity and quality goals of the 1980s, the AVF was an unqualified success. By the mid-1980s, however, the military compensation system had changed little since World War II. The AVF had inherited a common pay table for all personnel, little use of special and incentive pay, and a twenty-year retirement system that provided no benefits to personnel separating earlier. Interacting with this undifferentiated system was a long-term technological trend that was reducing the need for raw combat power and increasing the premium on skill.

Economists working for two presidential commissions, the 1976 Defense Manpower Commission and the 1978 President's Commission on Military Compensation (PCMC), had noted these issues. They recommended major changes to the compensation system, but the proposals were largely ignored because of resistance by the uniformed military. Consider first the issue of a common pay table. Military tradition was that everyone at the same rank and experience should receive the same pay regardless of occupation. A common pay table was believed to promote esprit de corps. This meant that many personnel ended up earning economic rents in the quest to attract marginal (supply-price) personnel into high-demand skills. Even by 2000 special and incentive pay never amounted to more than 5% of the basic pay budget.

The cost of the common-pay philosophy was aggravated by another unpleasant fact of life for the DOD. Although supply functions of military personnel were fairly elastic, they were not perfectly elastic. To attract more people into service or retain them in a skill, pay had to be raised. This meant that the military was in essence a monopsonist: the marginal cost of personnel was much higher than the average cost. Although much of this cost is a pure transfer from taxpayers to military personnel, it does mean that the DOD's personnel costs will expand at a very rapid rate in an attempt to attract and retain more personnel.

After the Cold War, 1990 to the Present

Downsizing. The fall of the Berlin wall in 1989 and the end of the Cold War raised an unexpected challenge—how to reduce the size of U.S. armed forces in the wake of reduced threats from the Soviet bloc. Planning for downsizing began in 1990. The target was a reduction in the active force from 2.1 million to 1.4 million persons. The Gulf War buildup and the war itself, lasting from August 1990 to March 1991, slowed the downsizing temporarily.

Military organizations are fed from the bottom—losses are replaced by young people who enter the lowest ranks with little prior work experience and then progress through the ranks on the basis of relative performance in a sequence of promotion tournaments (Rosen 1992; Asch and Warner 2001b). The main downsizing issue was how to reduce the size of an organization without lateral entry. Economists and economic thinking played a key role here.

The air force, with high retention, proposed to reduce its force by reducing accessions. The other services proposed to downsize through a combination of reduced accessions and reduced first-term reenlistment (which could be effected by a reduction in reenlistment bonuses). These proposals originated from the desire to keep faith with the more senior personnel who had been in service for a substantial period but who were not yet eligible for retirement. Involuntary layoffs of midcareer personnel would no doubt be seen as breaking the implicit contract that exists between the services and midcareerists that guaranteed a twenty-year career. In addition to being unfair to the group being involuntarily separated, such a break of faith would cause problems for future recruiting. On the other hand, a substantial reduction in the new entry flow would result in excessive experience growth in the short run and inability to staff the higher ranks in the long run.

Economists in the DOD, led by Christopher Jehn, the assistant secretary of defense for force management and personnel, designed a buyout program for midcareerists that induced a balanced force reduction brought about by voluntary separations. The program succeeded in producing the desired number of separations without excessive angst.[10] Although separatees were disappointed that their military careers ended prematurely, the downsizing proved that many of the assumed inflexibilities in the system could be addressed with better force-shaping tools.

Recruiting. Downsizing brought with it a reduction in the demand for new entrants from about 300,000 per year to about 180,000 per year. A key question for the DOD was whether supply shifted as the national security environment changed. Were youth less responsive to recruiting resources such as military pay and recruiters after the Cold War in the absence of the Soviet threat? Were they more responsive after September 11, 2001, and the emergence of a new threat? What was the effect of the Iraq War on enlistments? Similar questions emerged about retention. Were members less likely

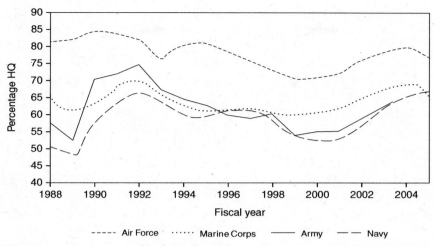

Figure 11.1 Percentage of high-quality enlistments, 1988–2005. *Source:* Percentages constructed by the authors from unpublished data provided by the Defense Manpower Data Center.

to stay in service as a result of more frequent, longer, and more dangerous deployments? Economic analysis informed answers to these questions.

The primary measure of recruiting success is the percentage of entrants who are "high quality." High-quality recruits possess a high-school degree and place in aptitude groups I–IIIA (AFQT of 50 or above). Figure 11.1 shows the percentage of high-quality recruits for the period 1988–2005. Research summarized in Asch, Hosek, and Warner (2007) has used post–Cold War data to provide econometric estimates of the recruiting effects of market factors (relative military pay and unemployment), demand as measured by recruiting goals, resource factors (recruiters and advertising), and enlistment incentives (bonuses and college-fund benefits). This research provides estimates of how factors affecting supply have shifted in the post–Cold War period and as a result of the Iraq War.

Research has found that high-quality enlistment is sensitive to the state of the civilian economy. This sensitivity is evident in Figure 11.1, where high-quality enlistment increased during the 1991–1993 recession period, declined in the 1995–1999 expansion, and increased sharply in the 2000–2003 recession. Estimates of the elasticity of high-quality recruiting with respect to unemployment range between 0.3 and 0.5, indicating a sizable responsiveness of military recruiting to the state of the business cycle.

One difference between studies with post–Cold War data and with earlier data is that the responsiveness of enlistment to military compensation does not appear to be as high. Recent estimates are in the range of 0.4 to 0.8, compared with the earlier 1.0–1.25 range. This change may be because a higher percentage of the youth population is enrolled in college today than before and during the Cold War.[11]

Figure 11.1 indicates that the high-quality percentage of recruits in the army began dropping in 2003, and the percentage in the Marine Corps started dropping in 2004. It is tempting to blame the Iraq War for those declines because the army and the Marine Corps have borne disproportionate casualties there. But part of the reason for the army's decline lies in management of the army's recruiter force. At the start of fiscal year 2002 the army had about 6,100 recruiters. For various reasons the army reduced its recruiter force, which fell steadily for the next seven quarters and bottomed out at 4,400 recruiters in the last quarter of fiscal year 2004. The army restored about two-thirds of this reduction in fiscal year 2005 (from 4,400 to 5,500).

Research with data from the period after the Cold War but before the Iraq War has also identified a downward trend in high-quality enlistment supply that seems caused by several adverse trends for the DOD. One of these is the rise in college attendance. The fraction of the population aged eighteen to twenty-four enrolled in college rose substantially after the Cold War and is now at about 69% of that population, the prime age range for military recruiting. If high-quality enlistments come only from the noncollege population, a rise in college attendance among those qualified for service from 69% to 74% would reduce the high-quality noncollege population by almost 170,000 and high-quality enlistments by 13,000 (about 7.5%).

Other trends have also been at work. According to Gilroy (2006), an astounding three-quarters of youth fail to meet minimum military entrance standards. Over half of those who fail to meet the standards do so for medical and physical reasons, and the percentage of youth failing to qualify for medical and physical reasons has been on the rise. Finally, Simon and Warner (2007), after controlling for other factors, estimate that the Iraq War has reduced Army high-quality enlistments by one-third.

Is There a Case for a Return to Conscription?

Despite the overall success of the AVF, some advocate a return to the draft. Interestingly, some recent calls for conscription are coming not from uniformed personnel but from elected officials. These calls for conscription seem motivated by (1) a belief that the U.S. armed forces are mercenary forces that are unrepresentative of American society, (2) an interest in reducing the budgetary costs of military manpower, and (3) opposition to the war in Iraq. We briefly address these concerns.

On the first issue, recruits have not been disproportionately drawn from minority groups. Furthermore, recruits do not come only from the lowest income classes. Data on the family incomes of military recruits do not exist, but some perspective on recruiting by income class can be had by looking at the distribution of recruiting by median family income in recruits' home zip codes. Using data from 1988 to 2000, Simon and Warner (2007) found that 60% of enlisted recruits came from families who resided in zip codes with median family incomes in the bottom half of the zip-code distribution of median family incomes. But this means that around 40% came from families living in the upper half of the zip-code distribution of median family incomes.

On the second issue, conscription is attractive to some members of Congress because the savings in military personnel costs could be directed to other uses. In part, the new interest in budgetary costs is driven by recent policies to increase the sizes of both the army and the Marine Corps. But this assumption of budgetary savings is based on faulty reasoning. Aside from the fact that the real cost of a mixed force is almost certain to be higher than the real cost of an AVF, the budgetary savings would likely be quite modest. Since 1973 defense manpower costs have fallen as a percentage of the DOD budget and as a percentage of gross domestic product (GDP) and are now about 27% of the DOD budget and 0.8% of GDP, respectively (Table 2 of Warner and Asch, 2001). A return to force levels of the Cold War era would raise military personnel costs to at most 2% of GDP, the level that prevailed in 1975.

More important, any simple calculation of savings based on multiplying the difference between volunteer pay and conscript pay by the number of personnel in uniform would be a gross exaggeration. First, it is highly unlikely that conscripts would be required to serve longer than two years. As described earlier, this would require substantial increases in training costs, in part because draftees are far less likely to reenlist.

Simon and Warner (2007) posed a hypothetical 100,000-person increase in the number of army enlisted personnel and calculated the actual budgetary savings, depending on whether volunteer enlistments turned out to be relatively strong or weak. The important conclusion from this work is that the annual budgetary savings from these realistic scenarios amount to only a few billion dollars (see Table 11.1). Such budgetary reductions and the reduction in tax distortions derived from them would not be sufficient to offset the real social cost reductions and productivity gains from an expanded volunteer force.

The third motivation for the interest of some members of Congress in reimposing conscription is opposition to the war in Iraq. In simple terms, they wish to increase the cost of the war and thereby reduce the support it garners. There are two aspects to this rationale. The first is the straightforward increase-cost-reduce-demand notion economists know so well. The second is more subtle, and that is to take advantage of the distribution of costs under conscription—and how this would work its way through the decision-making process.

Of the two, the distribution effect is probably the more important. As described earlier, the budgetary savings of conscription would be more than offset by increased costs elsewhere—the implicit tax on reluctant recruits, the diminution in performance, and the costs of employing the draft and maintaining a reasonable degree of compliance. But to judge by the rhetoric from conscription supporters such as Congressman Charles Rangel, a Democrat from New York, they believe that putting more sons and grandsons of members of Congress at risk would cool members' ardor for the war. The same argument obtains for the less direct means of putting the sons and grandsons of members' supporters at risk.

Concluding Remarks

Economists and the economic way of thinking were key in bringing about the end of the draft, in orchestrating the transition to the AVF, and in managing military personnel efficiently. Superb analysis by economists such as Hansen, Oi, and Weisbrod, forceful articulation of the case for the AVF by economists such as Friedman and Anderson, courageous leadership by DOD economists, and exemplary work by a legion of labor economists in academic institutions, research firms, and think tanks have cemented support for the institution. What is surprising is not that there are voices for a return to conscription, but that they are so muted, despite widespread disaffection with the war in Iraq.

But the elimination of the military draft and the advent of the AVF are yet another example of policy reforms that were adopted not only because the economic arguments and evidence were persuasive, but also because of the presence of significant angst among members of the public and their elected leaders. Had it not been for the controversy over the war in Vietnam, with demonstrations led by young men most at risk for being drafted, it is doubtful that the AVF would have come about.

Notes

1. Milton Friedman and John Kenneth Galbraith both endorsed the book and its conclusions; this was perhaps the only public policy issue about which they ever agreed.
2. Anderson (2004) recounts these events.
3. Warner and Asch (2001) show that a least-value-drafted-first (LDVF) system, such as prevailed in World War I, results in approximately the same people serving who would serve in a volunteer system. The same people also serve when draftees are allowed to buy their way out of service by hiring substitutes or paying a commutation fee to the government, as happened on both sides during the Civil War.
4. Quotation from *Report of the President's Commission* (1970, 23–24); the original source is not provided.
5. Milton Friedman and Congressman Pete McCloskey engaged in a heated debate about national service that is documented in Anderson (1982).
6. The rate of payroll cost growth varies inversely with the elasticity of supply of military personnel because the less elastic supply is, the more pay needs to be raised to reach a given desired force size.
7. Friedman (1967, 202–203) recognized this point when he wrote, "And to rely on volunteers under such conditions would then require very high pay in the armed services . . . It might turn out that the implicit tax of forced service is less bad than the alternative taxes that would be used to finance a volunteer army."
8. Interested readers are referred to Rostker (2006) for a detailed account of these periods. The U.S. DOD has sponsored three conferences to celebrate the three decades of the volunteer force. The conference volumes provide interesting and varied perspectives on the evolution of the AVF. See Bowman, Little and Sicilia (1986), Fredland et al. (1996), and Bicksler, Gilroy, and Warner (2004).
9. Annual enlisted turnover since the 1980s has averaged around 15%.
10. Mehay and Hogan (1998) and Asch and Warner (2001a) estimated the separation effects of the downsizing programs, and Warner and Pleeter (2001) derived estimates of personal discount rates from the choice between the lump sum and the annuity offered by the program.
11. According to data from the National Center for Educational Statistics, 58% of individuals graduating from high school in 1988 enrolled in college within the next twelve months. By 1996 that percentage had risen to 67%. It dropped to 62% in 2001–2003 but climbed back to 67% in 2004.

References

Altman, S., and R. Barro (1971). Officer supply—The impact of pay, the draft, and the Vietnam War. *American Economic Review* 61(4): 649–664.

Altman, S., and A. Fechter (1967). The supply of military personnel in the absence of a draft. *American Economic Review* 57(2): 19–31.

Anderson, M. (1982). *Registration and the Draft*. Stanford, Calif.: Hoover Institution Press.

Anderson, M. (2004). The making of the volunteer force. In B. Bicksler, C. Gilroy, and J. Warner, eds., *The All-Volunteer Force: Thirty Years of Service*. Washington, D.C.: Brassey's.

Asch, B., J. Hosek, and J. Warner (2007). The economics of military manpower in the post–Cold War era. In K. Hartley and T. Sandler, eds., *Handbook of Defense Economics*, vol. 2. Amsterdam: Elsevier: 1076–1118.

Asch, B., and J. Warner (2001a). *An Examination of the Effects of Voluntary Separation on Incentives*. Santa Monica, Calif.: Rand.

——— (2001b). A theory of compensation and personnel policy in hierarchical organizations with application to the U.S. military. *Journal of Labor Economics* 19: 523–562.

Bicksler, B., C. Gilroy, and J. Warner, eds. (2004). *The All-Volunteer Force: Thirty Years of Service*. Washington, D.C.: Brassey's.

Bowman, W., R. Little, and T. Sicilia (1986). *The All-Volunteer Force after a Decade: Retrospect and Prospect*. Washington, D.C.: Pergamon-Brassey's.

Browning, E. (1987). On the marginal welfare cost of taxation. *American Economic Review* 77(1): 11–23.

Fisher, A. (1969). The cost of the draft and the cost of ending the draft. *American Economic Review* 59(3): 239–254.

Ford, J. (2003). Looking back on the termination of the draft. Unpublished manuscript available from John Warner.

Fredland, J. E., C. Gilroy, R. Little, and W. S. Sellman, eds. (1996). *Professionals on the Front Line: Two Decades of the All-Volunteer Force*. Washington, D.C.: Brassey's.

Friedman, M. (1962). *Capitalism and Freedom*. Chicago: University of Chicago Press.

——— (1967). Why not a volunteer army? In Sol Tax, ed., *The Draft*. Chicago: University of Chicago Press, 200–207.

Gilroy, C. (2006). Recruiting an all-volunteer Force: What does enlistment supply look like? Briefing, Office of the Undersecretary of Defense (Personnel and Readiness), Washington, D.C., November 2.

Hansen, W. L., and B. A. Weisbrod (1967). Economics of a military draft. *Quarterly Journal of Economics* 81(3): 395–421.

Lee, D., and R. McKenzie (1992). A reexamination of the relative efficiency of the draft and the all-volunteer army. *Southern Economic Journal* 59: 646–654.

Mehay, S., and P. Hogan (1998). The effects of bonuses on voluntary quits: Evidence from the military's downsizing. *Southern Economic Journal* 65: 127–139.

Miller, J. (1968). *Why the Draft? The Case for a Volunteer Army*. Baltimore: Penguin Books.

Oi, Walter Y. (1967a). The costs and implications of an all-volunteer force. In Sol Tax, ed., *The Draft*. Chicago: University of Chicago Press, 221–251.

——— (1967b). The economic cost of the draft. *American Economic Review* 57(2): 39–62.

Report of the President's Commission on an All-Volunteer Armed Force (1970). London: Macmillan.

Rosen, S. (1992). The military as an internal labor market: Some allocation, productivity, and incentive problems. *Social Science Quarterly* 73(2): 227–237.

Ross, T. (1994). Raising an army: A positive theory of military recruitment. *Journal of Law & Economics* 37(1): 101–131.

Rostker, B. (2006). *I Want You! The Evolution of the All-Volunteer Force* Santa Monica, Calif.: Rand.

Simon, C., and J. Warner (2007). Managing the all-volunteer force in a time of war. *Economics of Peace and Security Journal* 2(1): 20–29.

Tollison, R. (1972). The political economy of the military draft. In J. Buchanan and R. Tollison, eds., *Theory of Public Choice: Political Applications of Economics*. Ann Arbor: University of Michigan Press, 302–316. [Reprinted from *Public Choice*, September 1970.]

Wagner, R. (1972). Conscription, voluntary service, and democratic fiscal choice. In J. Buchanan and R. Tollison, eds., *Theory of Public Choice: Political Applications of Economics*. Ann Arbor: University of Michigan Press, 136–152.

Warner, J., and M. Goldberg (1984). The influence of nonpecuniary factors on labor supply: The case of navy enlisted personnel. *Review of Economics and Statistics* 66(1): 26–35.

——— (1996). The economic theory of a military draft reconsidered. *Defence and Peace Economics* 7: 297–311.

——— (2001). The record and prospects of the all-volunteer military in the United States. *Journal of Economic Perspectives* 15 (Spring): 169–192.

Warner, J., and S. Negrusa (2005). Evasion costs and the theory of conscription. *Defence and Peace Economics* 16: 83–100.

Warner, J., and S. Pleeter (2001). The personal discount rate: Evidence from military downsizing programs. *American Economic Review* 91(1): 33–53.

COMMENT

Walter Y. Oi

A Free Society

"Freedom of action is granted to the individual not because it gives him greater satisfaction but if allowed to go on his own way, he will on the average serve the rest of us better than under any order that we know how to give."[1] The U.S. Army has historically embraced this autonomy principle except in times of major wars, when Congress turned to coercion.

The Conscription Tax

"The draft survives principally as a device by which we use compulsion to get young men to serve at less than the market rate of pay."[2] The draft places a conscription tax on those who are forced to serve, the difference between the rate of military pay and the opportunity cost of foregone civilian wages. In addition to this tax placed on those who are actually conscripted, men with a draft liability often incur costs to evade the draft: for example, becoming a father, staying in college, or moving to England. Larry Sjaastad and Ronald Hansen argue that evasion generates a huge cost of collecting the conscription tax, and that this cost could be avoided by ending conscription.[3] The use of cheap conscript labor results in adopting inefficient ways of producing defense.

The British Experience

The end of the Korean War and placing greater reliance on nuclear weapons led to a reduction in the size of the army. A 1956 study on the employment of National Service men (conscripts) found that man for man a civilian was more productive; three civilians could do the work of five National Service men. Further, 21.5% of National Service men were occupied in training. A member of the House of Commons said, "If anyone had suggested that conscription could be used to fight colonial wars, he would not have lasted five minutes."[4] The inefficiency of a mixed force of regulars and conscripts and the nature of the conflict in Vietnam contributed to the British decision to abolish the draft in 1956.[5]

The Lottery

Public support for Vietnam was fading. College students were demonstrating, burning draft cards, and shouting, "Hell No! We won't go." Lyndon Johnson appointed a presidential commission headed by Burke Marshall to reform the draft. Its report, *In Pursuit of Equity: Who Serves When Not All Serve,* was released in 1967. It recommended a lottery of nineteen-year-olds. The lottery allegedly achieved equity because everyone faced the same odds of being drafted. This is bad economics. The British said, "A system where losers serve 24 months, and others do none was not felt to be satisfactory."[6] Economics teaches us that the cost of risk bearing can vary across individuals. Risk-averse individuals buy insurance and pay a price to avoid risk. A lottery is inequitable because it does not equalize the cost of risk bearing. In the summer of 1969 the Richard Nixon administration forgot about the cost of risk bearing and introduced a lottery, which probably raised the cost of conscription.

The Gates Commission

In the 1968 campaign Richard Nixon promised that if elected, he would work to end the draft.[7] The transition team of Martin Anderson and Arthur Burns recommended the appointment of a presidential commission to be chaired by a former secretary of defense, Thomas S. Gates. The members of the Gates Commission agreed that the draft placed a large economic cost on young men that could be avoided by abolishing the draft. The report of the commission was prepared by its executive director, William H. Meckling, and was delivered to President Nixon in the Cabinet Room.[8]

The economists had done their work. They identified the unnecessary cost of conscription, estimated the supply curve of recruits to an all-volunteer force (AVF), and recommended raising entry-level pay. The next step was persuading Congress. The forty-one members of the House Armed Services Committee held Hearings in late February 1971. They were the first to act on the Gates Commission's recommendation to end the draft when the current draft authority expired on June 30, 1971. The members of the House Armed Services Committee had lived with a draft for most of their adult lives. Many believed that a draft and the threat of being drafted were needed to get recruits. John J. Ford observed, "They [the committee] had a sense of the moral rightness, if you will, of service to your country, or at least being liable for such service."[9] Walter Oi was the only member of the Gates Commission's staff to testify. He disagreed with the commission's recommendation for an immediate termination of the draft and argued for a one-year extension to smooth the transition to the AVF. Oi did not get his one-year extension, but his candor and questioning the DOD data made the committee a little more comfortable about the all-volunteer approach. The peacetime draft that had prevailed for over a quarter of a century was terminated on June 30, 1973.

Defense Economics

John Warner, James Miller, and Beth Asch advance the proposition that economics and the economic way of thinking played an important role in the decision to end conscription.[10] They are major contributors to the growing field of defense economics, which was started by Charles Hitch and Roland McKean.[11] The studies prepared by economists not only demonstrated the feasibility of an AVF but also contributed to policies to improve the efficiency of our regular and reserve forces. On the thirtieth anniversary of the AVF, Ford said that the success of the AVF was an amazing story thanks to the efforts of our military and political leaders and the writings of people like Beth Asch, James Hosek, and John Warner[12] and Bernard Rostker.[13]

Notes

1. H. B. Phillips, "On the Nature of Progress," *American Scientist* vol. 33 (1945), 255.

2. John Kenneth Galbraith, cited by Richard Gillam in *The Military Draft,* ed. Martin Anderson (Stanford, Calif: Hoover Institution Press, 1982), 113.

3. Larry A. Sjaastad and Ronald W. Hansen, "The Conscription Tax: An Empirical Analysis," in *Supplemental Studies for the Gates Commission,* vol. 2, Study 1 (Washington, D.C.: GPO, November 1970).

4. Patricia M. Flanary, "The British Decision to Abolish Peacetime Conscription," Supplemental Study 3.3 for the Gates Commission (Washington, D.C.: GPO, November 1970).

5. Ibid.

6. Ibid.

7. Richard M. Nixon, "The All-Volunteer Armed Force," in *The Military Draft,* ed. Martin Anderson (Stanford, Calif.: Hoover Institution Press, 1982), 603–609.

8. *The Report of the President's Commission on an All-Volunteer Armed Force* (Washington, D.C.: GPO, February 1970).

9. Ford, J. (2003). Looking back on the termination of the draft. Unpublished manuscript available from John Warner.

10. Beth J. Asch, James C. Miller III, and John T. Warner, chapter 11 in this volume.

11. Charles J. Hitch and Roland N. McKean, *The Economics of Defense in the Nuclear Age* (Cambridge, Mass.: Harvard University Press, 1960).

12. Beth J. Asch, James R. Hosek, and John T. Warner, The economics of military manpower in the post–Cold War era, in K. Hartley and T. Sandler, eds., *Handbook of Defense Economics,* vol. 2. Amsterdam: Elsevier, 1076–1118.

13. Bernard Rostker, *I Want You! The Evolution of the All-Volunteer Force* (Santa Monica, Calif.: Rand Corporation, 2006)

CHAPTER TWELVE

Public Policy and Saving for Retirement: The Autosave Features of the Pension Protection Act of 2006

John Beshears, James Choi, David Laibson, Brigitte C. Madrian, Brian Weller

On August 17, 2006, President George W. Bush signed the Pension Protection Act of 2006 (PPA) into law, following its passage by both houses of Congress in a strong showing of bipartisan support.[1] This law, probably the most sweeping piece of pension reform legislation since the Employee Retirement Income and Security Act of 1974 (ERISA), contains many pension reform provisions.[2] In this chapter we focus on a subset of measures within the PPA adopted specifically to promote better savings outcomes in defined-contribution savings plans.

The push for these provisions came in response to a growing body of economic research showing, first, that many individuals are not saving enough for retirement (despite a stated desire to save more), and second, that many individuals are largely passive in their retirement savings behavior. The "autosave" features encouraged in the PPA aim to harness the power of inertia to increase employee savings—if employees do nothing, the result will be that they are saving rather than that they are not. This chapter first summarizes the autosave features of the PPA, then describes the economic research that motivates them, and finally discusses how this research was translated into policy.

The Autosave Features of the Pension Protection Act

The PPA promotes employers' adoption of some or all of the following autosave features in their defined-contribution savings plans:

- Automatic enrollment—employees are automatically enrolled in the savings plan at a default contribution rate and default asset allocation unless they explicitly choose to opt out.
- Employer contribution—the employer makes a contribution to employee accounts, either on a noncontingent basis (independent of whether employees contribute anything) or as a match of employee contributions.
- Contribution escalation—participant contributions to the savings plan automatically increase over time.
- Qualified default investment alternative (QDIA)—contributions are defaulted into a diversified portfolio that includes exposure to both equity and fixed-income assets.

Encouragement for employers to incorporate these features into their savings plans comes in several forms. Although many employers recognized the potential benefit to employees of autopilot savings plans well before the PPA, some were reluctant to adopt these features because of various legal concerns. The PPA eliminated the legal underbrush on which many employer objections had rested.

One legal issue was an employer's potential liability for investment losses in the default fund under automatic enrollment. Section 404(c) of ERISA affords employers relief from legal liability for losses resulting when participants in employer-sponsored savings plans direct the asset allocation of their investments themselves. The PPA extends this protection to default investments under automatic enrollment (and in other circumstances when participants fail to make an explicit asset allocation election) if these defaults satisfy certain requirements, including exposure to more than one asset class.[3]

Finally, plans that adopt automatic enrollment with automatic contribution escalation[4] and a sufficiently generous employer contribution[5] are exempted from annual nondiscrimination testing. The nondiscrimination tests are regulations designed to ensure that the tax benefits of savings-plan participation do not accrue disproportionately to "highly compensated" employees. To pass the nondiscrimination tests, firms must demonstrate that the participation and savings rates of employees with compensation below the "highly compensated" income limit are sufficiently high relative to employees whose incomes are above the threshold.[6] Demonstrating compliance is costly to employers, and there are additional costs associated with restructuring savings plans to achieve compliance if a firm would not otherwise pass. If employers adopt conforming autosave features, they are exempt from having to demonstrate compliance. More generally, the exemption sends a signal to firms about what the Internal Revenue Service (IRS) and the Department of Labor (DOL), which jointly regulate employee benefit plans, deem acceptable and encouraged plan design features.

The Economic Research behind the Autosave Features of the Pension Protection Act

Understanding the significance of these PPA provisions requires some historical context. Until the 1970s most employers who provided retirement-income benefits for their workers did so through traditional defined-benefit pension plans. In 1975 there were 2.4 participants in defined-benefit pension plans for every 1 participant in a defined-contribution plan (Department of Labor 2007). In the 1980s, however, the pension landscape began to change because of a series of new laws and regulations starting with the 1974 passage of ERISA. This act made it more costly for employers to offer traditional defined-benefit pension plans to their workers. ERISA was followed by the addition of section 401(k) to the Internal Revenue Code in 1978. In 1981 an IRS clarification of the definition of taxable income allowed employers to exempt contributions to 401(k) savings plans from taxable income.

Although the 1978 legislation and the 1981 clarification were not intended to transform the U.S. pension landscape, this is in fact what ensued. Section 401(k) gave firms a tax-favored option for providing retirement-income benefits at a lower regulatory cost than that of traditional defined-benefit pensions in the post-ERISA environment. The 401(k) plan, originally intended as a supplemental savings vehicle, caused a complete upheaval in the employer-provided pension-plan system. By the mid-1980s both the number of defined-benefit pension plans and the number of participants in these plans had started a steady (and ongoing) decline. Defined-contribution savings plans—principally the 401(k) and its close cousins, the 403(b) and 457 plans—filled the breach. In 2006 the latest year for which data are available, defined-contribution participants outnumbered defined-benefit participants by a ratio of 3.3 to 1, a complete reversal of the situation thirty years earlier (Department of Labor 2008).

Employers initially adopted a "field of dreams" approach to defined-contribution savings plans in this new era: if we offer it, they will save. The initial philosophy was that individuals know what savings outcomes are in their best interest and will achieve these outcomes through their savings-plan choices. The hallmark of this first generation of defined-contribution savings plans was choice: individuals chose whether or not to participate, how much to save, and how to allocate their assets.

The foundations underlying this presumption began to crumble as research uncovered how poorly employees were actually using defined-contribution savings plans. In a series of surveys conducted periodically from 1991 to 2004, John Hancock Financial Services documented a striking lack of financial knowledge among defined-contribution-plan participants. In the most recent published version of this survey, 38% of respondents claimed that they had little or no investment knowledge, and two-thirds reported that they would be better off working with a financial advisor than managing their retirement investments on their own (John Hancock Financial Services 2002). This self-perceived lack of expertise is corroborated by more objective measures of financial knowledge (Lusardi and Mitchell 2006; Choi, Laibson, and Madrian 2007).

Financial ignorance need not be a problem if individuals can obtain reliable advice from those who are more knowledgeable and then can expeditiously implement that advice. In the age of defined-benefit pension plans, employers filled the role of a (paternalistic) retirement-savings advisor. Employers performed the complicated calculations required to determine how much money to set aside today to achieve the wealth needed to maintain consumption in retirement; employers contributed this amount to the pension plan without any active intervention by employees; and employers were responsible for managing the pension plan's asset allocation. All these tasks were done with the help of financial professionals. But in the transition from defined-benefit to defined-contribution savings plans, many employers stepped out of this paternalistic role.

Strong evidence of the poor personal financial management that ensued comes from research on savings outcomes under automatic enrollment (Madrian and Shea 2001; Choi et al. 2002, 2004, 2006; Beshears et al. 2008). Most defined-contribution savings plans have historically required employees to enroll proactively in order to initiate participation. As part of the enrollment process, employees choose a contribution rate and an asset allocation. In contrast, under automatic enrollment, employees are enrolled in the plan at a contribution rate and asset allocation prespecified by the employer unless they either explicitly opt out of participation or choose a different contribution rate and/or asset allocation. Automatic enrollment does not alter the set of options available to employees. It simply replaces one default (nonparticipation) with another (participation at a particular contribution rate and asset allocation). But this seemingly small procedural change generates significant differences in savings outcomes.

Figure 12.1 shows the relationship between employee tenure (the x-axis) and savings-plan participation rates (the y-axis) at a large chemicals firm for three groups of employees: those hired before automatic enrollment was introduced, those hired under automatic enrollment with a default contribution rate of 3% of pay, and those hired under automatic enrollment with a default contribution rate of 6% of pay. There is a large difference in participation rates between those hired before and those hired after automatic enrollment. Participation rates before automatic enrollment start below 50% for newly hired employees and gradually increase to about 75% for those with more than two years of tenure. In contrast, participation rates for employees hired after automatic enrollment exceed 90% once employees who do not opt out have been swept into the savings plan in their third month of employment. The participation rate under automatic enrollment does not appear to depend on whether the default contribution rate is 3% or 6%.

These differences are particularly surprising given the low costs of implementing a change in participation status. In survey responses employees in companies without automatic enrollment who have signed up for their

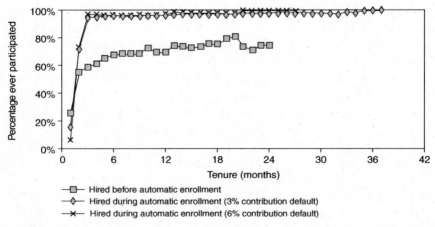

Figure 12.1 Automatic enrollment for new hires and savings-plan participation, company A. *Source:* Beshears et al. (2008); by permission of Oxford University Press.

employer's savings plan report that doing so took about an hour and a half; employees who have not signed up estimate that it would take them a similar amount of time to do so (Choi, Laibson, and Madrian 2007). These time costs are modest compared with the substantial financial consequences of participation, the largest of which is the employer matching contribution (for example, the company in Figure 12.1 offers a dollar-for-dollar match on employee contributions up to 6% of pay). Other benefits include favorable tax treatment and higher future consumption (which must be weighed against the cost of decreased current consumption).

It is not clear which of the tenure-participation profiles in Figure 12.1 most closely reflects the true savings preferences of employees. Other evidence, however, leads us to the conclusion that most employees prefer to be saving early in their tenure. First, the opt-out rate under automatic enrollment is low (Madrian and Shea 2001; Choi et al. 2002, 2006). Most of those who opt out do so almost immediately; few employees who are automatically enrolled decide later that they would rather not be contributing to the savings plan. In contrast, when the default is nonparticipation, the rate at which employees opt into savings-plan participation is initially high and persistently positive, even after several years. Second, when employees are required to make an active in-or-out savings-plan participation decision, around 70% of employees choose to join the plan (Carroll et al. 2007). In addition, when asked, most employees state a preference to save more than they currently are (Bernheim 1995; Farkas and Johnson 1997; Choi et al. 2002, 2006; Thaler and Benartzi 2004). Finally, a 2007 Harris Interactive poll finds that 98% of plan participants who were enrolled under automatic enrollment and did not opt out agree with the statement "You are glad your company offers automatic enrollment." More surprisingly, 79% of the employees who did opt out of the savings plan also agree. These various pieces of evidence suggest that most employees prefer to be participating in their employer-sponsored savings plan and that automatic enrollment is a useful mechanism for expediting enrollment. Hence there is a strong rationale for encouraging employer adoption of automatic enrollment through the PPA.

Automatic enrollment affects not only participation status but also contribution rates and asset allocation. Figure 12.2 shows the distribution of contribution rates for participants at a large food company before automatic enrollment, under automatic enrollment with a 3% default contribution rate, and under automatic enrollment with a 4% default contribution rate.[7] Like the company shown in Figure 12.1, this company provides a match on employee contributions up to 6% of pay. Before automatic enrollment, 84% of participants elected to contribute at or above the 6%

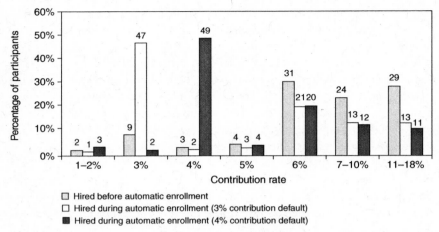

Figure 12.2 Distribution of 401(k) contribution rates for employees aged forty or more at hire, company D. *Source:* Choi et al. (2006); reprinted with permission.

match threshold, and very few had a contribution rate of 3% or 4%. Automatic enrollment dramatically shifts the distribution of contribution rates. When the default contribution rate is 3%, almost half the participants have a 3% contribution rate; when the default contribution rate is 4%, almost half have a 4% contribution rate. Under both automatic enrollment regimes, less than half of participants contribute at or above the match threshold—substantially fewer than the 84% at or above the threshold before automatic enrollment. The distribution of asset allocations, not shown in Figure 12.2 exhibits a similarly large shift toward the default asset allocation.

The default effect not only is large initially but persists for a long time. Figure 12.3 shows the relationship between tenure and the probability of simultaneously retaining both the default asset allocation and the default contribution rate at four companies with automatic enrollment. The percentage of participants at these defaults is initially very high but declines with tenure as participants begin to elect their own contribution rates and asset allocations. Despite this decline, a large fraction of participants remains at the default even at high levels of tenure (e.g., over three years). The default asset allocation, not shown in Figure 12.3, is slightly more persistent than the default contribution rate.

Figure 12.3 understates the persistence of the default asset allocation in one important dimension. Even when automatically enrolled participants trade out of the default fund, their new asset allocation tends to be closer to the default than the asset allocations chosen by participants who were hired before automatic enrollment (Madrian and Shea 2001; Beshears et al. 2008). The reason for this persistence may be that employees perceive the default as having been implicitly endorsed by the employer. This endorsement effect also appears after a company adopts automatic enrollment, in the form of higher allocations to the default fund among participants who were not themselves subject to automatic enrollment (because they were hired before automatic enrollment was implemented).[8]

Of course, the outcome that matters most is asset accumulation, which depends on all the variables discussed earlier: participation, contribution rates, and asset allocation. Here automatic enrollment can be a two-edged sword. Automatic enrollment clearly increases asset accumulation (at least within the savings plan) for employees who would not have participated otherwise, but how does it affect asset accumulation for employees who would have participated anyway? The answer to this question hinges critically on how the default compares to what employees would have chosen in the absence of automatic enrollment.

Choi et al. (2004) show that for some employees who would have participated in the absence of automatic enrollment, there is no effect on asset accumulation: these employees opt out of the automatic enrollment defaults early on and choose the same contribution rate and asset allocation that they would have chosen without automatic enrollment. But other employees are heavily influenced by the automatic enrollment defaults.

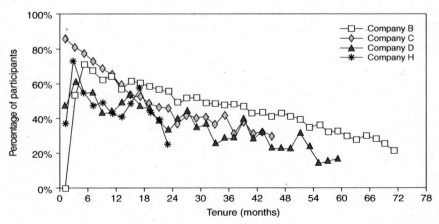

Figure 12.3 Percentage of participants hired during automatic enrollment who retain the automatic enrollment defaults. *Source:* Choi et al. (2006); reprinted with permission.

Automatic enrollment raises the contribution rates of the left tail of the savings distribution; those who would save nothing are induced to participate. But in the absence of automatic enrollment, many employees would have eventually enrolled at a contribution rate that is at or above the match threshold and with an asset allocation that is likely to contain substantial equity exposure. If the default contribution rate is below what employees would have chosen without automatic enrollment, and if the default asset allocation has a lower expected return than the asset allocation that employees would have chosen on their own, then the resulting low contribution rates and expected asset returns may outweigh the acceleration of participation under automatic enrollment, depressing the rate of asset accumulation.[9] In the long term these employees may actually be worse off as a result of automatic enrollment.

Whether automatic enrollment reduces asset accumulation depends on the defaults adopted by employers. Many employers have historically chosen defaults—low contribution rates and conservative default funds—that could work against long-term asset accumulation. This possibility provides the rationale for two of the other key autosave components of PPA: the adoption of contribution escalation as part of the safe harbor from nondiscrimination testing and the qualified default investment alternative (QDIA) guidelines.

Although the PPA exemption from nondiscrimination testing allows for a fixed default contribution rate of 6% or higher, the baseline specified in the legislation is automatic enrollment with a lower initial default contribution rate of 3% in conjunction with contribution escalation—specifically, automatic annual contribution rate increases of 1% continuing until participants have reached at least a 6% contribution rate but no more than a 10% contribution rate.

Thaler and Benartzi (2004) document the effectiveness of contribution escalation at increasing employee savings rates. At the firm they study, employees who chose an automatic annual 3% contribution increase saw their average contribution rate increase almost fourfold over the course of four years, from 3.5% of pay to 13.5% of pay. In contrast, employees who did not elect contribution escalation increased their average contribution rate by much less over the same period, from 5.3% to 7.5%. Interestingly, the latter group started out saving much more than those who chose contribution escalation, but their relative positions were reversed four years later. As might be expected, given the evidence on automatic enrollment, contribution escalation is much more effective if it is the default, harnessing employee inertia to increase contribution rates. In firms where contribution escalation is an option but is not the default, about 25% of savings-plan participants sign up; in contrast, when contribution escalation is the default, only 15% of participants opt out, so that 85% of participants are subject to future automatic contribution increases (Benartzi, Peleg, and Thaler 2007).

Combining automatic enrollment with contribution escalation mitigates the drag on long-term asset accumulation that results under automatic enrollment with a low default contribution rate. However, picking a higher initial default contribution rate is also an option (with or without contribution escalation). Relative to the PPA benchmark (3% initial contribution rate with contribution escalation), picking a higher initial contribution rate with contribution escalation will lead to the greatest level of asset accumulation, provided that it does not result in significantly higher opt-out rates. Picking a higher initial contribution rate without contribution escalation will lead to higher asset accumulation than the PPA baseline in the short run but may result in lower asset accumulation in the long run.

Like contribution escalation, the QDIA guidelines also mitigate the potential drag on long-term asset accumulation under automatic enrollment. In this case the pertinent issue is the lower expected investment returns that accompany a conservative default fund. The rationale employers have given for selecting conservative defaults has been a desire to forestall participant lawsuits if the default fund declines in value; by choosing a default fund designed to preserve principal, this risk is minimized (if not eliminated). The PPA diminishes this rationale by shielding plan sponsors from legal liability if the default fund they choose satisfies certain conditions, including diversification (which precludes using a single asset, such as employer stock, as a QDIA default) and exposure to both equity and fixed-income assets.

Moving from Research to Policy

The preceding discussion describes the evidence behind and rationale for the autosave and QDIA regulations that are part of the PPA. Another important part of the story, however, is how the provisions came to be incorporated into law.

McDonald's is commonly cited as the first company to have incorporated automatic enrollment into its 401(k) plan, starting in 1984.[10] By the mid-1990s a handful of other companies had also adopted automatic enrollment. The oft-cited motivation for doing so was to increase participation rates among lower-paid employees so that the firm's savings plan would pass the nondiscrimination tests and maintain its tax-qualified status.

There were some questions, however, about the permissibility of automatic enrollment. Could employers legally direct employee contributions to an employer-sponsored savings plan without the affirmative consent of employees, and could the absence of a "negative election" (that is, opting out) under automatic enrollment be construed as approval to make such contributions?

In 1997 a curious Treasury Department staffer requested an IRS decision on the permissibility of 401(k) automatic enrollment. The staffer's request was initially denied; investing scarce resources for the legal comfort of a few companies that had not formally requested such a decision did not appear warranted. But further reflection led Mark Iwry, then benefits tax counsel at the Treasury Department, to recognize that automatic enrollment had the potential to increase savings and improve retirement security for millions of Americans. An affirmative ruling on the permissibility of automatic enrollment might lead to more widespread adoption. So in 1998 the Treasury Department and the IRS issued Revenue Ruling 98-30, which described an acceptable scenario for 401(k) automatic enrollment.

In contrast to private rulings, which are issued in response to directed questions by private parties, revenue rulings are more general. The scenario in Ruling 98-30 involved a hypothetical company using automatic enrollment with a 3% default contribution rate invested in a balanced fund and an employer match that was not directed into employer stock. These seemingly ancillary details about the employer match were chosen quite purposefully. Mark Iwry and the staff at the Treasury Department had two concerns about automatic enrollment. First, they were worried that firms might substitute automatic enrollment for an employer match as a way to satisfy the nondiscrimination rules, a move that could nullify or even reverse the savings increases that might otherwise occur under automatic enrollment. Second, they were worried that employers might use automatic enrollment to funnel 401(k) contributions into employer stock in order to inflate its price. For firms interested in implementing automatic enrollment with the blessing of the IRS, the safest course of action would be to emulate the ruling's example precisely—that is, with the provision of an employer match that was not directed into employer stock.

This initial ruling was followed by a June 1998 speech by President Bill Clinton in which he endorsed automatic enrollment as a mechanism for increasing savings; Treasury Secretary Lawrence Summers also encouraged employer adoption of automatic enrollment in some of his public remarks. Despite a belief within the Treasury Department that automatic enrollment should be heavily endorsed, there were concerns that moving too quickly could backfire politically. Automatic enrollment could be perceived as being overtly paternalistic or yet another burdensome employer obligation. Either of these outcomes could result in congressional action to block 401(k) automatic enrollment programs. Thus the Treasury Department and the IRS began issuing a series of successively more expansive rulings meant to illustrate the different types of plans and automatic enrollment schemes deemed acceptable. The hope was that this gradual expansion would nudge employers toward automatic enrollment schemes with desirable features without stirring up too much political controversy.

These actions by the Treasury Department coincided with the emergence of the first research findings on how automatic enrollment and contribution escalation affect savings outcomes. Although Treasury officials had worried about automatic enrollment displacing employer matches and being used to direct savings-plan assets into employer stock, neither of these fears seemed to have been realized in practice. The biggest drawback to automatic enrollment was unanticipated: the persistence of the default options chosen by employers. As discussed previously, low default contribution rates reduce the contribution rates of individuals in the right tail of the savings distribution, and individuals do not quickly move away from these low defaults. Thus 401(k) automatic enrollment could have a neutral or even negative net effect on aggregate retirement-asset accumulation. Similarly, if employers adopted conservative default funds with expected returns below those of the assets employees would otherwise choose for themselves, account balances would grow more slowly in expectation.

Although all the revenue rulings issued by the Treasury Department and the IRS used a balanced fund as the default investment option, most early adopters of automatic enrollment opted for much more conservative money-market or stable-value default funds. Employers were concerned that a default fund that declined in value could give rise to a participant class-action lawsuit. The Treasury Department could do little more on this front, given that its existing revenue rulings already specified more aggressive defaults (balanced funds), but it could encourage higher initial default contribution rates and contribution escalation. One of the revenue rulings in 2000 specified a 4% default contribution rate, in contrast to the 3% default rate specified in earlier rulings. This was followed in 2004 by an IRS general information letter that clarified that employers have substantial discretion in structuring default contributions under automatic enrollment, including default contribution rates that are higher (or lower) than those used in previous revenue rulings, default contribution rates that are higher (or lower) than the employer match threshold, and default contribution rates that increase over time—that is, automatic contribution escalation.[11]

As the results of the academic research began to diffuse, automatic enrollment and contribution escalation gained traction with employers, savings-plan administrators, and benefits consultants. The staunchest opponents were those who felt that automatic enrollment and contribution escalation were too paternalistic, but these concerns were largely allayed by the argument that with or without automatic enrollment and contribution escalation, a company savings plan has a default; the question is simply what that default should be.

The discomfort some employers felt in adopting automatic enrollment was not entirely philosophical. Several legal issues made many employers reluctant to adopt so-called autopilot savings plans. Some employers did not feel adequately shielded from state laws that prohibit employers from withholding money from an employee's paycheck without consent. Other companies were concerned about potential legal liability associated with choosing a default fund that would likely hold a significant fraction of the plan's assets going forward. Still others were concerned about the tax implications of automatic enrollment for employees who did not want to participate in the savings plan but who did not opt out of participation before the opt-out deadline. These employees would incur a 10% tax penalty if they tried to recover the contributions they had made inadvertently. Congressional action was required to address these concerns.

Peter Orszag and Mark Iwry of the Retirement Security Project took the lead in incorporating into the PPA provisions that would encourage employers to adopt automatic enrollment and contribution escalation (including clearing out the legal underbrush mentioned earlier) and in pushing the legislation through Congress. They were helped by groups such as the Profit Sharing/401(k) Council of America (representing the interests of employers), the American Association of Retired Persons (AARP) (representing the interests of older individuals), and the nonpartisan Employee Benefit Research Institute. The sell was not a difficult one; most key political constituencies were quickly convinced that automatic enrollment was aligned with their own interests. Employee support for automatic enrollment was widespread, leading to the backing of labor unions.[12] Employers were generally in favor; the proposed legislation would grant relief from legal liability for investment losses in qualifying default funds, and it would also grant relief from nondiscrimination testing to employers that adopted sufficiently generous forms of automatic enrollment. Employers were also not required to adopt automatic enrollment if they did not want to. The financial sector recognized that automatic enrollment and contribution escalation would increase assets that it would manage. The failure of Social Security reform spurred an interest in promoting increased private savings among both conservatives and liberals, and although liberals were generally more inclined to support strengthening traditional defined-benefit pension schemes, they were swayed by the evidence that automatic enrollment had the largest beneficial impact on the savings outcomes of lower-income individuals and minority groups. In the words of Peter Orszag, automatic enrollment "had become like apple pie on Capitol Hill—everyone was for it."[13]

Orszag attributes the success of the autosave features in the PPA to three factors.[14] First, there was clear and compelling evidence that automatic enrollment was an effective means of increasing savings and improving economic well-being, particularly of minorities and of the poor. The evidence and the theory behind automatic enrollment and contribution escalation were transparent and convincing. Second, the results of the economic research on the isolated adoption of automatic enrollment and contribution escalation were clearly scalable and conformed to intuition and to experience. Third, as noted earlier, the effects of automatic enrollment appealed to both sides of the political aisle.

The United States is not the only country to recognize the impact that automatic enrollment can have on savings outcomes. In New Zealand the KiwiSaver Act adopted in 2006 creates a new national program based on automatic enrollment to supplement the existing superannuation scheme. On the other side of the Atlantic, the United Kingdom's Pensions Act of 2007 also incorporates automatic enrollment as part of its pension system reforms. Although it is too early to determine the efficacy of these programs, widespread take-up of 401(k) automatic enrollment in the United States is encouraging and has inspired Orszag to declare the autosave features of the PPA "a stunning example of the success of behavioral economics in affecting public policy."[15]

Notes

We thank Hewitt Associates for providing the data analyzed in this chapter. We are particularly grateful to Lori Lucas, Pam Hess, and Yan Xu, some of our many current and former contacts at Hewitt. We thank Mark Iwry, Peter Orszag, Robert Shiller, and John Siegfried for helpful conversations on this chapter. We acknowledge financial support from the National Institute on Aging (NIA) (grant R01-AG021650) and the U.S. Social Security Administration (grant 10-P-98363-1 to the National Bureau of Economic Research [NBER] as part of the Social Security Administration [SSA] Retirement Research Consortium). The opinions and conclusions expressed are solely those of the authors and do not represent the opinions or policy of the NIA, the SSA, any other agency of the U.S. federal government, or the NBER.

1. The bill was passed by the Senate in a 93–5 vote and by the House of Representatives in a 279–131 vote.
2. See the U.S. Department of Labor's pension reform website for more details on the Pension Protection Act (including the complete text of the 393-page act): www.dol.gov/EBSA/pensionreform.html.
3. These qualified default investment alternative (QDIA) regulations specifically endorse three different long-term investment options: life-cycle or target-retirement-date funds, balanced funds, and professionally managed accounts (see www.dol.gov/ebsa/pdf/fsQDIA.pdf and www.dol.gov/ebsa/regs/fedreg/final/07-5147.pdf).
4. The default contribution rate must be 3% or higher initially and then escalate by 1% each year until it reaches a rate of at least 6% and no more than 10%. Contribution escalation can presumably continue beyond the 10% level with a participant's affirmative election.
5. Employers can choose either a noncontingent contribution of 3% of pay for all employees (regardless of whether the employees choose to contribute themselves) or an employer match of 100% on the first 1% of pay contributed to the plan and 50% on further contributions up to 6% of pay (for a total matching contribution of 3.5% of pay if employees contribute at least 6% of their pay to the plan). A more generous noncontingent contribution or employer match is also acceptable.
6. The income threshold for classification as a "highly compensated employee" has increased over time, and is set at $110,000 for 2009.
7. Because of concurrent 401(k) eligibility changes for employees under the age of forty at this company, we restrict the analysis to employees aged forty or over at the time of hire. These employees were immediately eligible to participate in the 401(k) plan both before and after the switch to automatic enrollment.
8. A similar endorsement effect may influence employee allocations to employer stock, which are higher in firms that direct the employer match into employer stock than in firms where employer stock is simply available as an investment option.(Benartzi 2001; Brown, Liang, and Weisbenner 2007).
9. Of course, lower expected asset returns may be acceptable or even desirable if they are associated with less risk. However, standard economic theory suggests that individuals should be willing to accept at least some stock-market risk, so that some exposure to the higher expected return of equities is attractive from a normative standpoint.
10. Interestingly, McDonald's abandoned automatic enrollment in 2002, just as it was gaining popularity among other employers.
11. A general information letter is a device used by the IRS when a ruling does not seem necessary because a point is sufficiently obvious but may require clarification.
12. See Harris Interactive (2007) for evidence on widespread employee support of automatic enrollment.

13. Interview with Peter Orszag, July 3, 2007.
14. Ibid.
15. Ibid.

References

Benartzi, Shlomo (2001). "Excessive Extrapolation and the Allocation of 401(k) Accounts to Company Stock." *Journal of Finance* 56(5): 1747–1764.

Benartzi, Shlomo, Ehud Peleg, and Richard H. Thaler (2007). "Choice Architecture and Retirement Savings Plans." UCLA working paper.

Bernheim, B. Douglas (1995). "Do Households Appreciate Their Financial Vulnerabilities? An Analysis of Actions, Perceptions, and Public Policy." In Charles E. Walker, Mark A. Bloomfield, and Margo Thorning, eds., *Tax Policy and Economic Growth*. Washington, D.C.: American Council for Capital Formation, 1–30.

Beshears, John, James J. Choi, David Laibson, and Brigitte C. Madrian (2008). "The Importance of Default Options for Retirement Saving Outcomes: Evidence from the United States." In Stephen J. Kay and Tapen Sinha, eds., *Lessons from Pension Reform in the Americas*. Oxford: Oxford University Press, 59–87.

Brown, Jeffrey R., Nellie Liang, and Scott Weisbenner (2007). "Individual Account Investment Options and Portfolio Choice: Behavioral Lessons from 401(k) Plans." *Journal of Public Economics* 91(10): 1992–2013.

Carroll, Gabriel D., James J. Choi, David Laibson, Brigitte C. Madrian, and Andrew Metrick (forthcoming). "Optimal Defaults and Active Decisions." *Quarterly Journal of Economics*.

Choi, James M., David Laibson, and Brigitte C. Madrian (2007). "$100 Bills on the Sidewalk: Suboptimal Investment in 401(k) Plans." NBER Working Paper 11554.

Choi, James M., David Laibson, Brigitte C. Madrian, and Andrew Metrick (2002). "Defined Contribution Pensions: Plan Rules, Participant Decisions, and the Path of Least Resistance." In James Poterba, ed., *Tax Policy and the Economy*. Cambridge, MA: National Bureau of Economic Research, 67–114.

────── (2004). "For Better or for Worse: Default Effects and 401(k) Savings Behavior." In David A. Wise, ed., *Perspectives on the Economics of Aging*. Chicago: University of Chicago Press, 81–121.

────── (2006). "Saving for Retirement on the Path of Least Resistance." In Edward J. McCaffrey and Joel Slemrod, eds., *Behavioral Public Finance: Toward a New Agenda*. New York: Russell Sage Foundation, 304–351.

Department of Labor. Employee Benefit Security Administration (2007). "Private Pension Plan Bulletin Historical Tables." www.dol.gov/ebsa/pdf/private-pensionplanbulletinhistoricaltables.pdf (accessed December 13, 2007).

Department of Labor. Employee Benefit Security Administration (2008). "Private Pension Plan Bulletin: Abstract of 2006 Form 5500 Annual Reports." www.dol.gov/ebsa/pdf/2006pensionplanbulletin.pdf (accessed April 20, 2009).

Farkas, Steve, and Jean Johnson (1997). *Miles to Go: A Status Report on Americans' Plans for Retirement.* New York: Public Agenda.

Harris Interactive (2007). "Retirement Made Simpler." www.retirementmadesimpler.org/Library/FINAL%20RMS%20Topline%20Report%201-5-07.pdf (accessed December 28, 2007).

John Hancock Financial Services (2002). *Insight into Participant Investment Knowledge and Behavior: Eighth Defined Contribution Plan Survey.* Boston: John Hancock Financial Services. www.jhancockstructures.com/gsfp/survey2002 .pdf (accessed December 28, 2007).

Lusardi, Annamaria, and Olivia Mitchell (2006). "Financial Literacy and Planning: Implications for Retirement Wellbeing." Pension Research Council Working Paper 2006-1.

Madrian, Brigitte C., and Dennis F. Shea (2001). "The Power of Suggestion: Inertia in 401(k) Participation and Savings Behavior." *Quarterly Journal of Economics* 116: 1149–1187.

Thaler, Richard H., and Shlomo Benartzi (2004). "Save More Tomorrow: Using Behavioral Economics to Increase Employee Savings." *Journal of Political Economy* 112 (1, pt. 2): S164–S187.

COMMENT

Robert J. Shiller

The new "autosave" features of the U.S. Pension Protection Act of 2006, which the authors and some of their colleagues originally proposed, are a very important, if little-noted, advance that is of the first magnitude for improving national welfare. As has happened throughout history with good ideas, the autosave features have been copied in other countries, for example, New Zealand and the United Kingdom. We might well expect that these autosave plans will become a new worldwide standard. The authors should be congratulated for a change that marks one of the triumphs of economic research for public policy in recent years.

The autosave features creatively address an important problem: many people seem to have trouble making elementary saving decisions; in fact, many actually postpone for their entire lifetimes making an active, informed decision. Yet the government should not be making savings decision for people. People should be making their own decisions in light of their own information. There is no better expert on any person's situation than that person. How can we design a system that performs reasonably well for all people? We need a system that prevents most people from making massive mistakes but allows people who have good reason to adjust for their own circumstances to do so.

That is the question to which these authors have found a reasonably good answer. The simple idea, which the PPA made feasible, is that people whose employer offers a defined-contribution pension plan should be automatically enrolled in a standard plan with contribution rates and portfolio allocations that are reasonable for the generic person, and they can freely drop out, reduce their contribution, or change their portfolio allocation if they choose to do so. Thus those people who are inert and unresponsive will end up with a plan that is reasonable for the average person, and people with good reasons and the initiative to deviate from such a plan, and presumably with the better information that these people often have, may then do so.

The switch in the United States and other countries from the defined-benefit pension system to the defined-contribution pension system that has occurred over the past few decades did not recognize the problem that many people will not participate at a high-enough level, or with an aggressive-enough portfolio, or at all. The authors and their colleagues have helped avert what would otherwise become a first-order national problem when the new defined-contribution generations retire, that a good percentage of them would not have adequate savings to have a reasonable standard of living in retirement.

That is a simple idea that may sound obvious. Part of the reason autosave was not adopted long ago is that the 401(k) pension plans came to the general public almost as an accident and as an initially small part of a larger pension system. Section 401(k) was adopted in 1978 with the idea that it would be used for certain executives, not for the general public. The government Social Security system, in which participation is compulsory, was then much larger and more important, as was also the defined-benefit pension system. So the 401(k) plans initially seemed like plans for a small elite group or for people for whom the defects of the plans would not be serious problems. The defects of the plans only became apparent as the plans expanded to cover a large part of the population.

But there is another part of the reason that the autosave idea was missed. Autosave was not adopted earlier because its potential advantages were not obvious to the lawmakers who would need to facilitate such a plan until the research that is reported in this chapter was done. This research shows that in fact the percentage of those who participate is much higher under the automatic enrollment plan, and that the contribution rates and allocations reflect the defaults, even years afterward.

The roots of this revolution in pensions go back very far, with recognition that people often will not prepare for the distant and difficult-to-see future when they are impressed instead by the exigencies and realities of the here and now. Indeed, when the first social pension plans were being debated in Europe in the 1870s, there was a recognition that the plans could not be entirely voluntary, for "it is very doubtful that any substantial number of workers would on their own sign up for a pension plan."[1] In

1928 Frank Ramsey spoke of a "weakness of the imagination" in planning for the distant future.[2] In 1929 A. C. Pigou spoke of a "faulty telescopic faculty."[3] In 1980 Richard Thaler spoke of an "endowment effect" that encouraged people to accept whatever it is that they now appear to have. But these early recognitions of problems that might beset voluntary pension plans were only casual observations. The work that is reported in this chapter represents serious research.

I do not think that the Pension Protection Act of 2006 is the final word on the automatic enrollment feature. It represents a significant step forward, but it is more a suggestion of a whole new approach to public policy than a fait accompli.

Specifically, there are national issues about how high the default contribution rate should be. The rate should probably vary through time, and the incentives should therefore be changed through time. The implementation of this plan can have general equilibrium effects. Widely encouraging people to enter the stock market, for example, could have the effect of bidding up the prices in this market and lowering the returns that people can expect.

There is little agreement in the finance profession on what the default portfolio allocation should be, and how it should depend on the ages of the individual and family members. When one actually sets up a portfolio-optimization problem for the representative individual, one finds that one can get widely different optimal allocations over the life cycle. We need more research that will help enlighten the choice of such allocations.

Beyond that, there are likely to be many other directions for the general idea of encouraging better public policy by properly defining default options and procedures that people can be asked to go through to deviate from these defaults. I think, therefore, that this chapter is not only a wonderful example of economic research promoting better living but also an inspiration for much more such research in the future.

Notes

1. G. Behm, *Schriften des Vereins für Sozialpolitik* (1874).
2. Ramsey (1928): 543.
3. Pigou (1928): 25 (chapter 2, section 3).

References

Behm, G. "Uber Alters- und Invalidencassen fur Arbeiter." *Schriften des Vereins für Sozialpolitik* 5(1874): 141–142.

Pigou, A. C. *The Economics of Welfare.* New Brunswick, N.J.: Transactions, 1928.

Ramsey, Frank P. "A Mathematical Theory of Saving." *Economic Journal* 38(152) (December 1928): 543–559.

Thaler, Richard. "Toward a Positive Theory of Consumer Choice." *Journal of Economic Behavior and Organization* 1 (March 1980): 39–60.

Contributors
Index

Contributors

Beth J. Asch, senior labor economist, Rand Corporation

Elizabeth E. Bailey, John C. Hower Professor of Business and Public Policy, Wharton School of Business, University of Pennsylvania

John Beshears, Ph.D. candidate, Department of Business Economics, Harvard University

Rebecca M. Blank, Under Secretary for Economic Affairs, U.S. Department of Commerce

Michael J. Boskin, T. M. Friedman Professor of Economics and Senior Fellow, Hoover Institution, Stanford University

Jeremy Bulow, Richard Stepp Professor of Economics, Stanford University

James Choi, Assistant Professor of Finance, School of Management, Yale University

Peter Cramton, Professor of Economics, University of Maryland

Kenneth G. Elzinga, Robert C. Taylor Professor of Economics, University of Virginia

Nancy Folbre, Professor of Economics, University of Massachusetts

Daniel S. Hamermesh, Sue Killam Professor in the Foundations of Economics, University of Texas at Austin

Jerry Hausman, John and Jennie S. MacDonald Professor of Economics, Massachusetts Institute of Technology

V. Joseph Hotz, Arts and Sciences Professor of Economics, Duke University

Douglas A. Irwin, Robert E. Maxwell '23 Professor of Arts and Sciences, Dartmouth College

Anne O. Krueger, Professor of International Economics, Johns Hopkins University

David Laibson, Professor of Economics, Harvard University

Brigitte C. Madrian, Aetna Professor of Public Policy and Corporate Management, Kennedy School of Government, Harvard University

R. Preston McAfee, J. Stanley Johnson Professor of Business, Economics, and Management, California Institute of Technology

John McMillan, formerly Jonathan B. Lovelace Professor of Economics and Senior Fellow, Institute for Economic Policy Research, Stanford University

Laurence H. Meyer, Distinguished Scholar, Center for Strategic and International Studies, and Vice Chairman, Macroeconomic Advisers

James C. Miller III, Senior Fellow (by courtesy), Hoover Institution, and Senior Fellow, Center for Public Choice and Mercatus Center, both at George Mason University

Robert A. Moffitt, Krieger-Eisenhower Professor of Economics, Johns Hopkins University

Daniel Newlon, Economics Program Director, National Science Foundation

Wallace E. Oates, Professor of Economics, University of Maryland

Walter Y. Oi, Elmer B. Milliman Professor of Economics, University of Rochester

Charles R. Plott, Edward S. Harkness Professor of Economics and Political Science, California Institute of Technology

Nancy L. Rose, Professor of Economics, Massachusetts Institute of Technology

Alvin E. Roth, George Gund Professor of Economics and Business Administration, Harvard University

Robert J. Shiller, Arthur M. Okun Professor of Economics, Yale University

John J. Siegfried, Professor of Economics, Vanderbilt University, and Secretary-Treasurer, American Economic Association

John B. Taylor, Mary and Robert Raymond Professor of Economics, Stanford University, and Bowen H. and Janice Arthur McCoy Senior Fellow, Hoover Institution

Thomas H. Tietenberg, Mitchell Family Professor of Economics Emeritus, Colby College

John T. Warner, Professor of Economics, Clemson University

Brian Weller, graduate student, University of Chicago Graduate School of Business

Lawrence J. White, Arthur E. Imperatore Professor of Economics, Stern School of Business, New York University

Simon Wilkie, Executive Director, Center for Communications Law and Policy, and Senior Fellow, Annenberg Center for Communications, University of Southern California

Index

lobbying in spectrum allocation, 182n4
local synergies in spectrum license
allocation, 171
location of emissions, 44, 53–54
Long, Russell, 96
Long Boom, 146–147
long-run investment markets, 225
loss function, 156
lotteries for spectrum licence allocation, 169
lottery draft, 256–257, 271
lower-level substitution bias, 72
Lucas, Robert, 41
LVDF (least-value-drafted-first), 267n2

MacAvoy, Paul, 10, 204
macroeconomics: policy, 11–13; researchers,
41; theory and regime shift, 165
malnutrition. *See* health and nutrition
Malthus, Thomas, 249
managed accounts, 288n3
many-to-one matching model. *See*
college-admissions model
marginal abatement cost in emissions
trading, 43
marginal cost pricing, 8–9
marital status: in deferred-acceptance
algorithms, 212–215; and the EITC, 102;
and work incentives, 95–97, 99–100,
134–135. *See also* demographics;
marriage model
marketable permits system in emissions
trading, 43–44
market definition, remaining challenges,
239
market income, 144–145. *See also* per
capita income
market organization: auction markets,
223–225; deferred-acceptance algorithms,
207; labor markets for doctors, 211–215;
S-C-P model, 234; for success, 217–218;
unraveling and failure, 211, 218n5; via
clearinghouse, 209–210, 212
Markusen, Ann, 22
marriage model, 207–209, 218n6. *See also*
marital status
Marshall, Alfred, 249
Marshall, Burke, 271
Mason, Edward, 228, 233
matching, 223–225
matching algorithms, 206
Matsushita v. Zenith (1986), 238
McAfee, Preston, 169, 172
McCloskey, Pete, 267n5

McDonald's, 283, 288n10
MCI, 182n4
McKean, Roland, 272
McMillan, John, 169, 172
MDRC, 135–136
means-tested transfer programs, 99
Meckling, William, 254, 272
Medicaid, costs compared with the EITC,
99
medical market organization, 211–215
Medicare, 25
mergers: antitrust policy, 227; approval
questions, 239–240; enforcement of, 9;
influence of economics, 234–235; welfare
effects versus efficiency, 238–239. *See also*
monopolies
Mexico, economic development, 120
Meyer, Bruce, 107
Meyer, John, 8
Michigan Panel of Income Dynamics, 26
microdata simulation modeling, 27
middle class, rise in China and India, 126
Milgrom, Paul: on the activity rule, 175; on
ascending auctions, 173; on auction
design and bidding strategy, 169; on bid
increment size, 178
military adventurism, 257
military downsizing, 261–262, 267n10
military expenditure and regional economic
growth, 22
military personnel: management of an AVF,
260–264; payroll cost, 267n6; personnel
productivity, 271; quality, draft versus
AVF, 257–258, 263–264; reenlistment
rate, 267n9
Miller, James, 8, 190, 204, 251, 254
Miller-Tydings Act (1937), 242–243n27
Mincer, Joseph, 23
minimum wage policy, 37, 137
Modigliani, Franco, 25
Moffitt, Robert, 137
monetary economics, 146–167; Great
Awakening, 156–159; Great Moderation,
148–152; Great Regime Shift, 150,
153–154; overview of benefits, 146–147;
theory and policy, 159–160
monetary policy: basis in economics
principles, 13; in developing countries,
114; improved performance of, 155–156;
recession (of 2007–2009/2010), 147; rule
and regime shift, 153–155; transparency
and regime shift, 153
monopolies, 112, 226–227. *See also* mergers

Harvard University Press is a member of Green Press Initiative
(greenpressinitiative.org), a nonprofit organization working to
help publishers and printers increase their use of recycled paper
and decrease their use of fiber derived from endangered forests.
This book was printed on 100% recycled paper containing
50% post-consumer waste and processed chlorine free.